CULLEN BUNN

BONE PARISH

JONAS SCHARF   ALEX GUIMARÁES

VOLUME THREE

BOOM!
STUDIOS

BOOM! STUDIOS

BONE PARISH Volume Three, December 2019. Published by BOOM! Studios, a division of Boom Entertainment, Inc. Bone Parish is ™ & © 2019 Cullen Bunn. Originally published in single magazine form as BONE PARISH No. 9-12. ™ & © 2019 Cullen Bunn. All rights reserved. BOOM! Studios™ and the BOOM! Studios logo are trademarks of Boom Entertainment, Inc., registered in various countries and categories. All characters, events, and institutions depicted herein are fictional. Any similarity between any of the names, characters, persons, events, and/or institutions in this publication to actual names, characters, and persons, whether living or dead, events, and/or institutions is unintended and purely coincidental. BOOM! Studios does not read or accept unsolicited submissions of ideas, stories, or artwork.

BOOM! Studios, 5670 Wilshire Boulevard, Suite 400, Los Angeles, CA 90036-5679. Printed in China. First Printing.

ISBN: 978-1-68415-426-5, eISBN: 978-1-64144-543-6

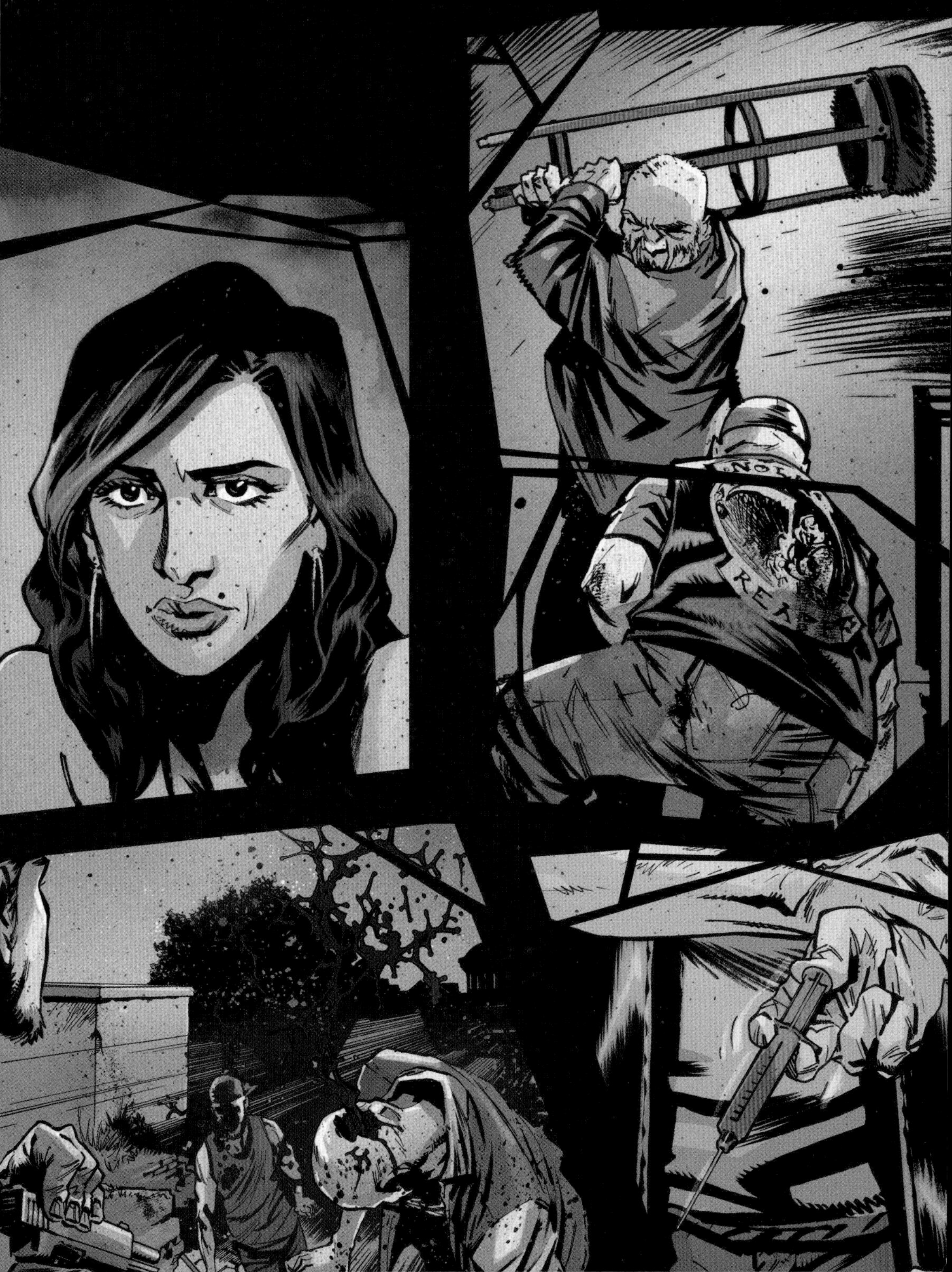

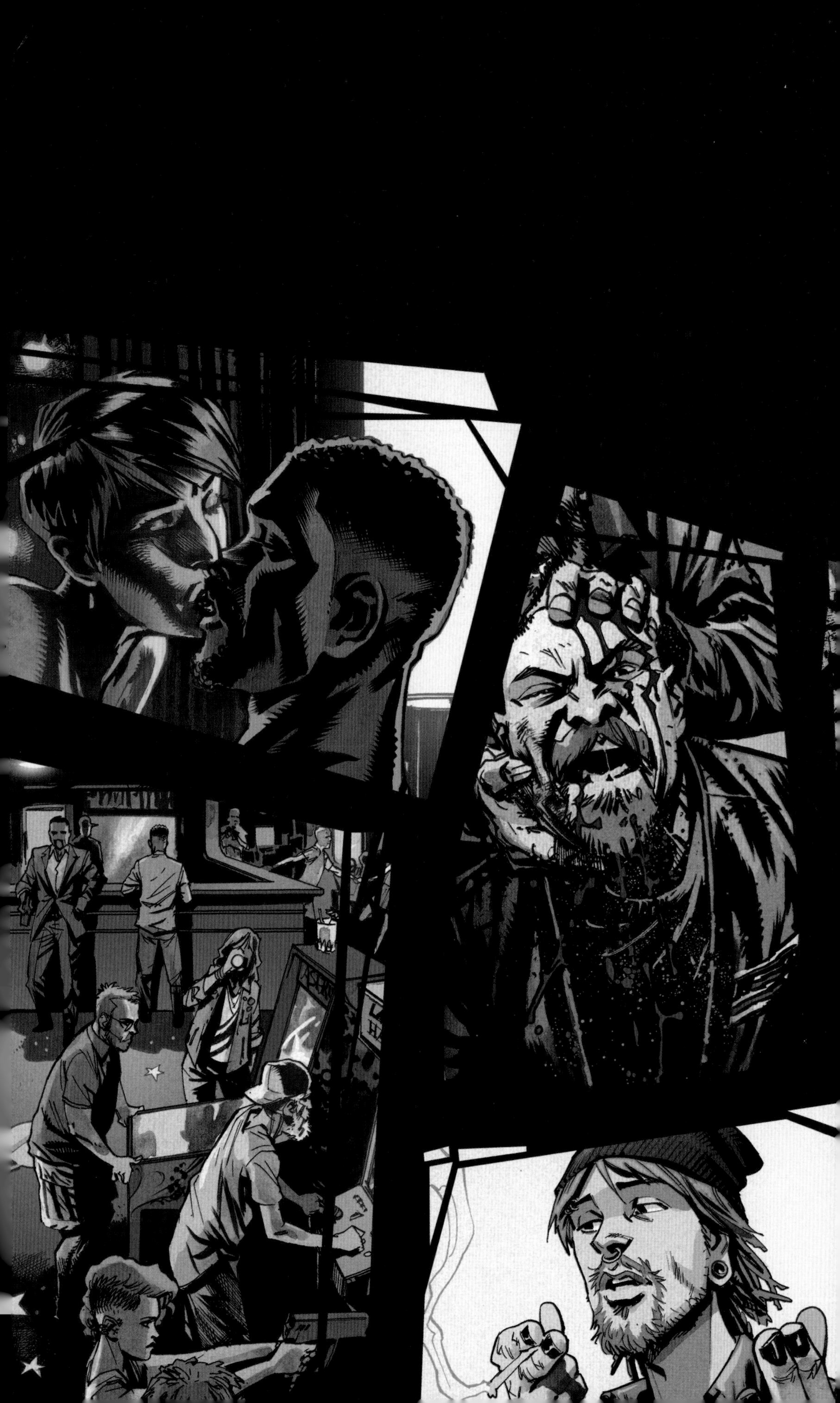

Written by
CULLEN BUNN

Illustrated by
JONAS SCHARF

Colored by
ALEX GUIMARÃES

Lettered by
ED DUKESHIRE

Cover by
LEE GARBETT

Series Designer
MICHELLE ANKLEY

Collection Designer
JILLIAN CRAB

Editor
ERIC HARBURN

BONE PARISH Created by
CULLEN BUNN & JONAS SCHARF

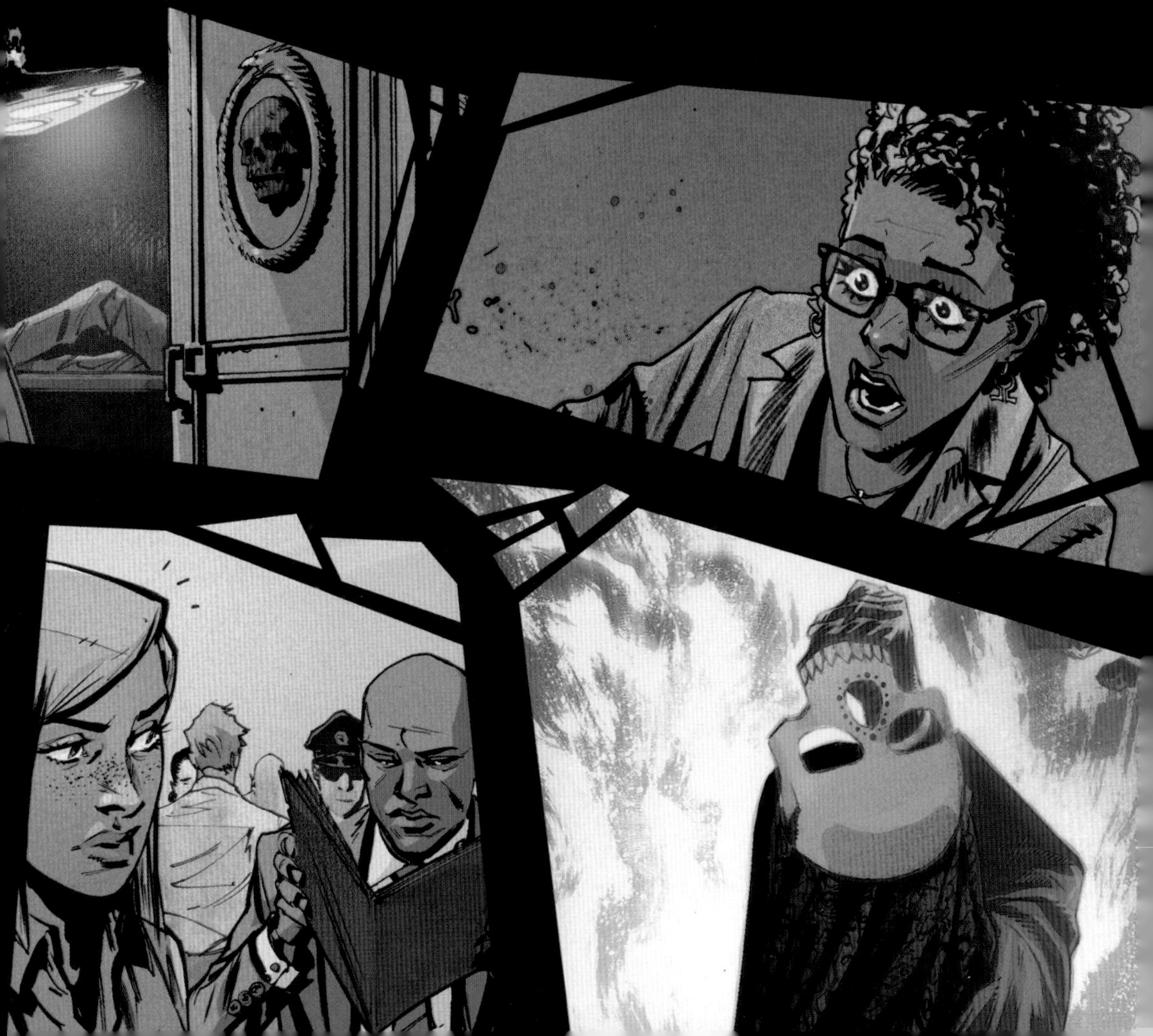

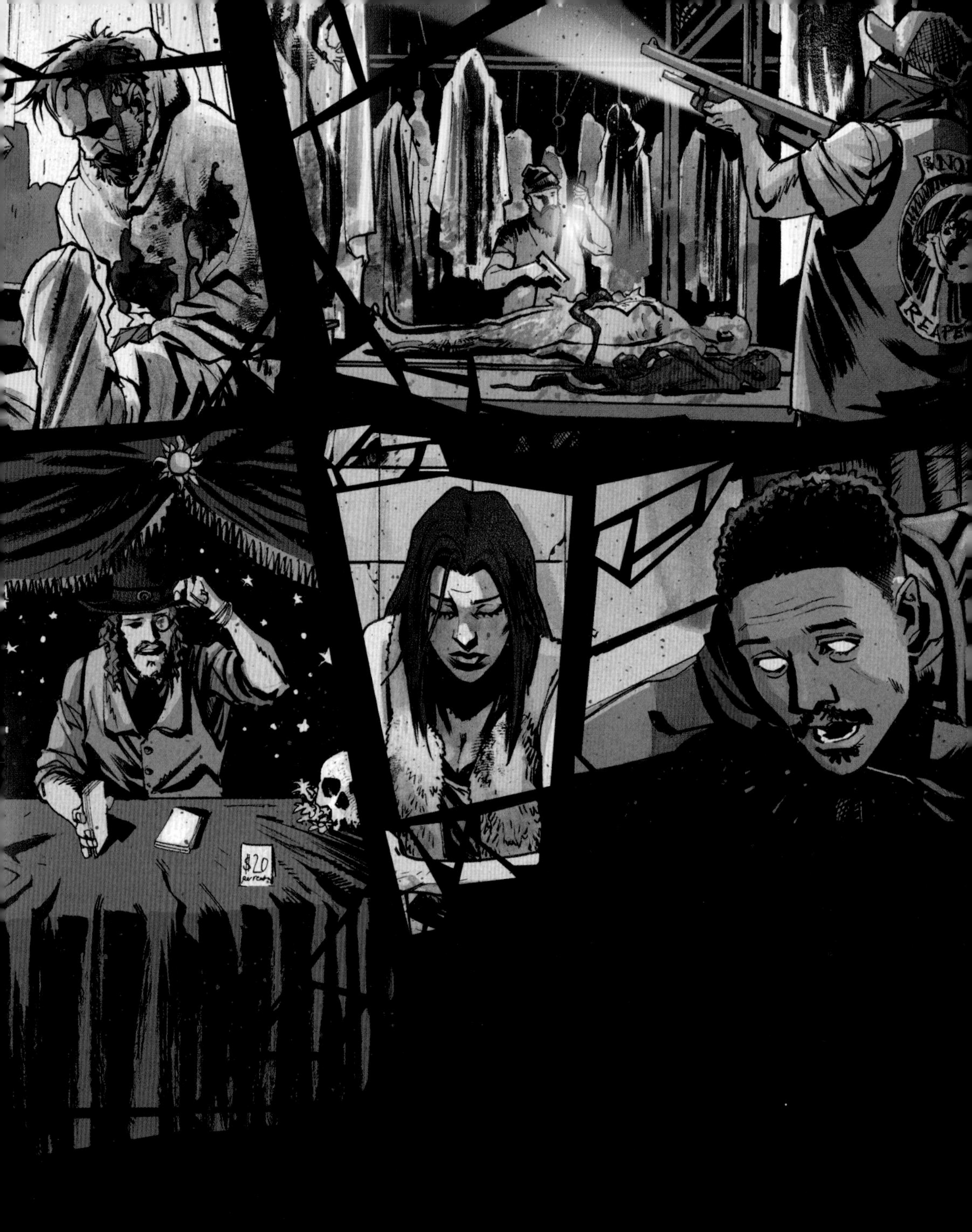
$20

Chapter Nine

THICKER THAN WATER

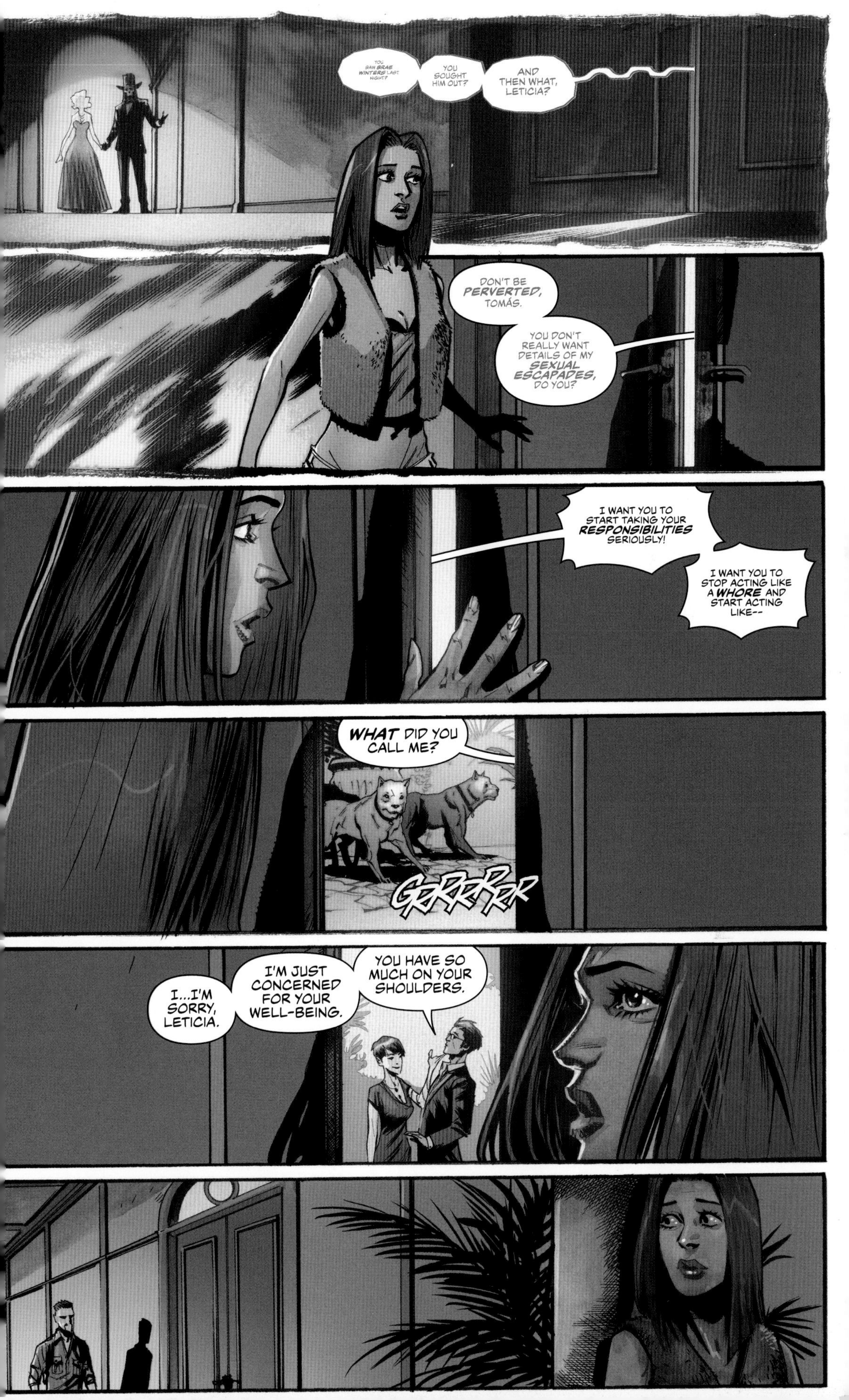
YOU SAW BRAE WINTERS LAST NIGHT?
YOU SOUGHT HIM OUT?
AND THEN WHAT, LETICIA?
DON'T BE PERVERTED, TOMÁS.
YOU DON'T REALLY WANT DETAILS OF MY SEXUAL ESCAPADES, DO YOU?
I WANT YOU TO START TAKING YOUR RESPONSIBILITIES SERIOUSLY!
I WANT YOU TO STOP ACTING LIKE A WHORE AND START ACTING LIKE--
WHAT DID YOU CALL ME?
GRRRRRR
I...I'M SORRY, LETICIA.
I'M JUST CONCERNED FOR YOUR WELL-BEING.
YOU HAVE SO MUCH ON YOUR SHOULDERS.

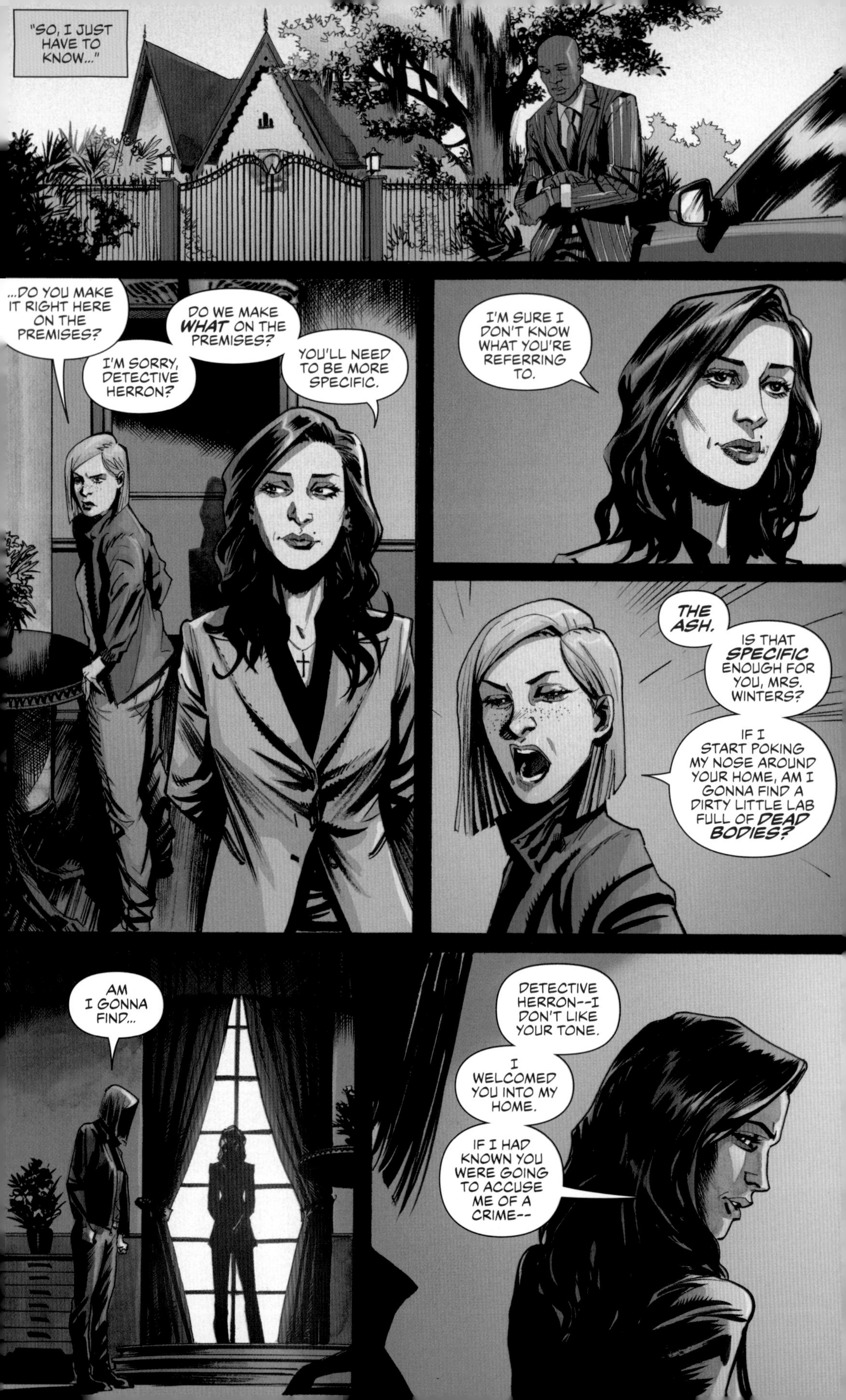
"SO, I JUST HAVE TO KNOW..."
...DO YOU MAKE IT RIGHT HERE ON THE PREMISES?
I'M SORRY, DETECTIVE HERRON?
DO WE MAKE *WHAT* ON THE PREMISES?
YOU'LL NEED TO BE MORE SPECIFIC.
I'M SURE I DON'T KNOW WHAT YOU'RE REFERRING TO.
THE ASH.
IS THAT *SPECIFIC* ENOUGH FOR YOU, MRS. WINTERS?
IF I START POKING MY NOSE AROUND YOUR HOME, AM I GONNA FIND A DIRTY LITTLE LAB FULL OF *DEAD BODIES?*
AM I GONNA FIND...
DETECTIVE HERRON--I DON'T LIKE YOUR TONE.
I WELCOMED YOU INTO MY HOME.
IF I HAD KNOWN YOU WERE GOING TO ACCUSE ME OF A CRIME--

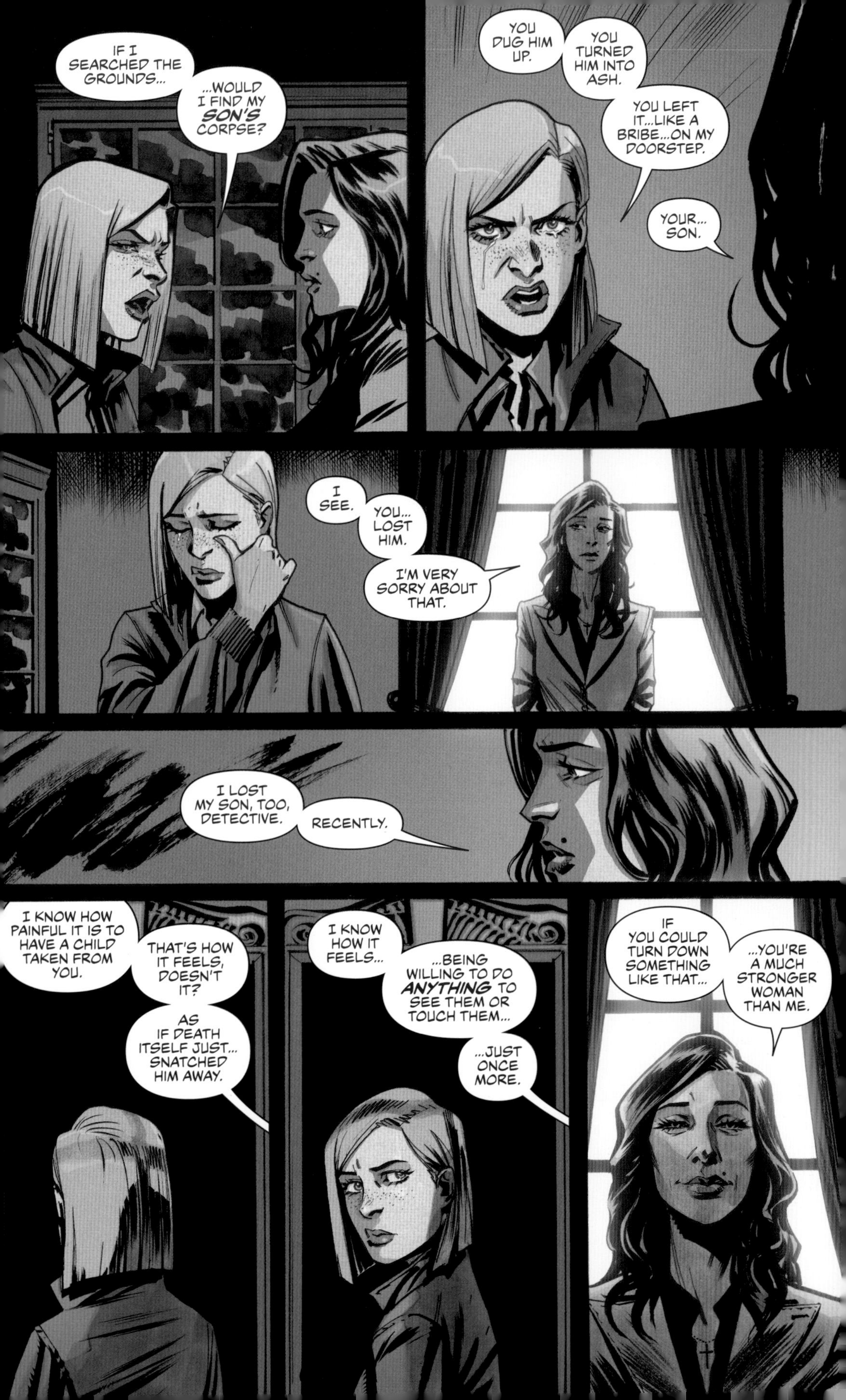
IF I SEARCHED THE GROUNDS...
...WOULD I FIND MY SON'S CORPSE?
YOU DUG HIM UP.
YOU TURNED HIM INTO ASH.
YOU LEFT IT...LIKE A BRIBE...ON MY DOORSTEP.
YOUR... SON.
I SEE.
YOU... LOST HIM.
I'M VERY SORRY ABOUT THAT.
I LOST MY SON, TOO, DETECTIVE.
RECENTLY.
I KNOW HOW PAINFUL IT IS TO HAVE A CHILD TAKEN FROM YOU.
THAT'S HOW IT FEELS, DOESN'T IT?
AS IF DEATH ITSELF JUST... SNATCHED HIM AWAY.
I KNOW HOW IT FEELS...
...BEING WILLING TO DO ANYTHING TO SEE THEM OR TOUCH THEM...
...JUST ONCE MORE.
IF YOU COULD TURN DOWN SOMETHING LIKE THAT...
...YOU'RE A MUCH STRONGER WOMAN THAN ME.

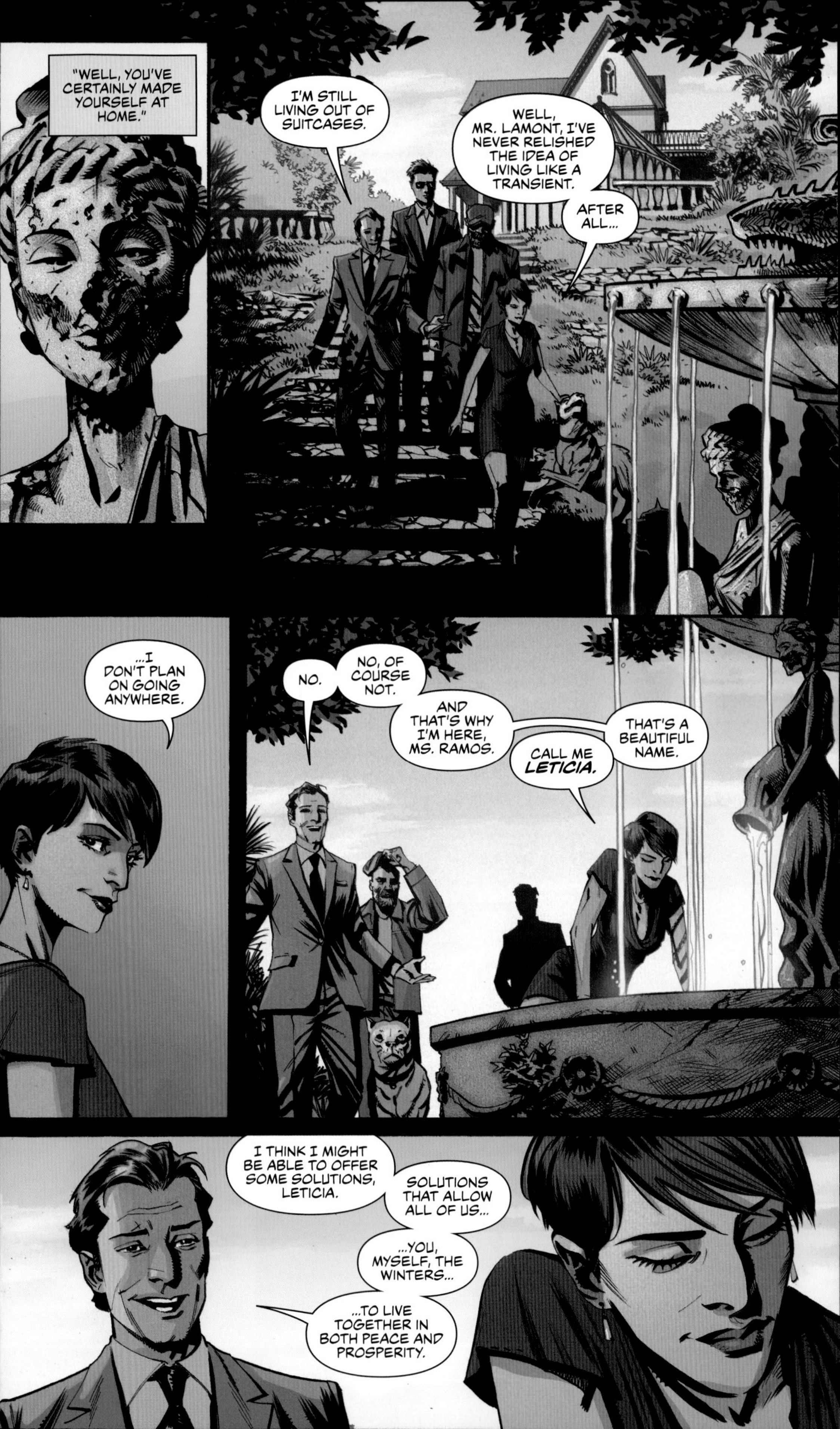
"WELL, YOU'VE CERTAINLY MADE YOURSELF AT HOME."
I'M STILL LIVING OUT OF SUITCASES.
WELL, MR. LAMONT, I'VE NEVER RELISHED THE IDEA OF LIVING LIKE A TRANSIENT.
AFTER ALL...
...I DON'T PLAN ON GOING ANYWHERE.
NO.
NO, OF COURSE NOT.
AND THAT'S WHY I'M HERE, MS. RAMOS.
CALL ME *LETICIA.*
THAT'S A BEAUTIFUL NAME.
I THINK I MIGHT BE ABLE TO OFFER SOME SOLUTIONS, LETICIA.
SOLUTIONS THAT ALLOW ALL OF US...
...YOU, MYSELF, THE WINTERS...
...TO LIVE TOGETHER IN BOTH PEACE AND PROSPERITY.

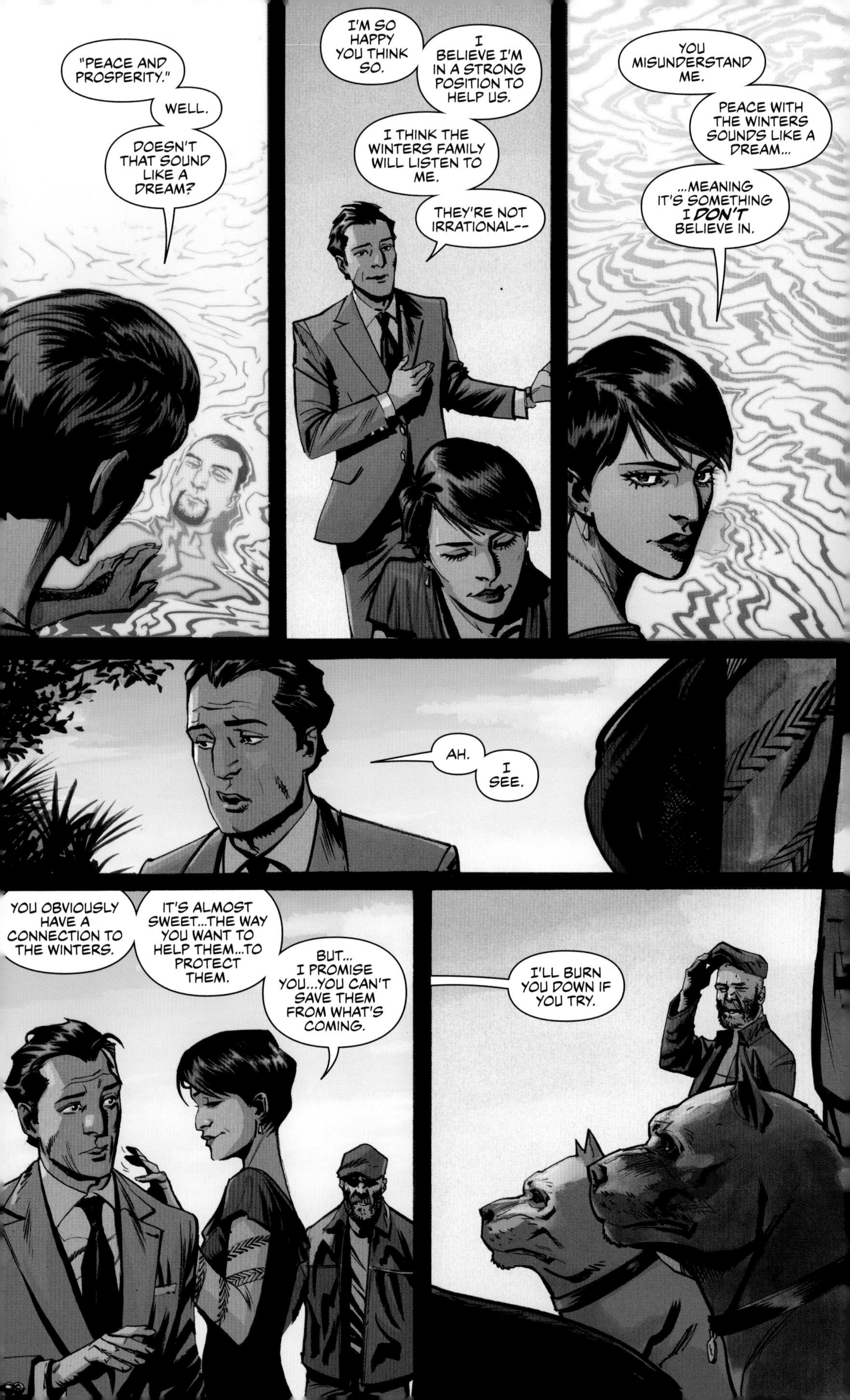

"PEACE AND PROSPERITY."
WELL.
DOESN'T THAT SOUND LIKE A DREAM?
I'M SO HAPPY YOU THINK SO.
I BELIEVE I'M IN A STRONG POSITION TO HELP US.
I THINK THE WINTERS FAMILY WILL LISTEN TO ME.
THEY'RE NOT IRRATIONAL--
YOU MISUNDERSTAND ME.
PEACE WITH THE WINTERS SOUNDS LIKE A DREAM...
...MEANING IT'S SOMETHING I *DON'T* BELIEVE IN.
AH.
I SEE.
YOU OBVIOUSLY HAVE A CONNECTION TO THE WINTERS.
IT'S ALMOST SWEET...THE WAY YOU WANT TO HELP THEM...TO PROTECT THEM.
BUT... I PROMISE YOU...YOU CAN'T SAVE THEM FROM WHAT'S COMING.
I'LL BURN YOU DOWN IF YOU TRY.

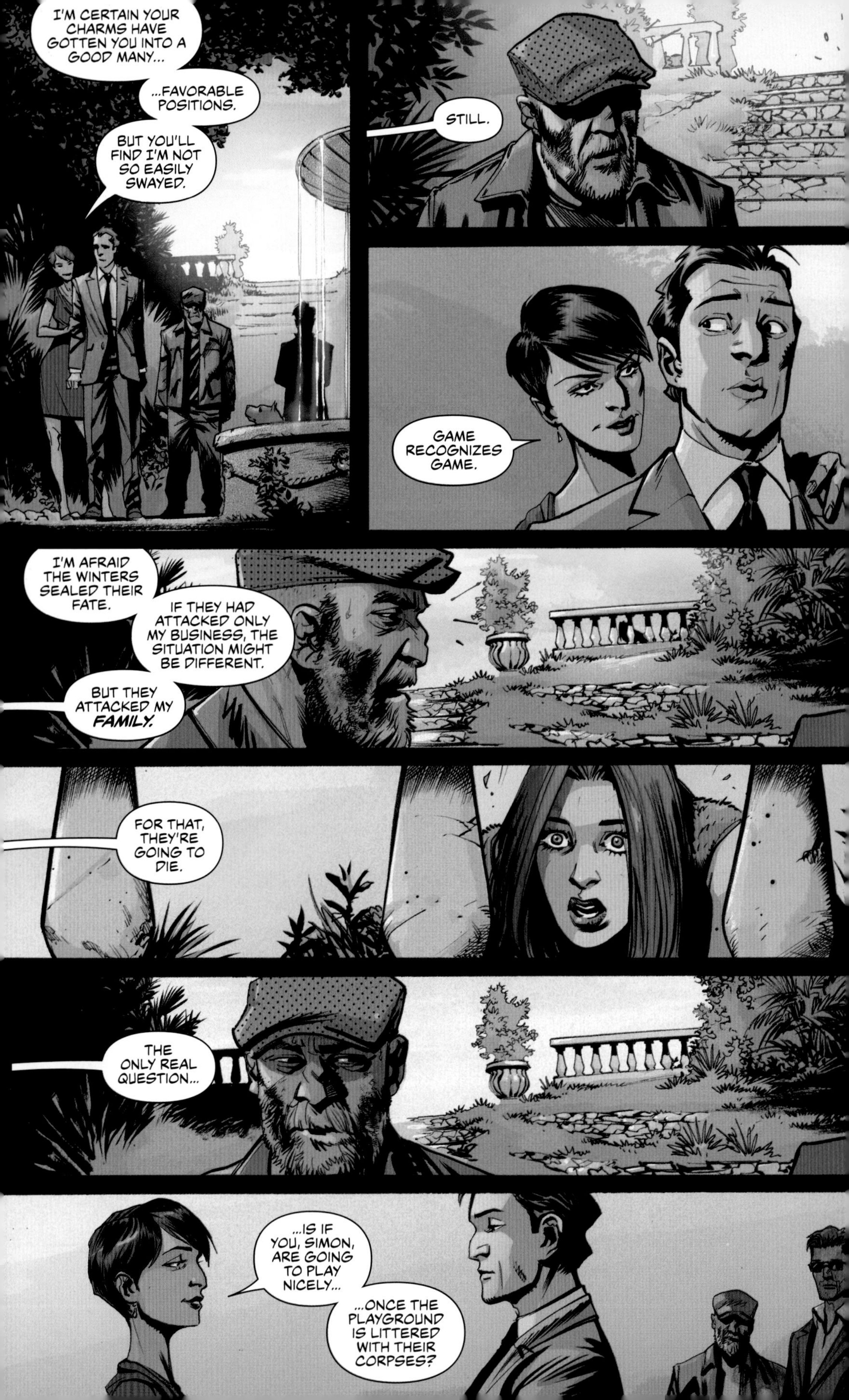
I'M CERTAIN YOUR CHARMS HAVE GOTTEN YOU INTO A GOOD MANY...
...FAVORABLE POSITIONS.
BUT YOU'LL FIND I'M NOT SO EASILY SWAYED.
STILL.
GAME RECOGNIZES GAME.
I'M AFRAID THE WINTERS SEALED THEIR FATE.
IF THEY HAD ATTACKED ONLY MY BUSINESS, THE SITUATION MIGHT BE DIFFERENT.
BUT THEY ATTACKED MY *FAMILY.*
FOR THAT, THEY'RE GOING TO DIE.
THE ONLY REAL QUESTION...
...IS IF YOU, SIMON, ARE GOING TO PLAY NICELY...
...ONCE THE PLAYGROUND IS LITTERED WITH THEIR CORPSES?

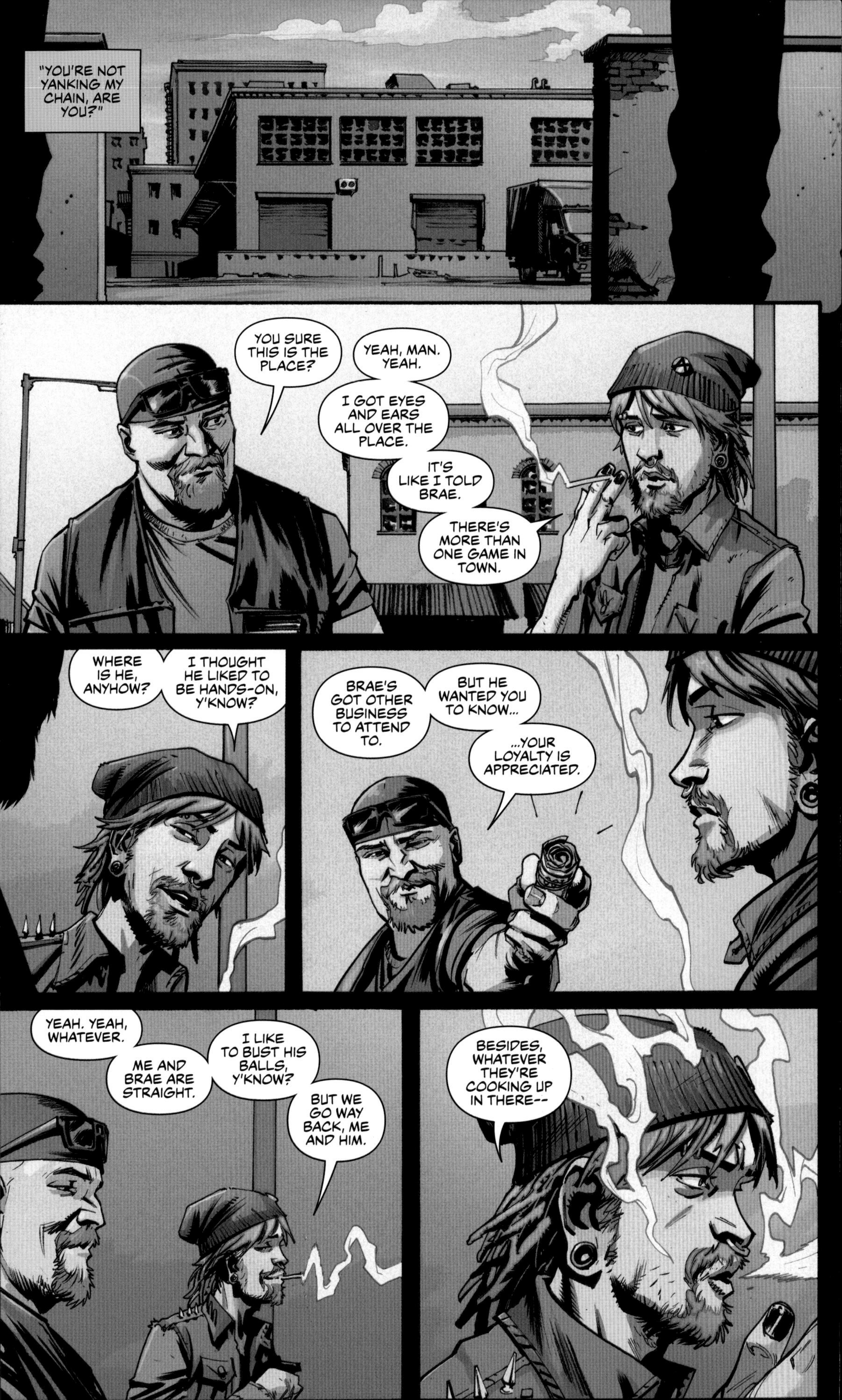
"YOU'RE NOT YANKING MY CHAIN, ARE YOU?"
YOU SURE THIS IS THE PLACE?
YEAH, MAN. YEAH.
I GOT EYES AND EARS ALL OVER THE PLACE.
IT'S LIKE I TOLD BRAE.
THERE'S MORE THAN ONE GAME IN TOWN.
WHERE IS HE, ANYHOW?
I THOUGHT HE LIKED TO BE HANDS-ON, Y'KNOW?
BRAE'S GOT OTHER BUSINESS TO ATTEND TO.
BUT HE WANTED YOU TO KNOW...
...YOUR LOYALTY IS APPRECIATED.
YEAH. YEAH, WHATEVER.
ME AND BRAE ARE STRAIGHT.
I LIKE TO BUST HIS BALLS, Y'KNOW?
BUT WE GO WAY BACK, ME AND HIM.
BESIDES, WHATEVER THEY'RE COOKING UP IN THERE--

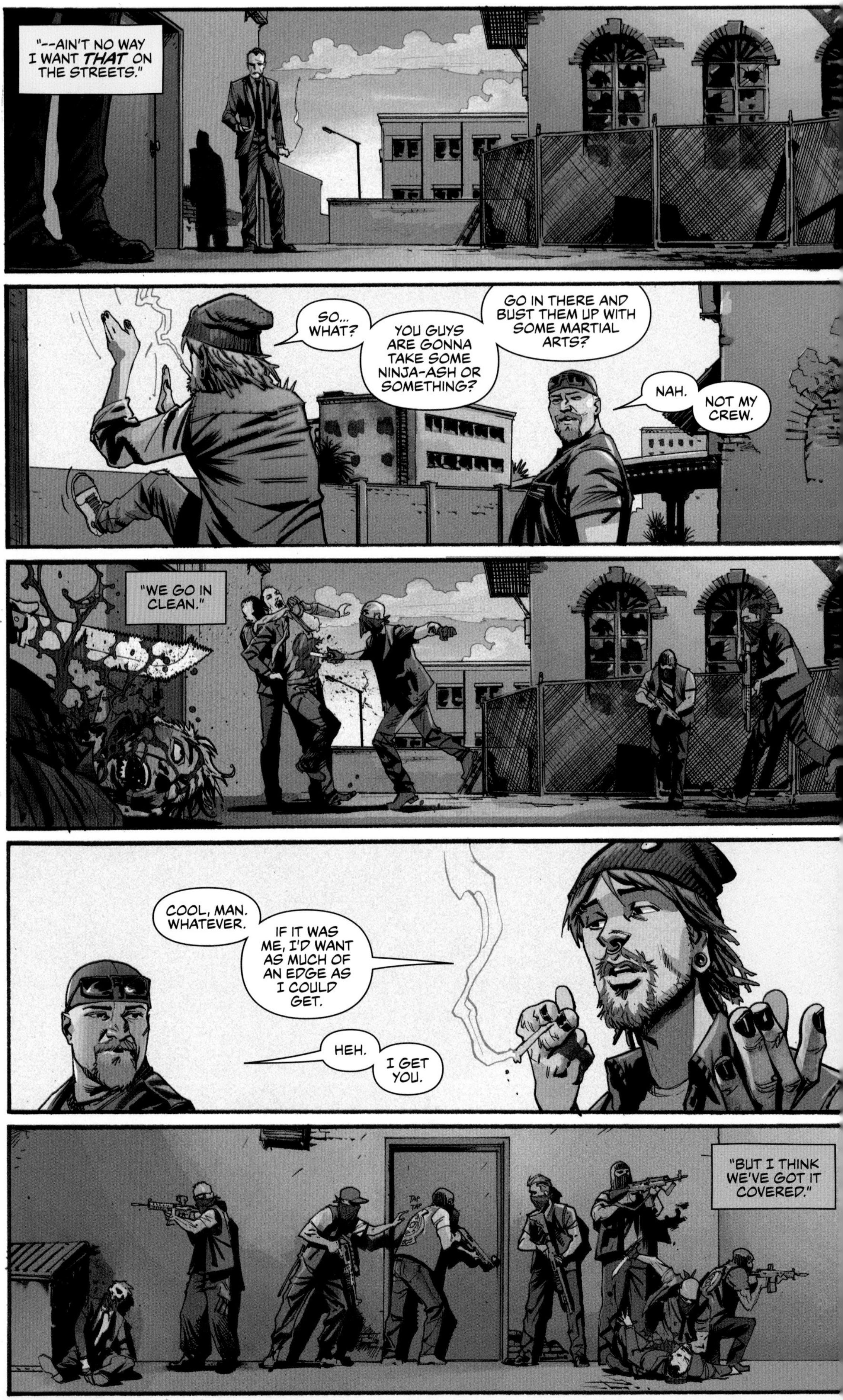
"--AIN'T NO WAY I WANT THAT ON THE STREETS."
SO... WHAT?
YOU GUYS ARE GONNA TAKE SOME NINJA-ASH OR SOMETHING?
GO IN THERE AND BUST THEM UP WITH SOME MARTIAL ARTS?
NAH.
NOT MY CREW.
"WE GO IN CLEAN."
COOL, MAN. WHATEVER.
IF IT WAS ME, I'D WANT AS MUCH OF AN EDGE AS I COULD GET.
HEH.
I GET YOU.
TAP TAP
"BUT I THINK WE'VE GOT IT COVERED."

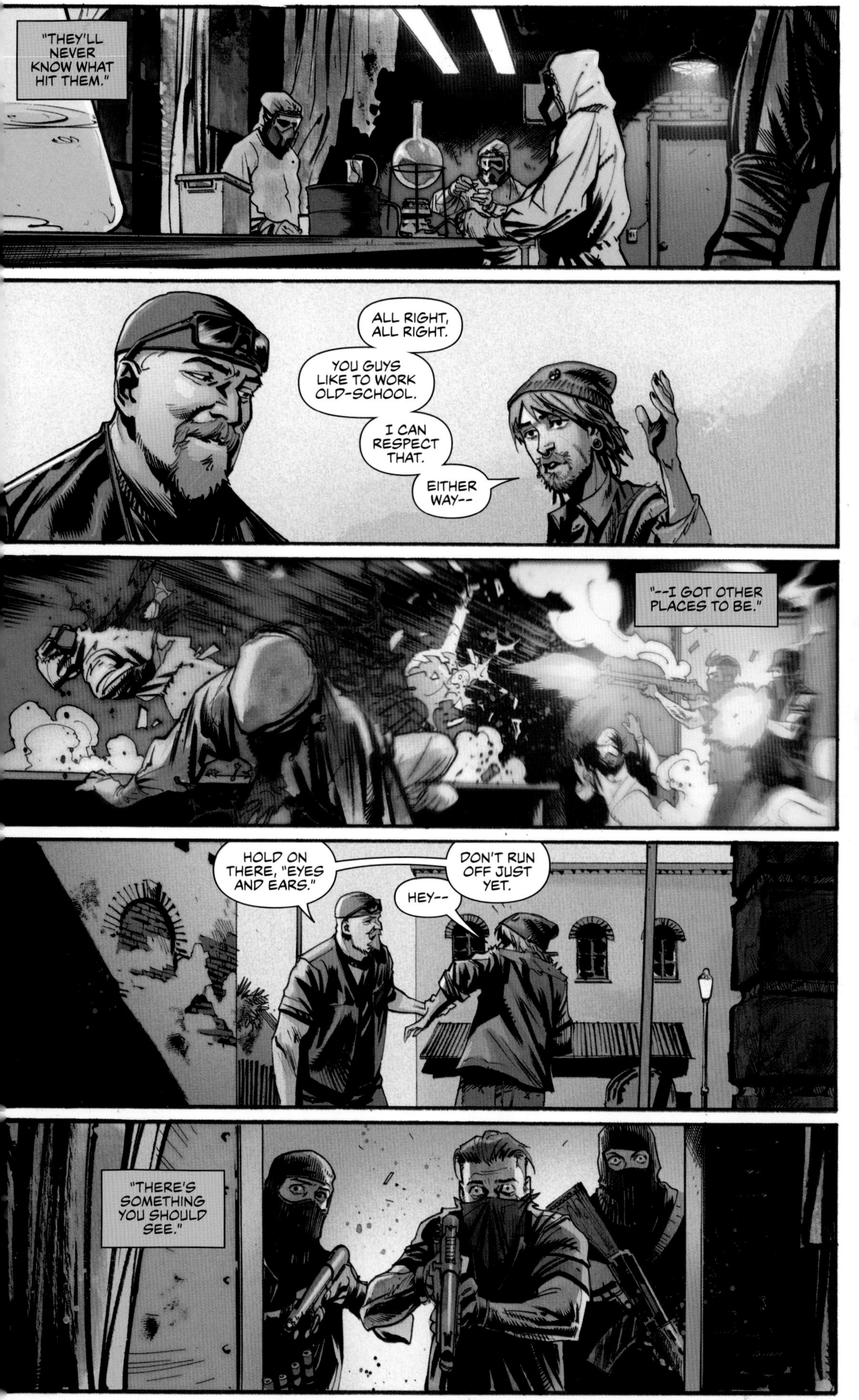
"THEY'LL NEVER KNOW WHAT HIT THEM."
ALL RIGHT, ALL RIGHT.
YOU GUYS LIKE TO WORK OLD-SCHOOL.
I CAN RESPECT THAT.
EITHER WAY--
"--I GOT OTHER PLACES TO BE."
HOLD ON THERE, "EYES AND EARS."
DON'T RUN OFF JUST YET.
HEY--
"THERE'S SOMETHING YOU SHOULD SEE."

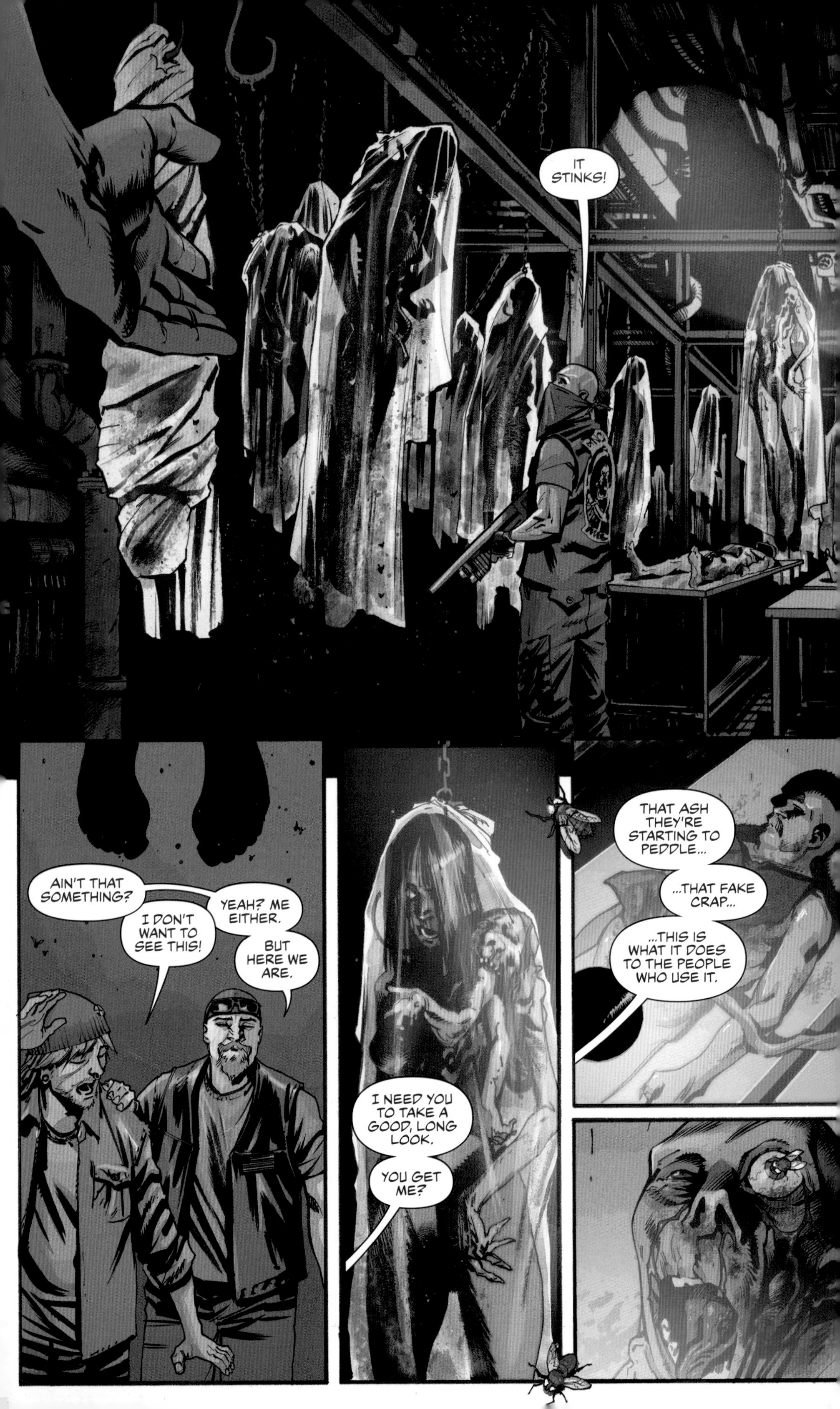
IT STINKS!
AIN'T THAT SOMETHING?
I DON'T WANT TO SEE THIS!
YEAH? ME EITHER.
BUT HERE WE ARE.
I NEED YOU TO TAKE A GOOD, LONG LOOK.
YOU GET ME?
THAT ASH THEY'RE STARTING TO PEDDLE...
...THAT FAKE CRAP...
...THIS IS WHAT IT DOES TO THE PEOPLE WHO USE IT.

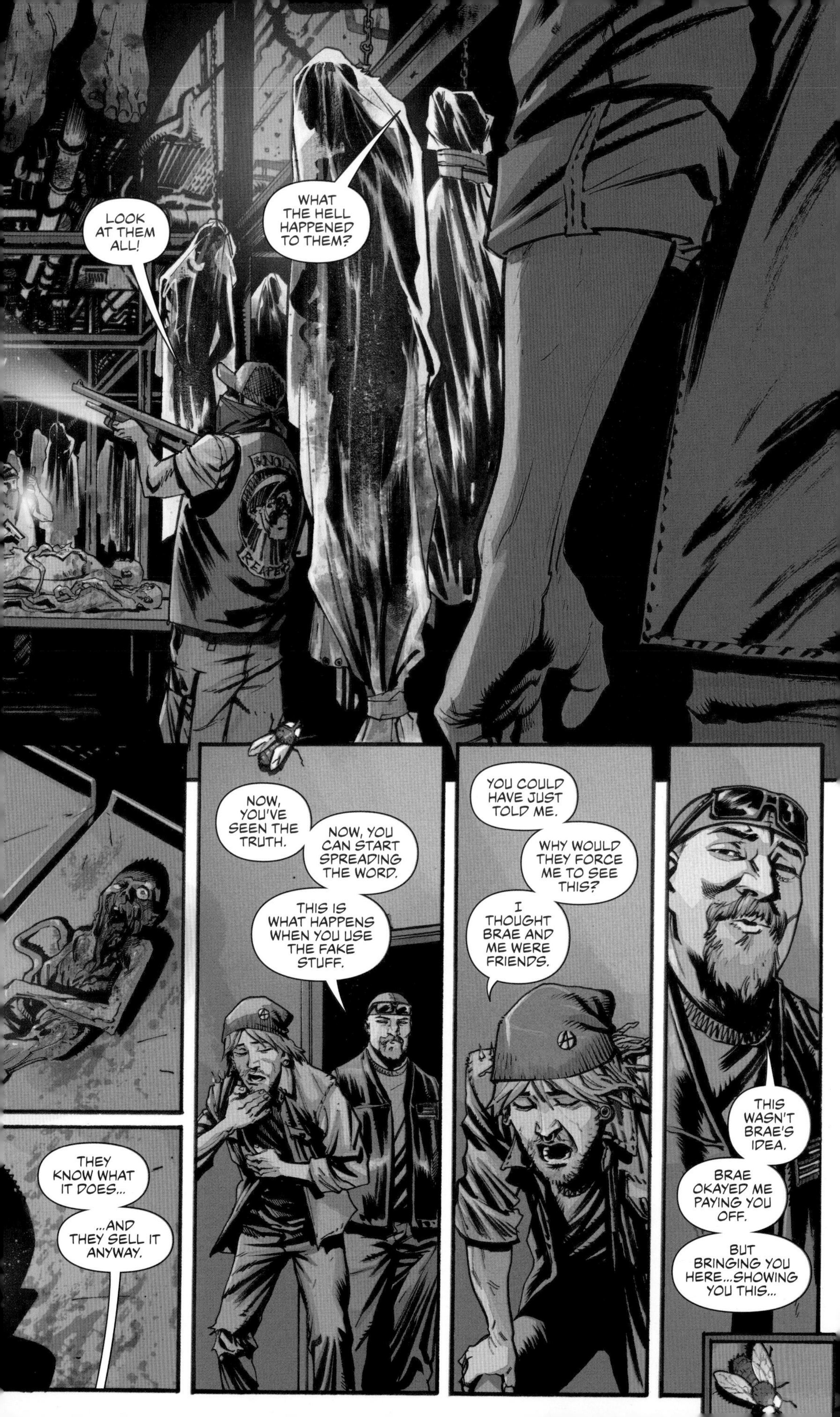
LOOK AT THEM ALL!
WHAT THE HELL HAPPENED TO THEM?
REAPERS
THEY KNOW WHAT IT DOES...
...AND THEY SELL IT ANYWAY.
NOW, YOU'VE SEEN THE TRUTH.
NOW, YOU CAN START SPREADING THE WORD.
THIS IS WHAT HAPPENS WHEN YOU USE THE FAKE STUFF.
YOU COULD HAVE JUST TOLD ME.
WHY WOULD THEY FORCE ME TO SEE THIS?
I THOUGHT BRAE AND ME WERE FRIENDS.
THIS WASN'T BRAE'S IDEA.
BRAE OKAYED ME PAYING YOU OFF.
BUT BRINGING YOU HERE...SHOWING YOU THIS...

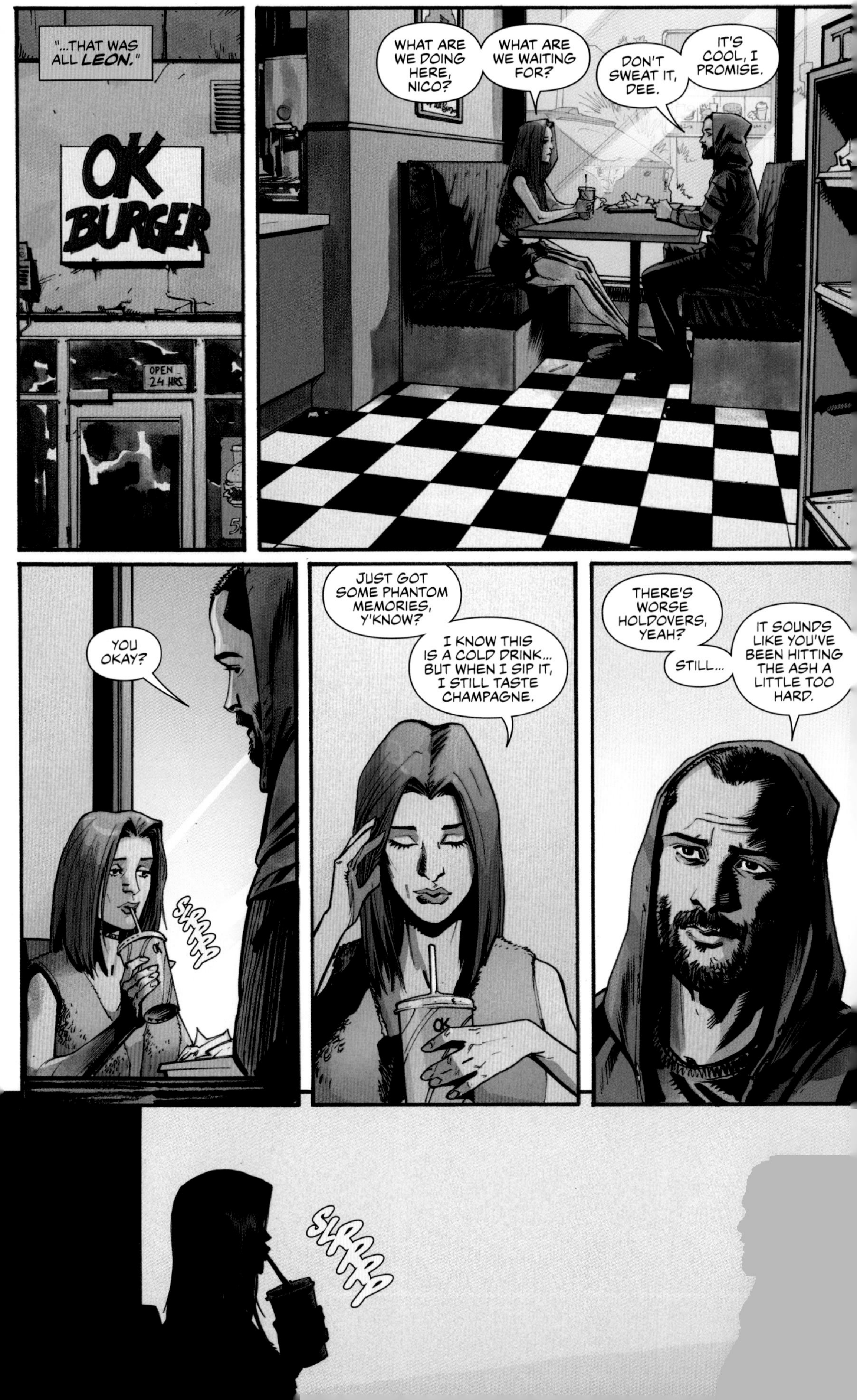

"...THAT WAS ALL LEON."
OK BURGER
OPEN 24 HRS
WHAT ARE WE DOING HERE, NICO?
WHAT ARE WE WAITING FOR?
DON'T SWEAT IT, DEE.
IT'S COOL, I PROMISE.
YOU OKAY?
SLRRRP
JUST GOT SOME PHANTOM MEMORIES, Y'KNOW?
I KNOW THIS IS A COLD DRINK... BUT WHEN I SIP IT, I STILL TASTE CHAMPAGNE.
THERE'S WORSE HOLDOVERS, YEAH?
STILL...
IT SOUNDS LIKE YOU'VE BEEN HITTING THE ASH A LITTLE TOO HARD.
SLRRRP

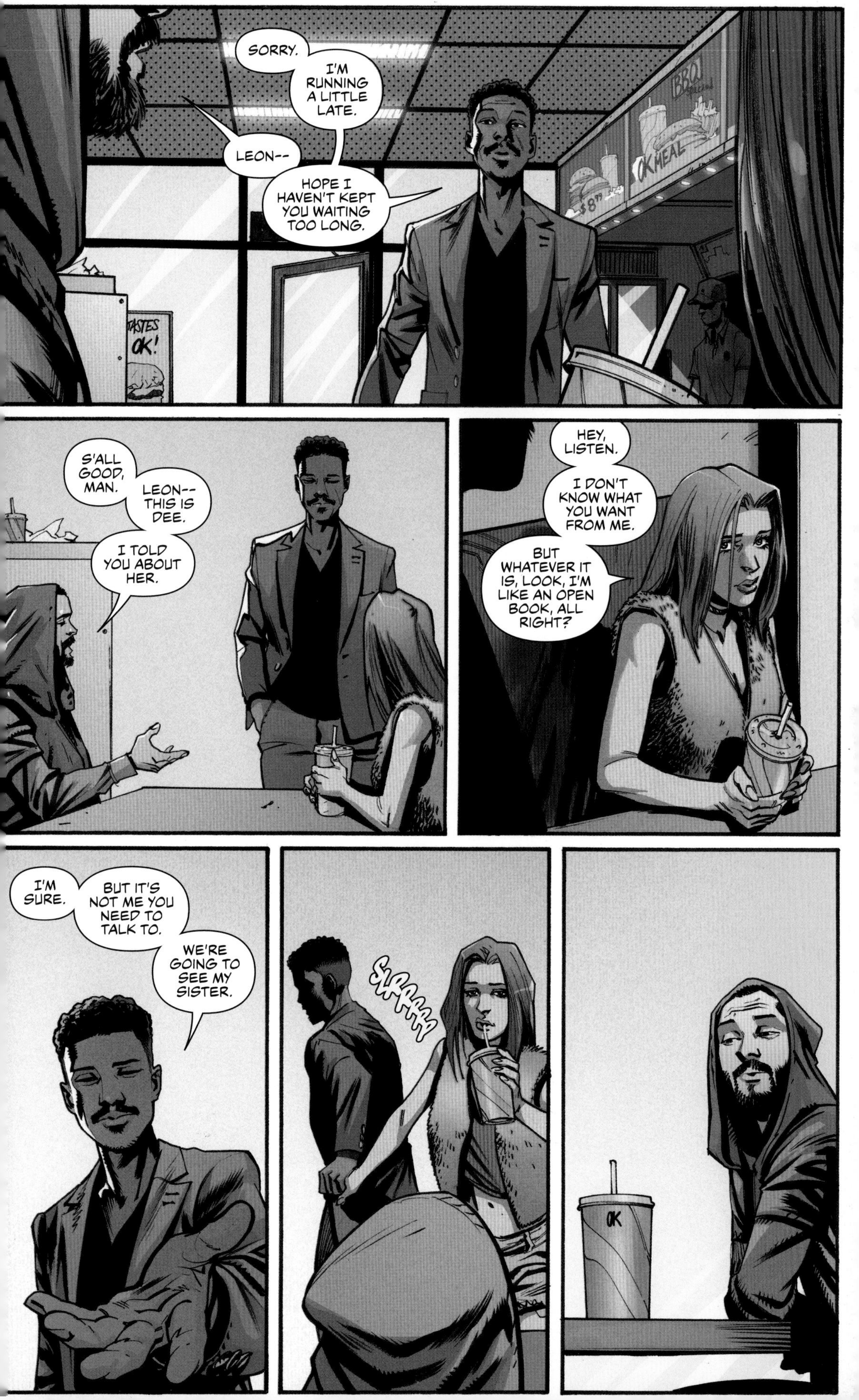
SORRY.
I'M RUNNING A LITTLE LATE.
LEON--
HOPE I HAVEN'T KEPT YOU WAITING TOO LONG.
BBQ
OK MEAL
$8.99
TASTES OK!
S'ALL GOOD, MAN.
LEON-- THIS IS DEE.
I TOLD YOU ABOUT HER.
HEY, LISTEN.
I DON'T KNOW WHAT YOU WANT FROM ME.
BUT WHATEVER IT IS, LOOK, I'M LIKE AN OPEN BOOK, ALL RIGHT?
I'M SURE.
BUT IT'S NOT ME YOU NEED TO TALK TO.
WE'RE GOING TO SEE MY SISTER.
SLRRRRP
OK

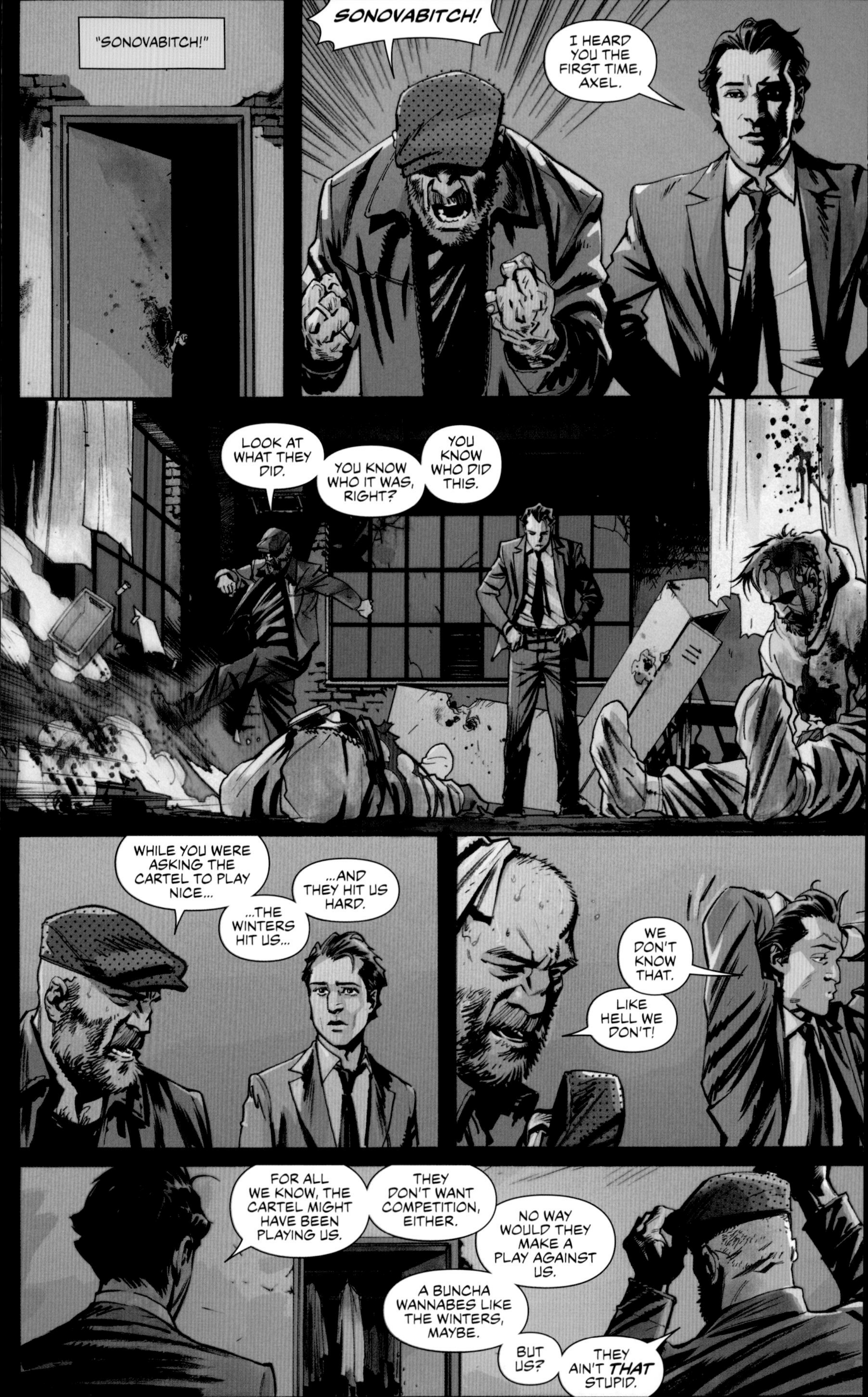
"SONOVABITCH!"
SONOVABITCH!
I HEARD YOU THE FIRST TIME, AXEL.
LOOK AT WHAT THEY DID.
YOU KNOW WHO IT WAS, RIGHT?
YOU KNOW WHO DID THIS.
WHILE YOU WERE ASKING THE CARTEL TO PLAY NICE...
...THE WINTERS HIT US...
...AND THEY HIT US HARD.
WE DON'T KNOW THAT.
LIKE HELL WE DON'T!
FOR ALL WE KNOW, THE CARTEL MIGHT HAVE BEEN PLAYING US.
THEY DON'T WANT COMPETITION, EITHER.
NO WAY WOULD THEY MAKE A PLAY AGAINST US.
A BUNCHA WANNABES LIKE THE WINTERS, MAYBE.
BUT US?
THEY AIN'T THAT STUPID.

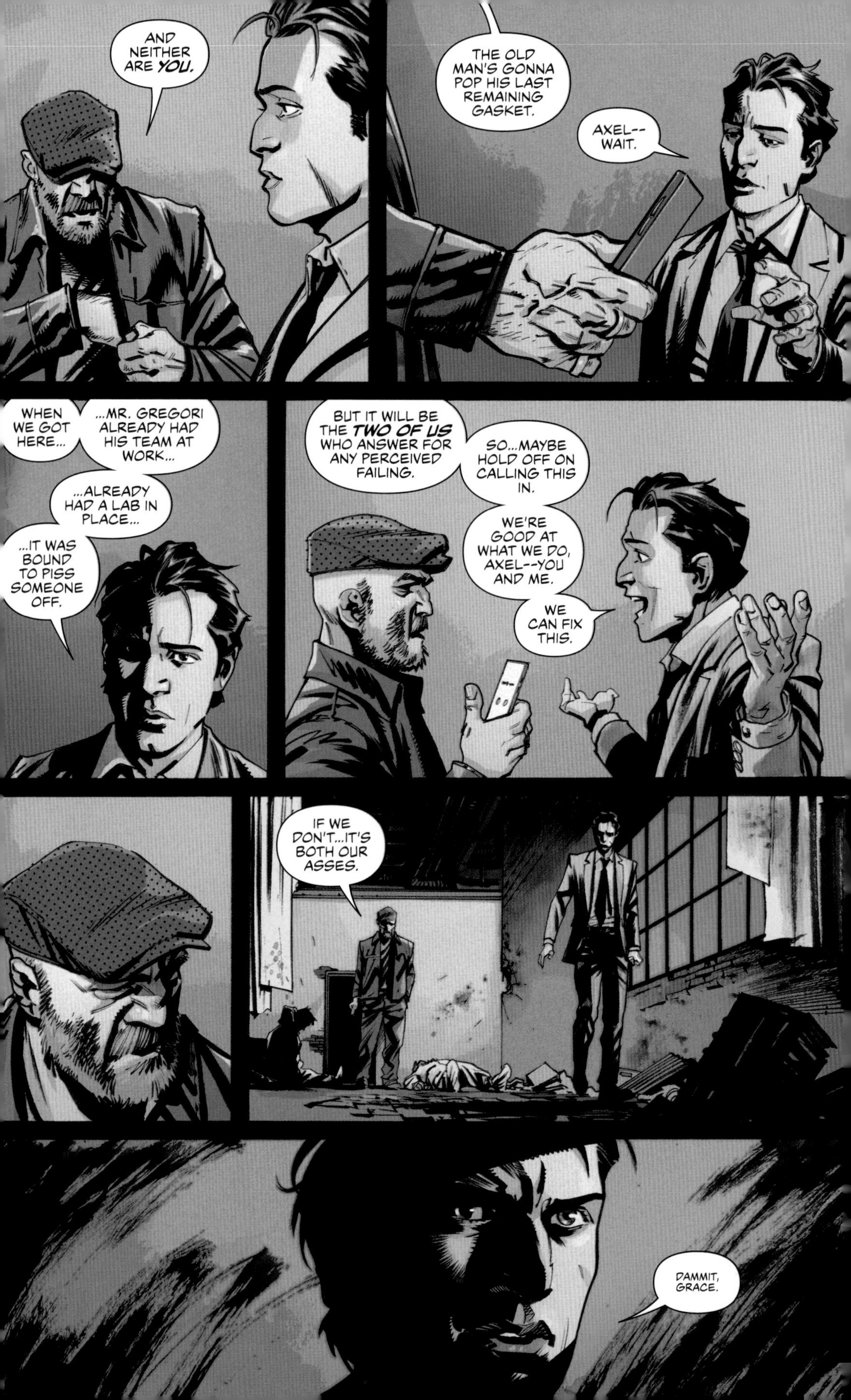
AND NEITHER ARE YOU.
THE OLD MAN'S GONNA POP HIS LAST REMAINING GASKET.
AXEL-- WAIT.
WHEN WE GOT HERE...
...MR. GREGORI ALREADY HAD HIS TEAM AT WORK...
...ALREADY HAD A LAB IN PLACE...
...IT WAS BOUND TO PISS SOMEONE OFF.
BUT IT WILL BE THE TWO OF US WHO ANSWER FOR ANY PERCEIVED FAILING.
SO...MAYBE HOLD OFF ON CALLING THIS IN.
WE'RE GOOD AT WHAT WE DO, AXEL--YOU AND ME.
WE CAN FIX THIS.
IF WE DON'T...IT'S BOTH OUR ASSES.
DAMMIT, GRACE.

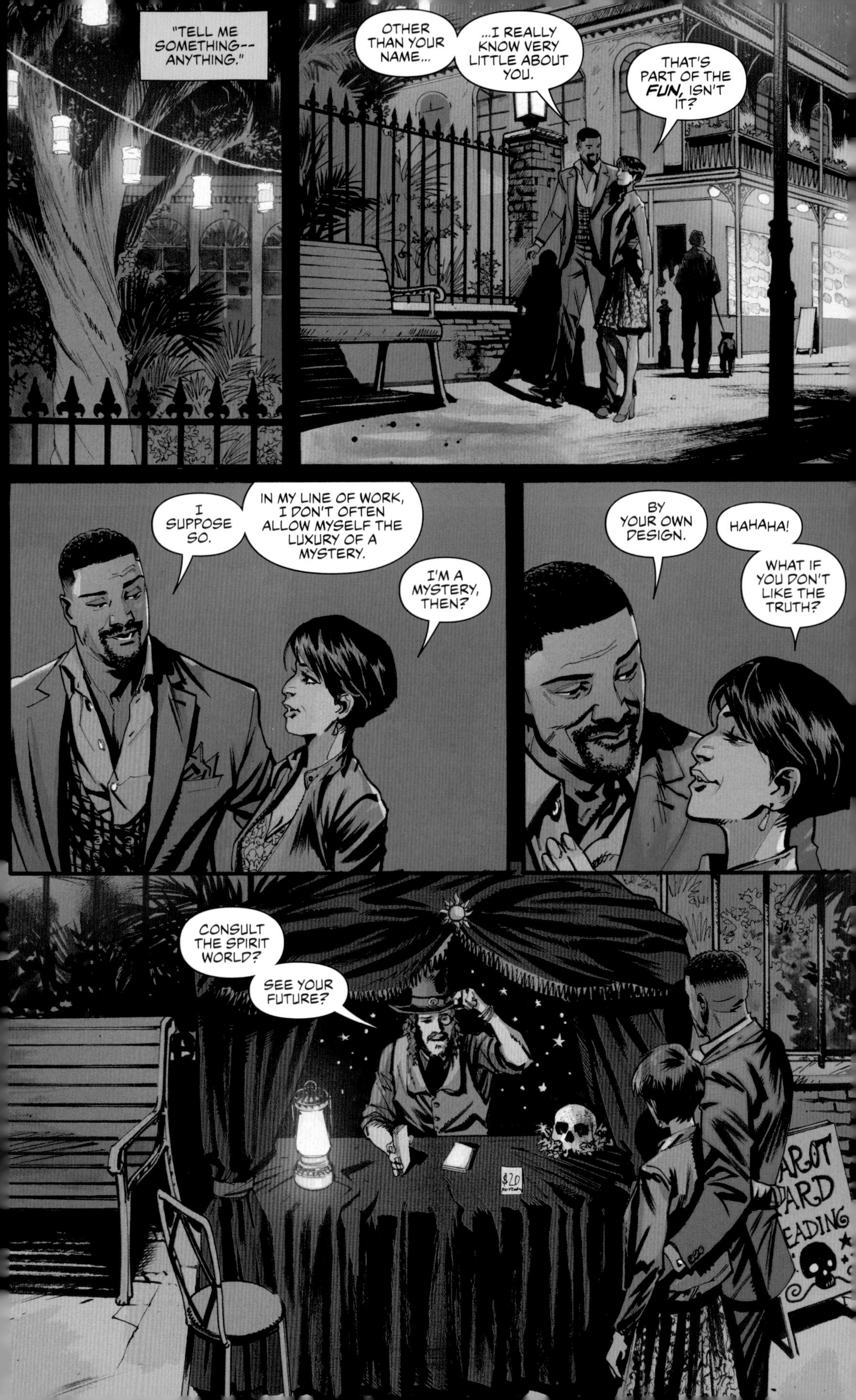
"TELL ME SOMETHING--ANYTHING."
OTHER THAN YOUR NAME...
...I REALLY KNOW VERY LITTLE ABOUT YOU.
THAT'S PART OF THE FUN, ISN'T IT?
I SUPPOSE SO.
IN MY LINE OF WORK, I DON'T OFTEN ALLOW MYSELF THE LUXURY OF A MYSTERY.
I'M A MYSTERY, THEN?
BY YOUR OWN DESIGN.
HAHAHA!
WHAT IF YOU DON'T LIKE THE TRUTH?
CONSULT THE SPIRIT WORLD?
SEE YOUR FUTURE?
$20

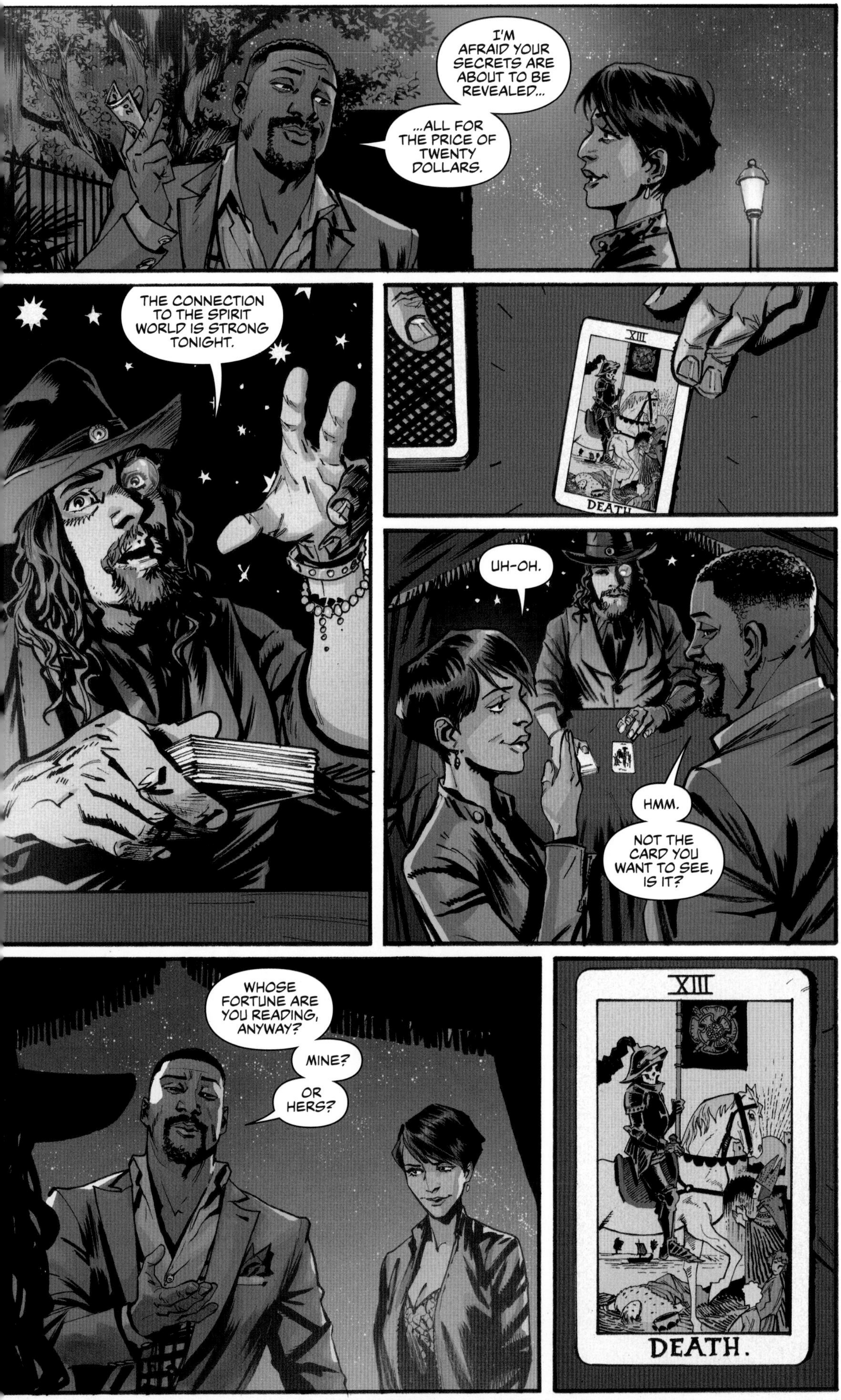

I'M AFRAID YOUR SECRETS ARE ABOUT TO BE REVEALED...
...ALL FOR THE PRICE OF TWENTY DOLLARS.
THE CONNECTION TO THE SPIRIT WORLD IS STRONG TONIGHT.
XIII
DEATH
UH-OH.
HMM.
NOT THE CARD YOU WANT TO SEE, IS IT?
WHOSE FORTUNE ARE YOU READING, ANYWAY?
MINE?
OR HERS?
XIII
DEATH.

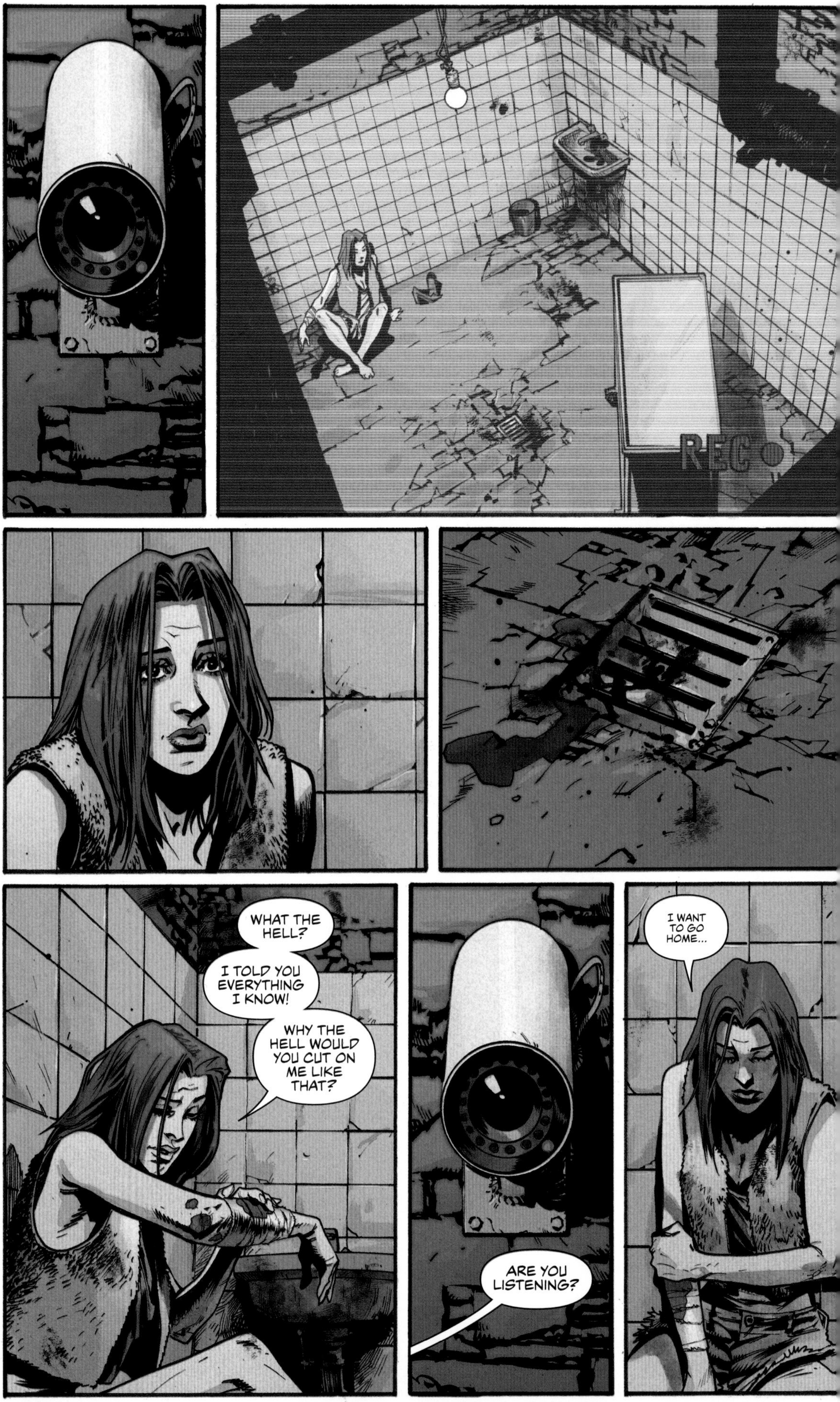
REC
WHAT THE HELL?
I TOLD YOU EVERYTHING I KNOW!
WHY THE HELL WOULD YOU CUT ON ME LIKE THAT?
ARE YOU LISTENING?
I WANT TO GO HOME...

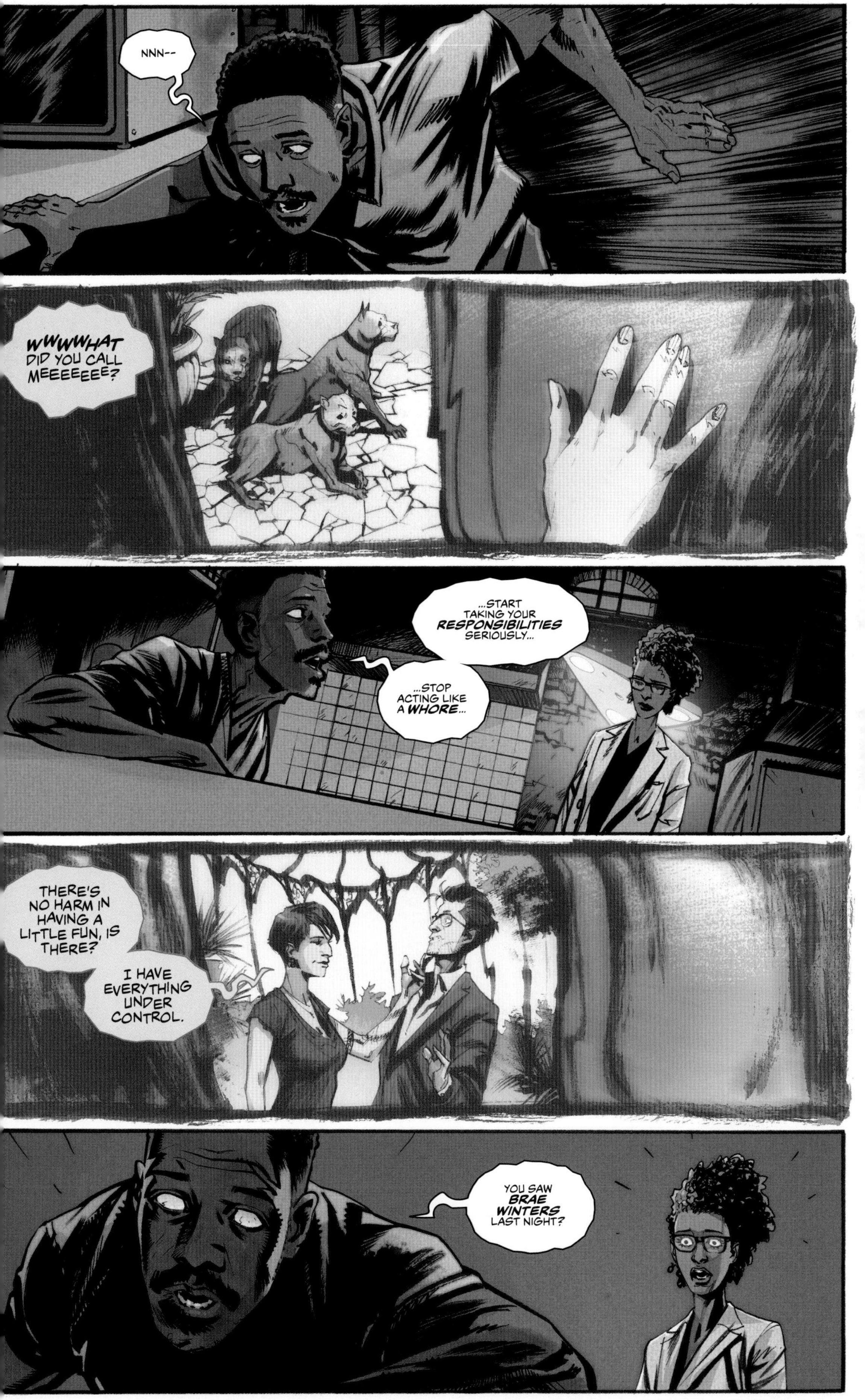
NNN--
WWWWHAT DID YOU CALL MEEEEEEE?
...START TAKING YOUR RESPONSIBILITIES SERIOUSLY...
...STOP ACTING LIKE A WHORE...
THERE'S NO HARM IN HAVING A LITTLE FUN, IS THERE?
I HAVE EVERYTHING UNDER CONTROL.
YOU SAW BRAE WINTERS LAST NIGHT?

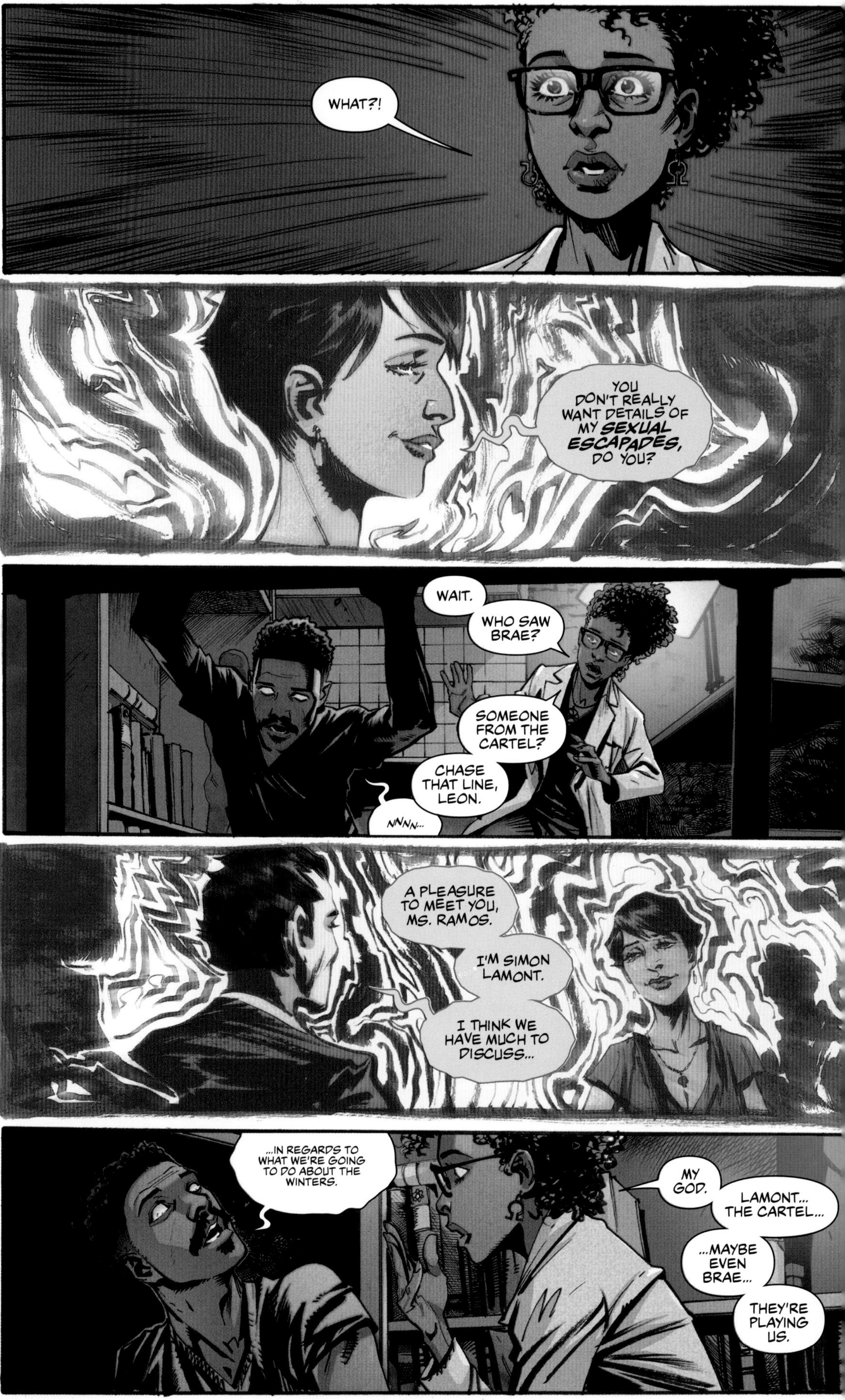
WHAT?!
YOU DON'T REALLY WANT DETAILS OF MY SEXUAL ESCAPADES, DO YOU?
WAIT.
WHO SAW BRAE?
SOMEONE FROM THE CARTEL?
CHASE THAT LINE, LEON.
NNNN...
A PLEASURE TO MEET YOU, MS. RAMOS.
I'M SIMON LAMONT.
I THINK WE HAVE MUCH TO DISCUSS...
...IN REGARDS TO WHAT WE'RE GOING TO DO ABOUT THE WINTERS.
MY GOD.
LAMONT... THE CARTEL...
...MAYBE EVEN BRAE...
THEY'RE PLAYING US.

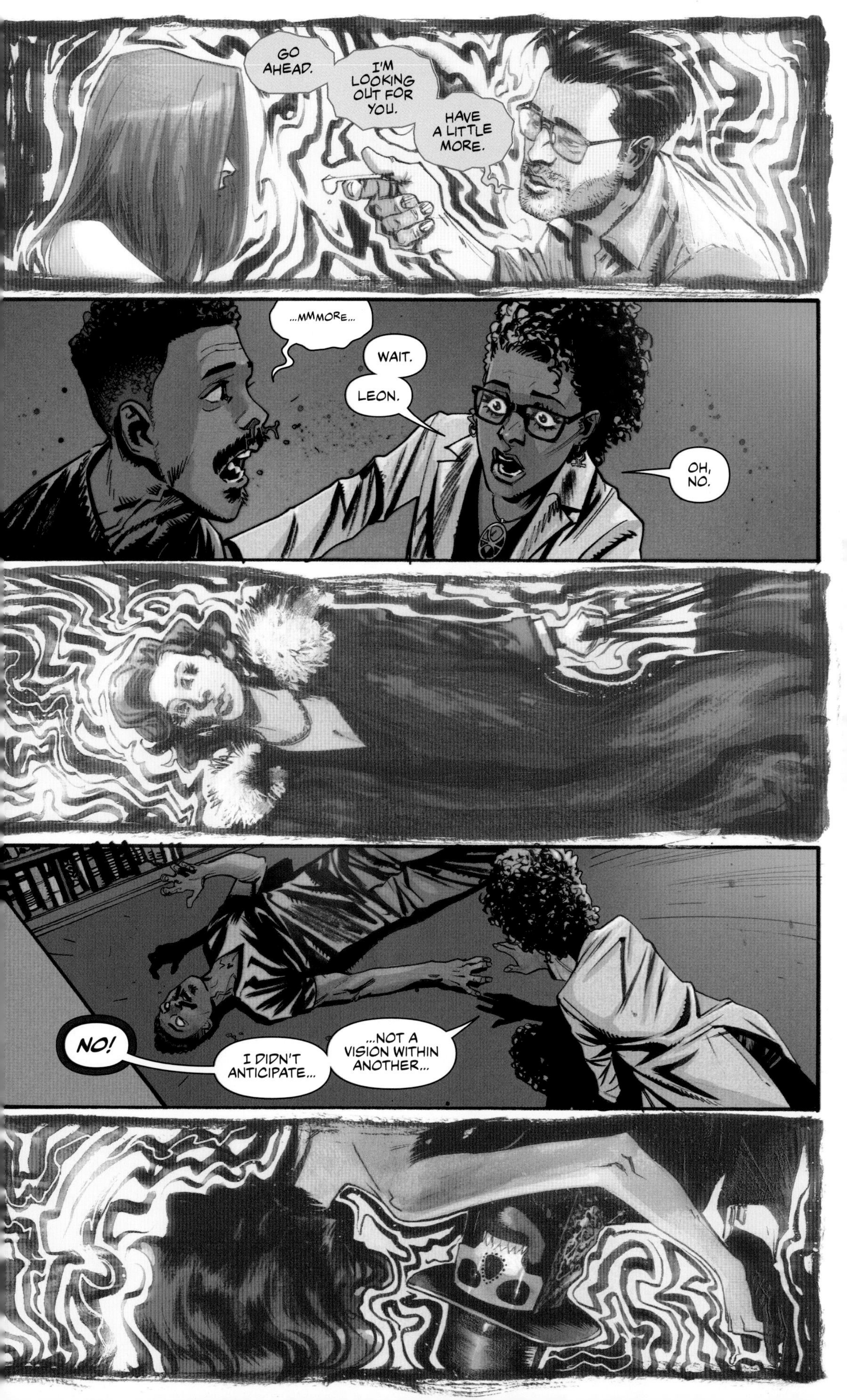
GO AHEAD.
I'M LOOKING OUT FOR YOU.
HAVE A LITTLE MORE.
...MMMORE...
WAIT.
LEON.
OH, NO.
NO!
I DIDN'T ANTICIPATE...
...NOT A VISION WITHIN ANOTHER...

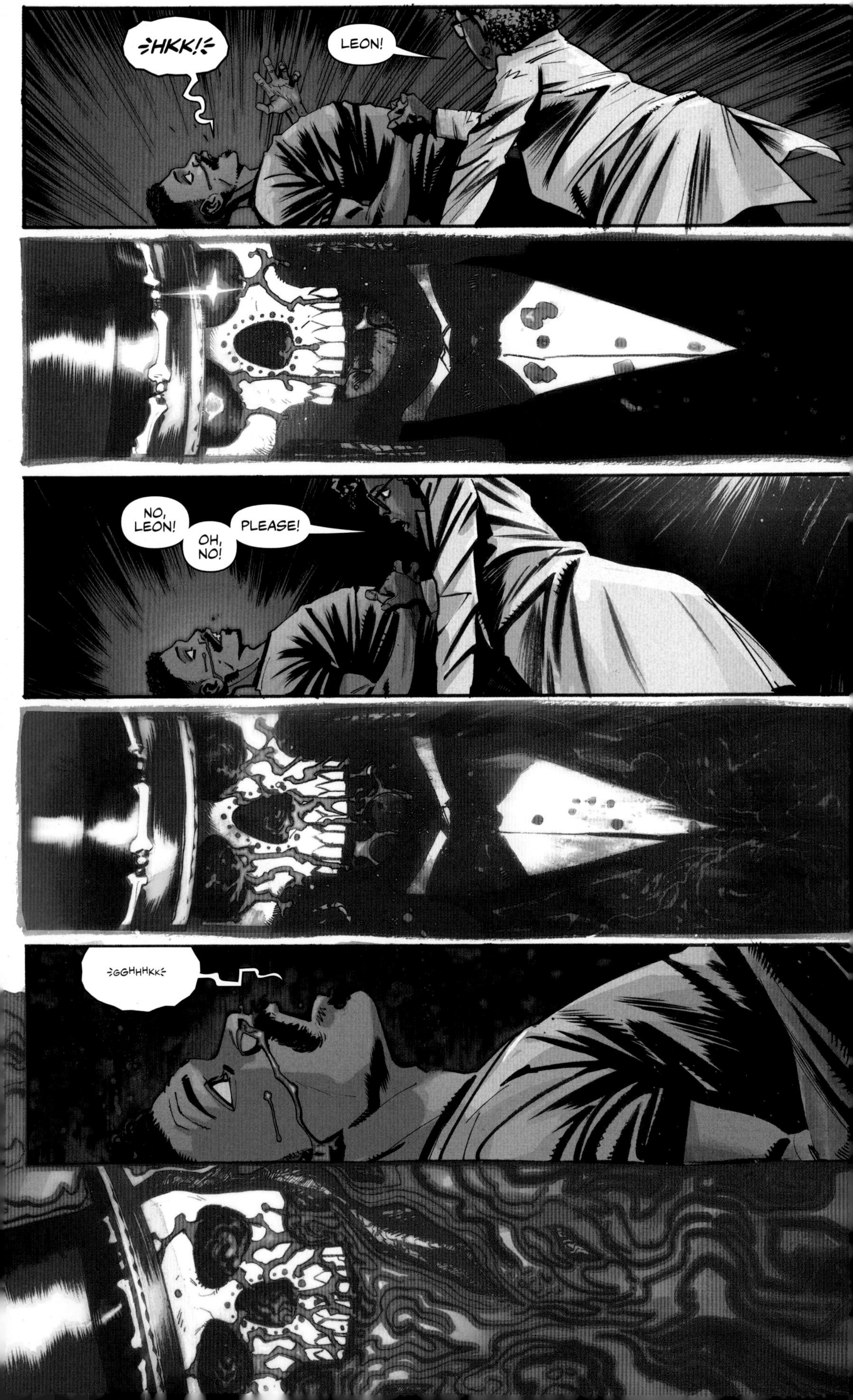
HKK!
LEON!
NO, LEON!
OH, NO!
PLEASE!
GGHHHKK

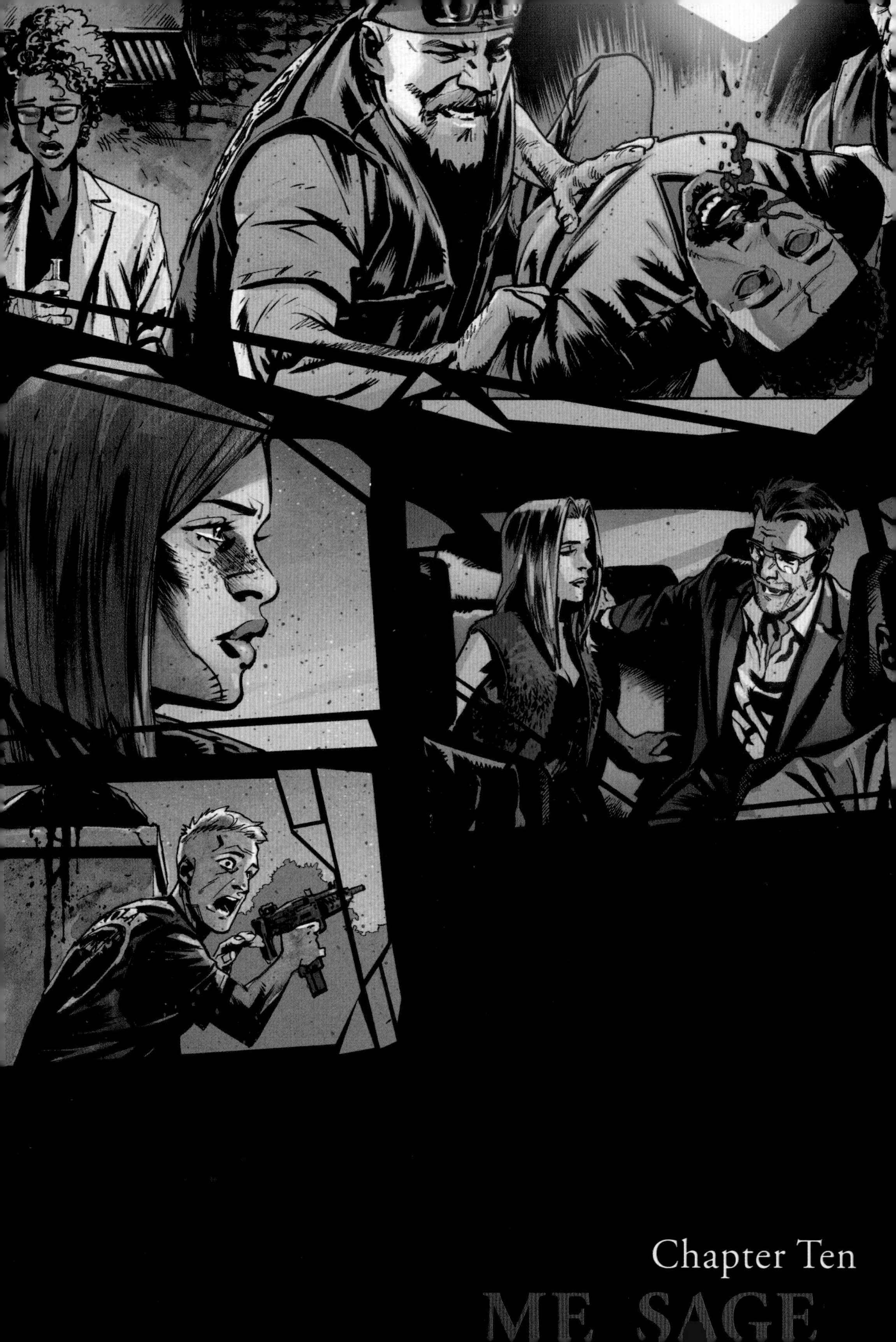

Chapter Ten

ME SAGE

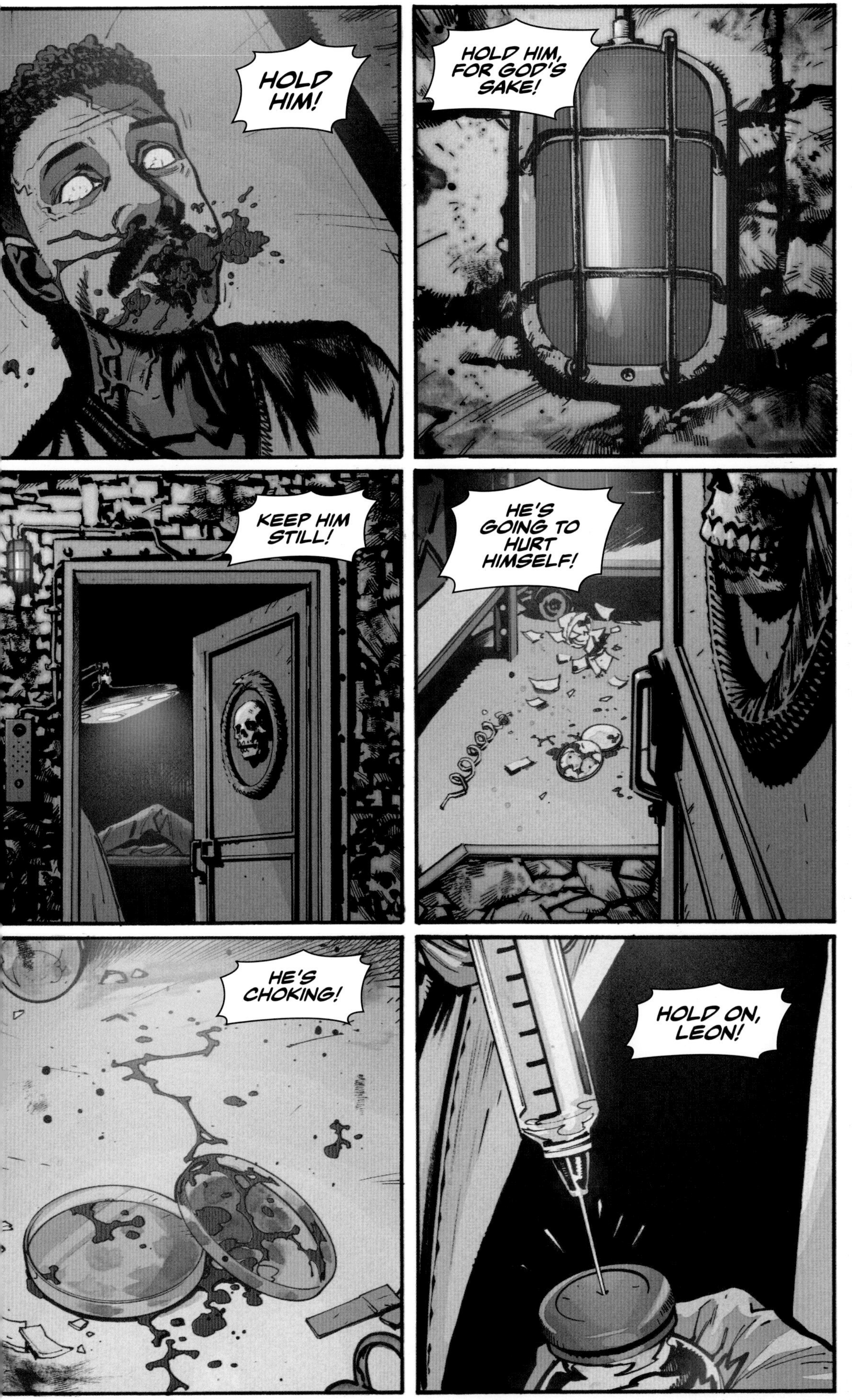
HOLD HIM!
HOLD HIM, FOR GOD'S SAKE!
KEEP HIM STILL!
HE'S GOING TO HURT HIMSELF!
HE'S CHOKING!
HOLD ON, LEON!

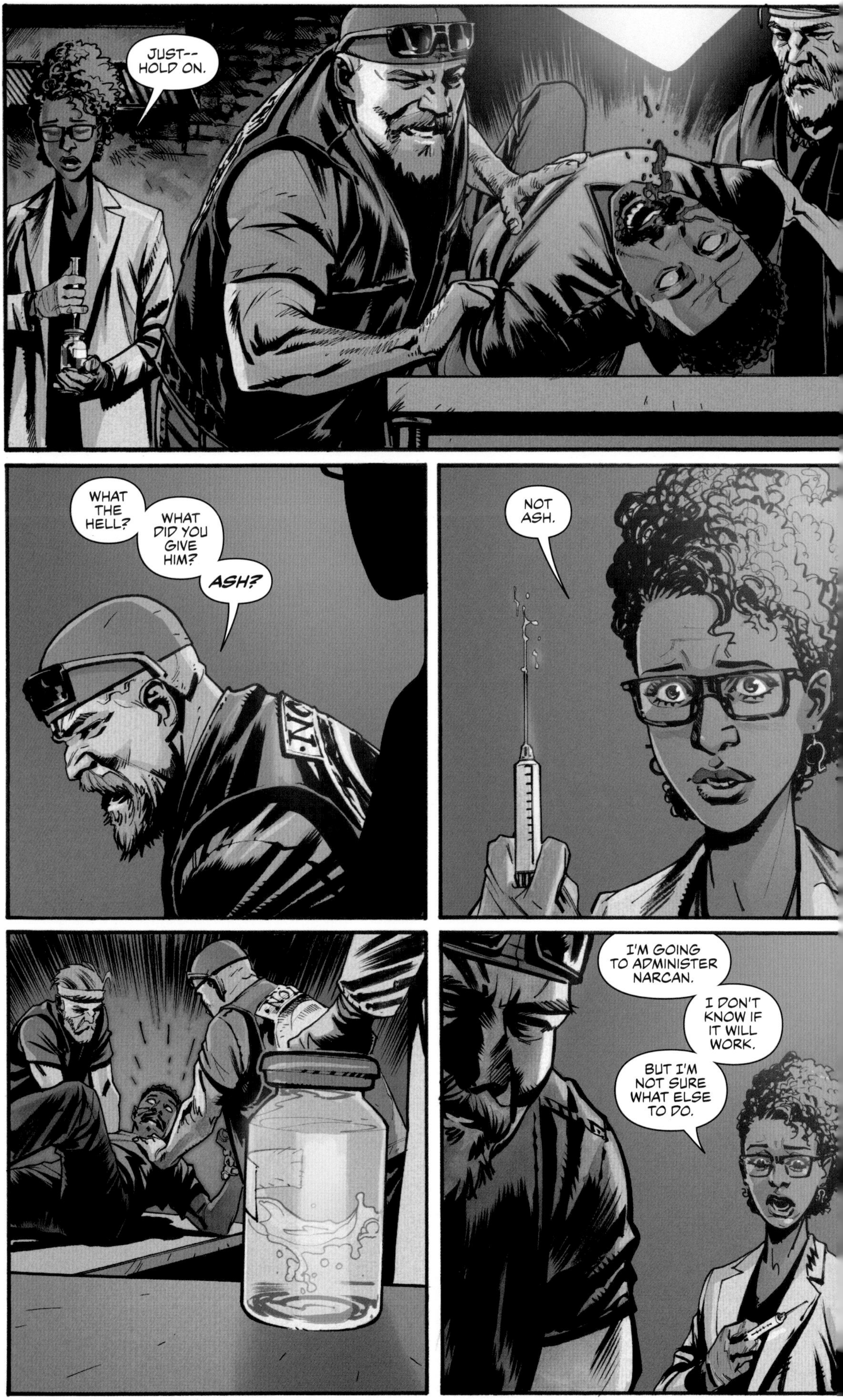
JUST--
HOLD ON.
WHAT THE HELL?
WHAT DID YOU GIVE HIM?
ASH?
NOT ASH.
I'M GOING TO ADMINISTER NARCAN.
I DON'T KNOW IF IT WILL WORK.
BUT I'M NOT SURE WHAT ELSE TO DO.

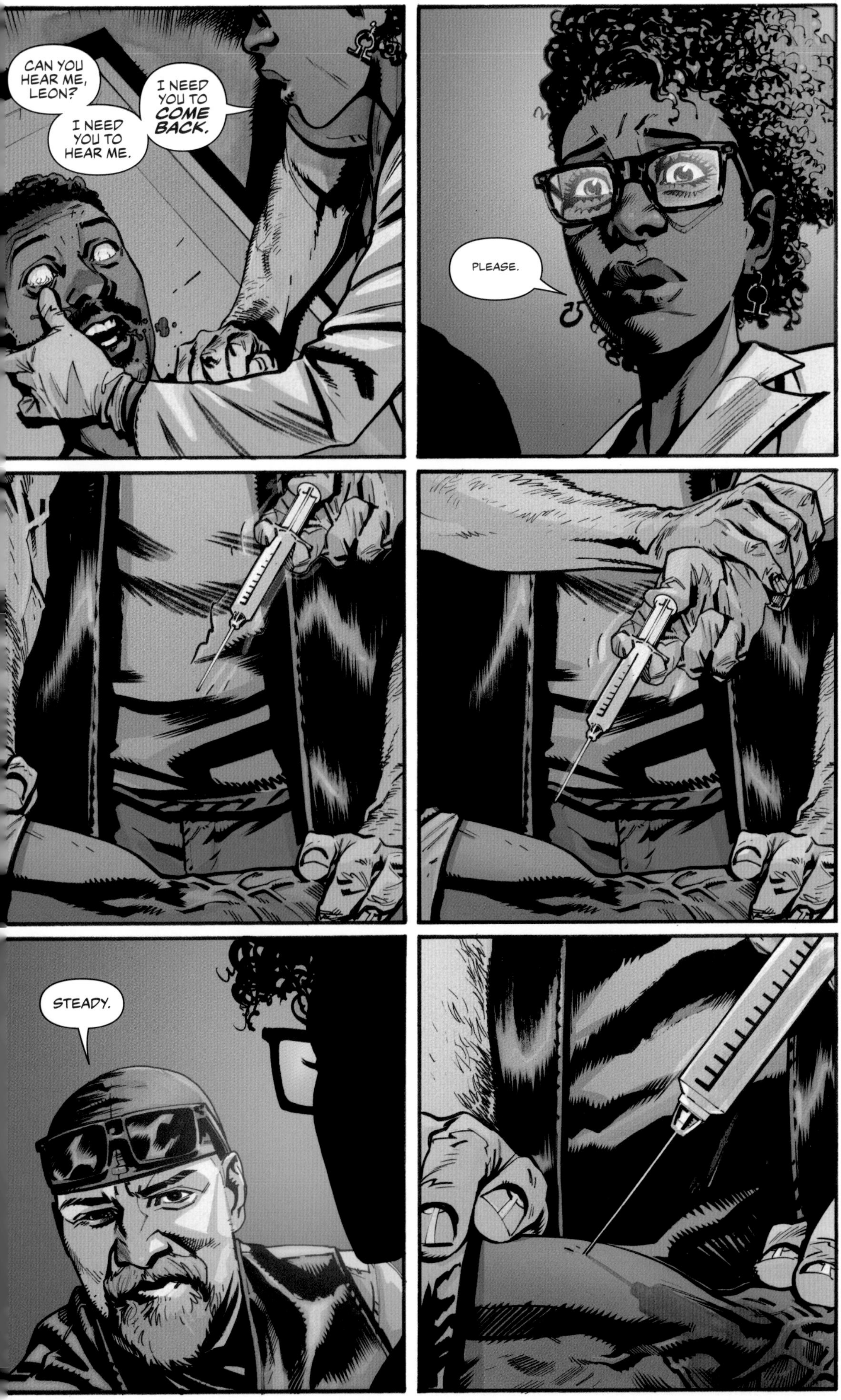
CAN YOU HEAR ME, LEON?
I NEED YOU TO HEAR ME.
I NEED YOU TO COME BACK.
PLEASE.
STEADY.

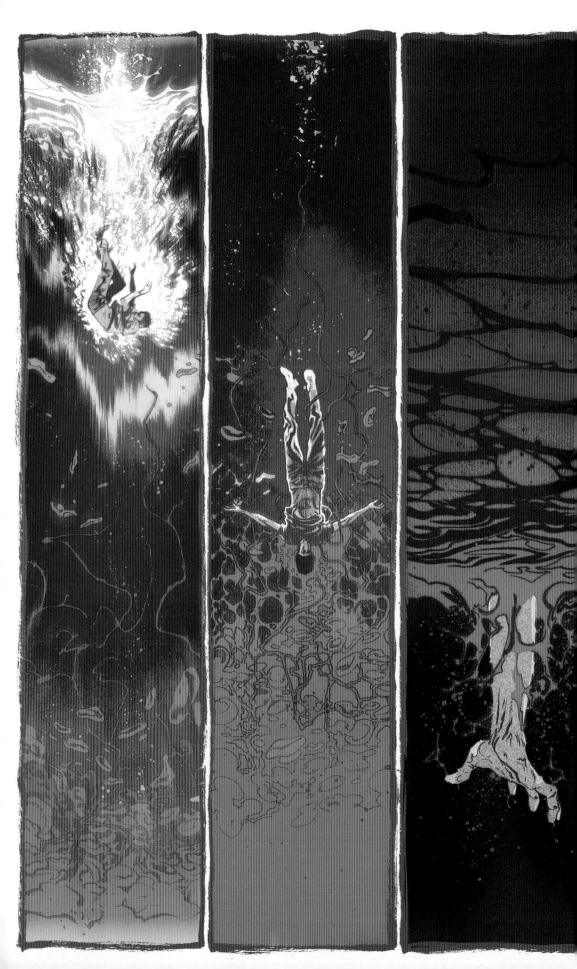

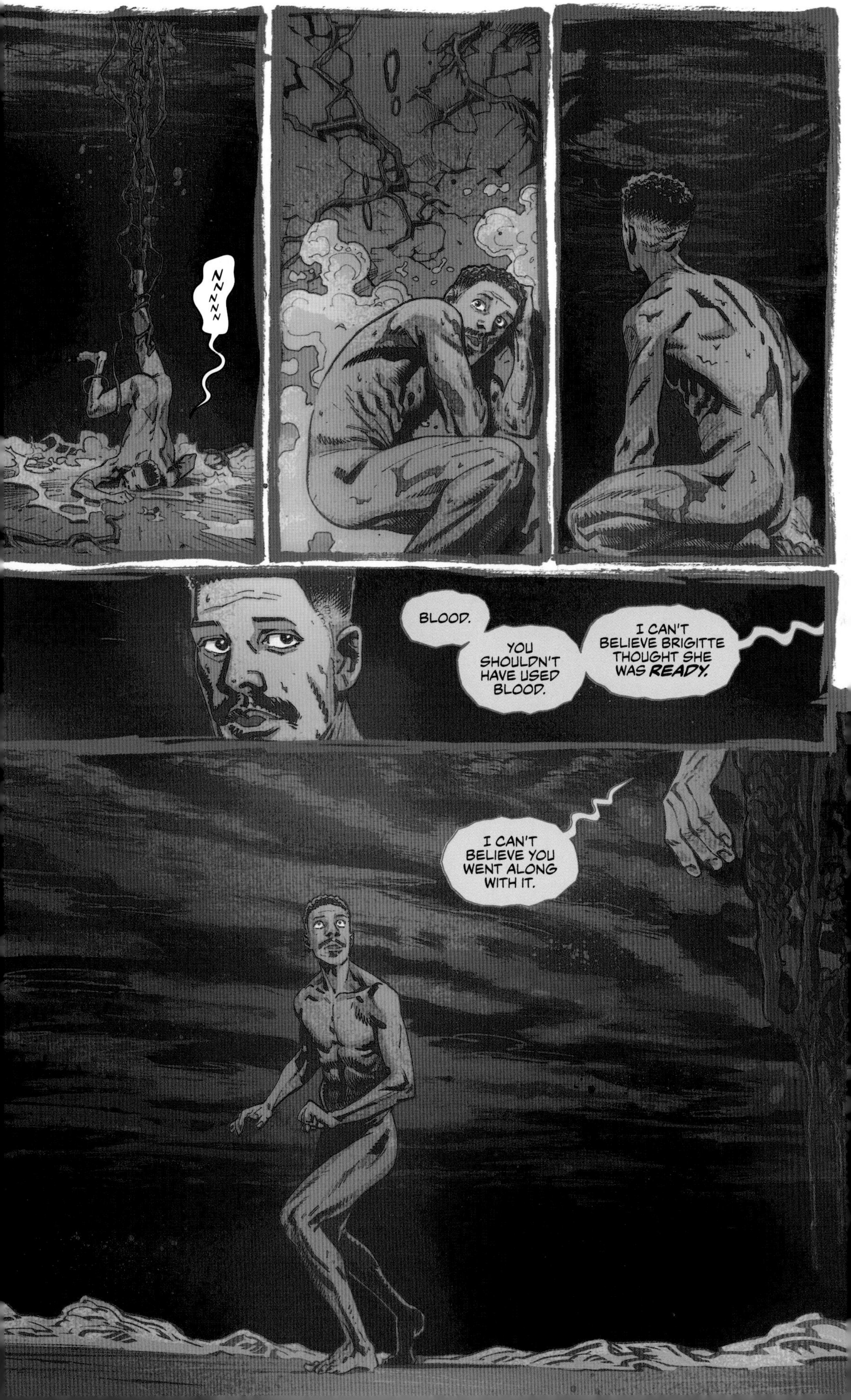
NNNNN
!
BLOOD.
YOU SHOULDN'T HAVE USED BLOOD.
I CAN'T BELIEVE BRIGITTE THOUGHT SHE WAS READY.
I CAN'T BELIEVE YOU WENT ALONG WITH IT.

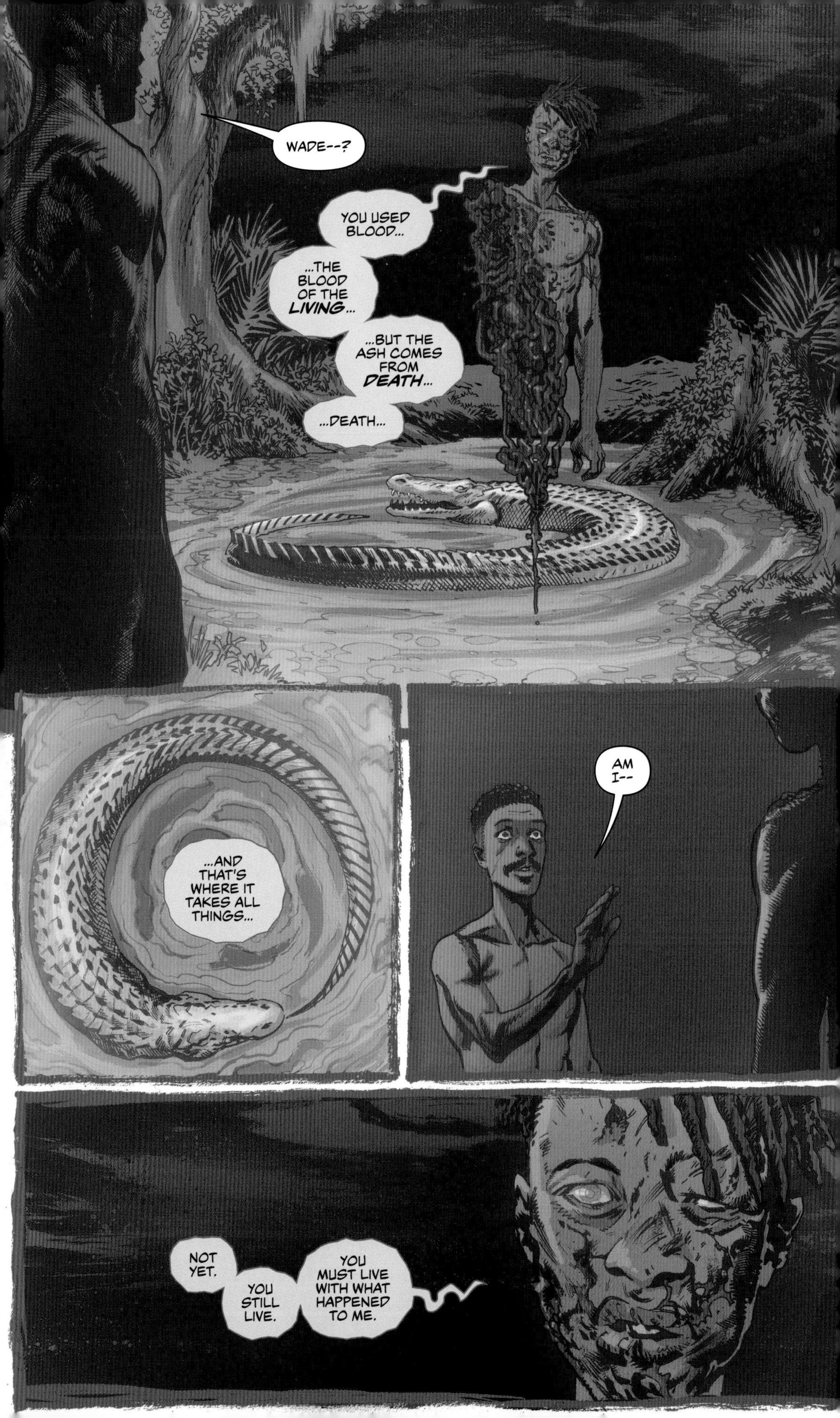
WADE--?
YOU USED BLOOD...
...THE BLOOD OF THE *LIVING*...
...BUT THE ASH COMES FROM *DEATH*...
...DEATH...
...AND THAT'S WHERE IT TAKES ALL THINGS...
AM I--
NOT YET.
YOU STILL LIVE.
YOU MUST LIVE WITH WHAT HAPPENED TO ME.

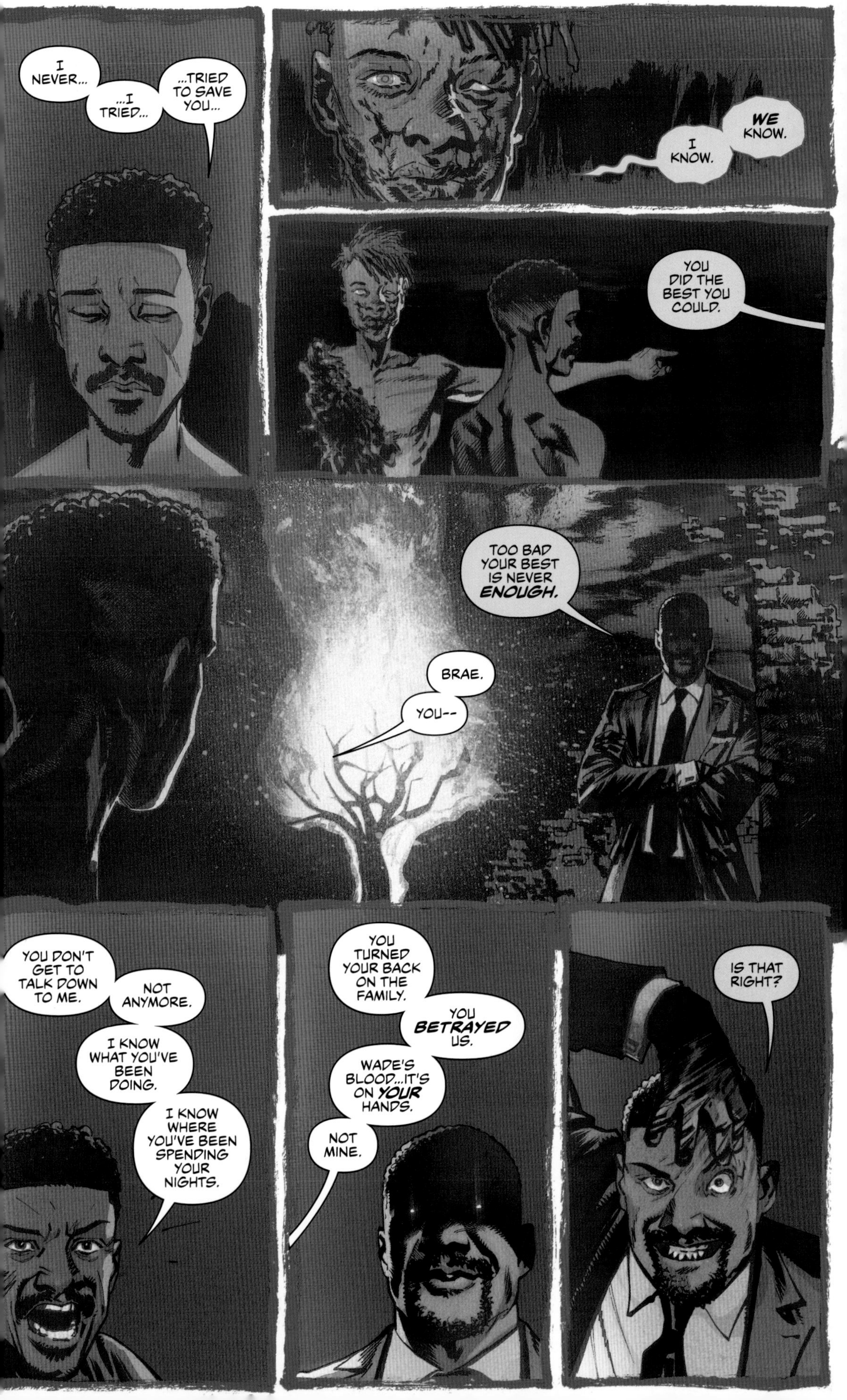
I NEVER...
...I TRIED...
...TRIED TO SAVE YOU...
I KNOW.
WE KNOW.
YOU DID THE BEST YOU COULD.
TOO BAD YOUR BEST IS NEVER ENOUGH.
BRAE.
YOU--
YOU DON'T GET TO TALK DOWN TO ME.
NOT ANYMORE.
I KNOW WHAT YOU'VE BEEN DOING.
I KNOW WHERE YOU'VE BEEN SPENDING YOUR NIGHTS.
YOU TURNED YOUR BACK ON THE FAMILY.
YOU BETRAYED US.
WADE'S BLOOD...IT'S ON YOUR HANDS.
NOT MINE.
IS THAT RIGHT?

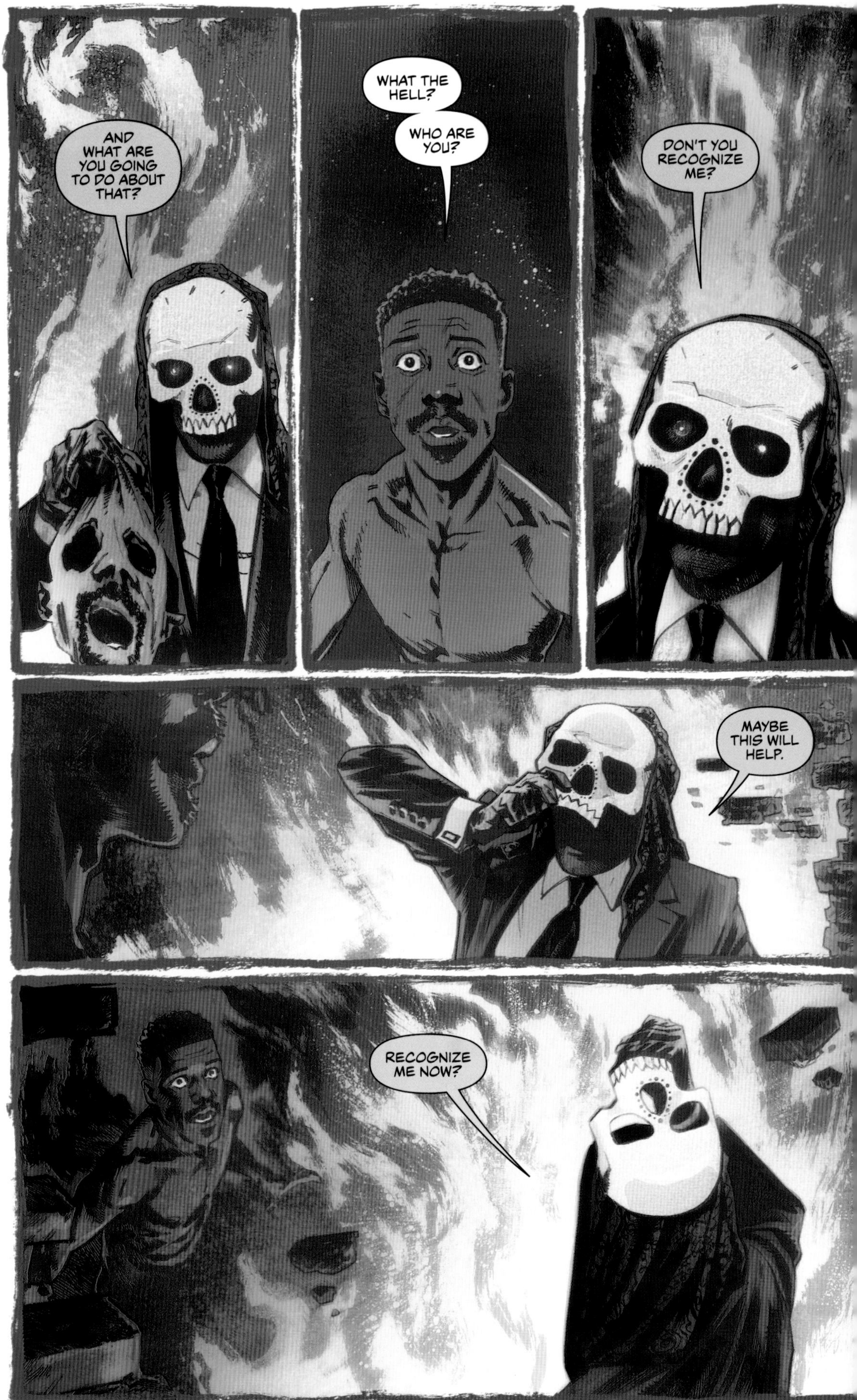
AND WHAT ARE YOU GOING TO DO ABOUT THAT?
WHAT THE HELL?
WHO ARE YOU?
DON'T YOU RECOGNIZE ME?
MAYBE THIS WILL HELP.
RECOGNIZE ME NOW?

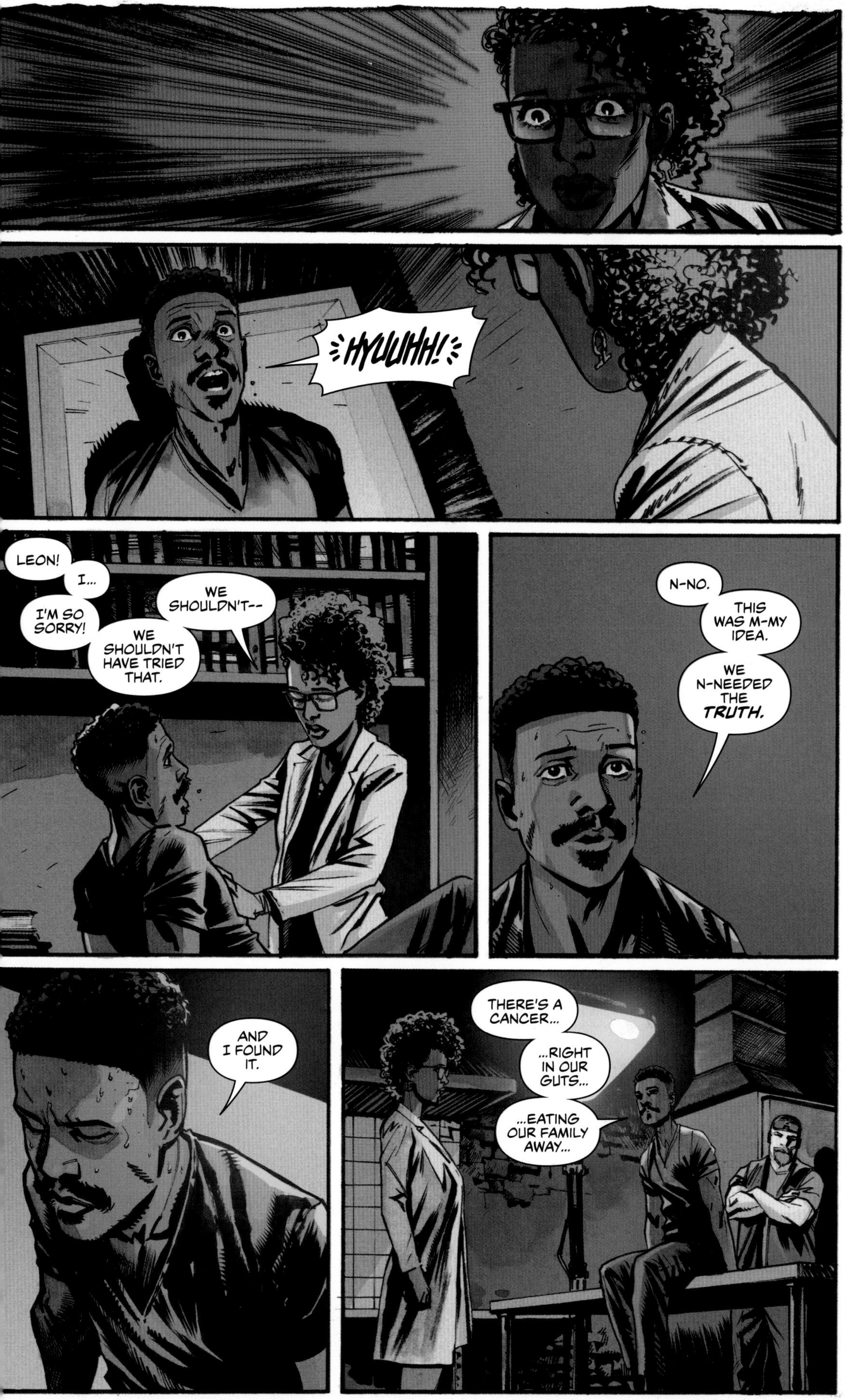
HYUUHH!
LEON!
I...
I'M SO SORRY!
WE SHOULDN'T--
WE SHOULDN'T HAVE TRIED THAT.
N-NO.
THIS WAS M-MY IDEA.
WE N-NEEDED THE *TRUTH.*
AND I FOUND IT.
THERE'S A CANCER...
...RIGHT IN OUR GUTS...
...EATING OUR FAMILY AWAY...

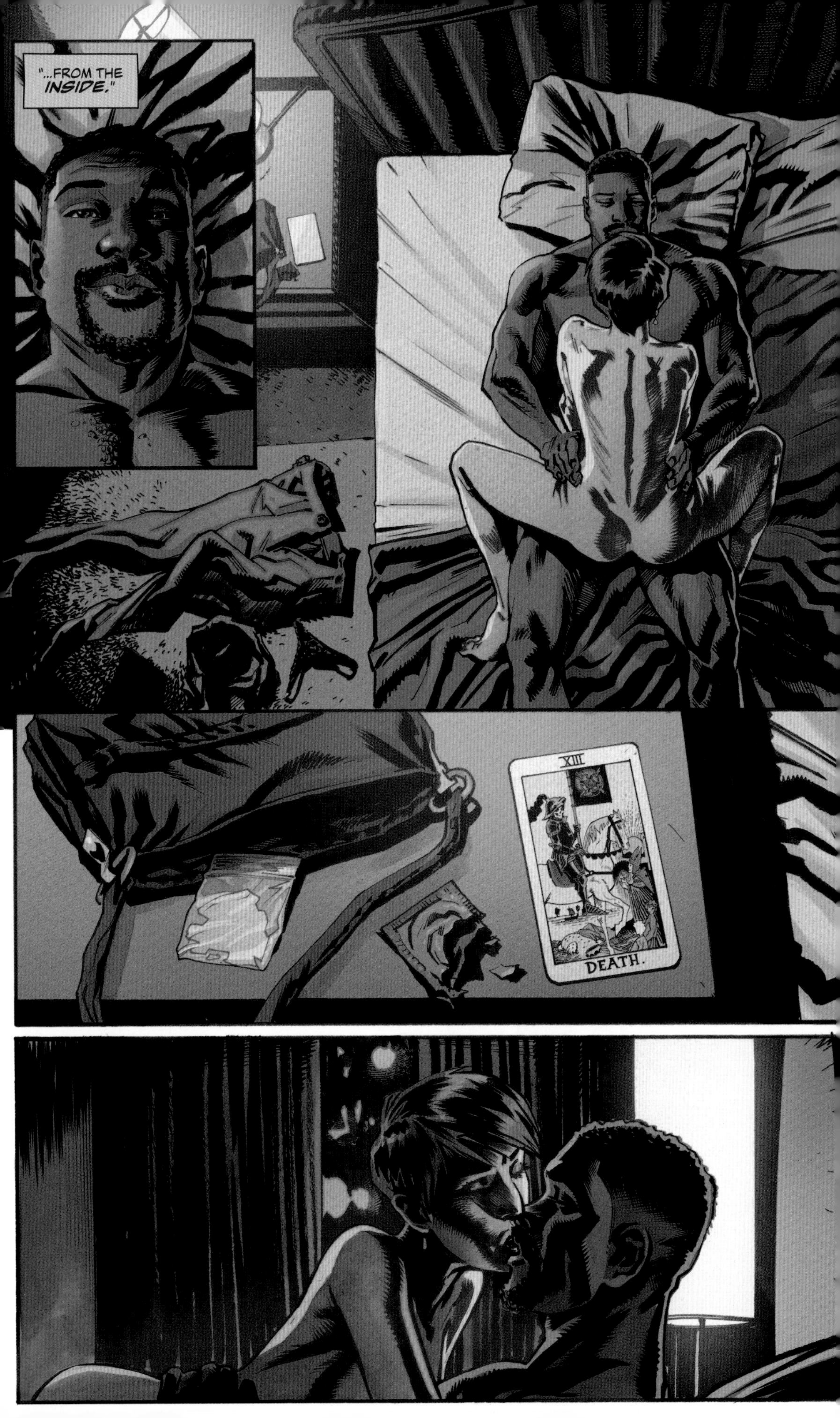
"...FROM THE *INSIDE.*"
XIII
DEATH.

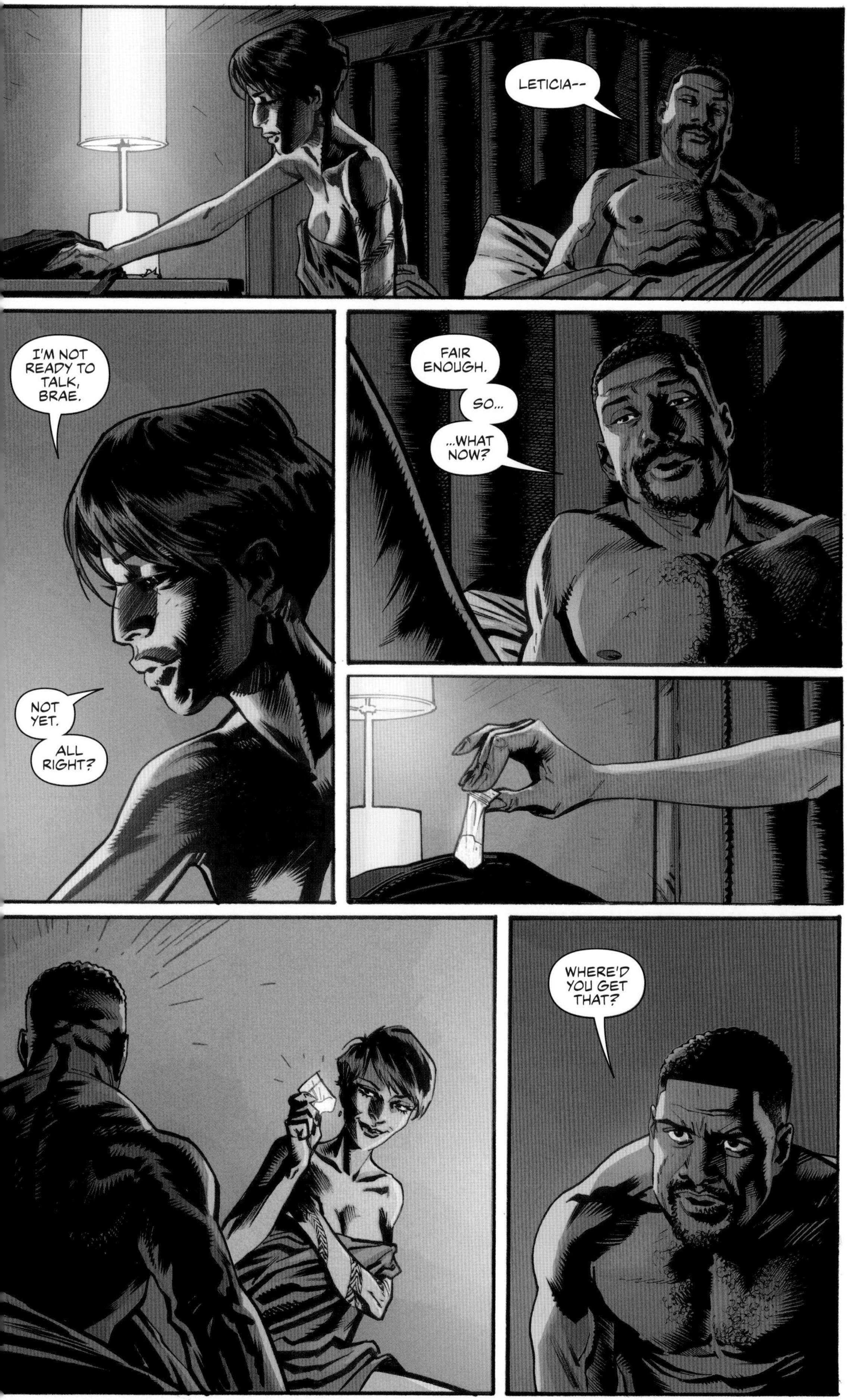
LETICIA--
I'M NOT READY TO TALK, BRAE.
NOT YET.
ALL RIGHT?
FAIR ENOUGH.
SO...
...WHAT NOW?
WHERE'D YOU GET THAT?

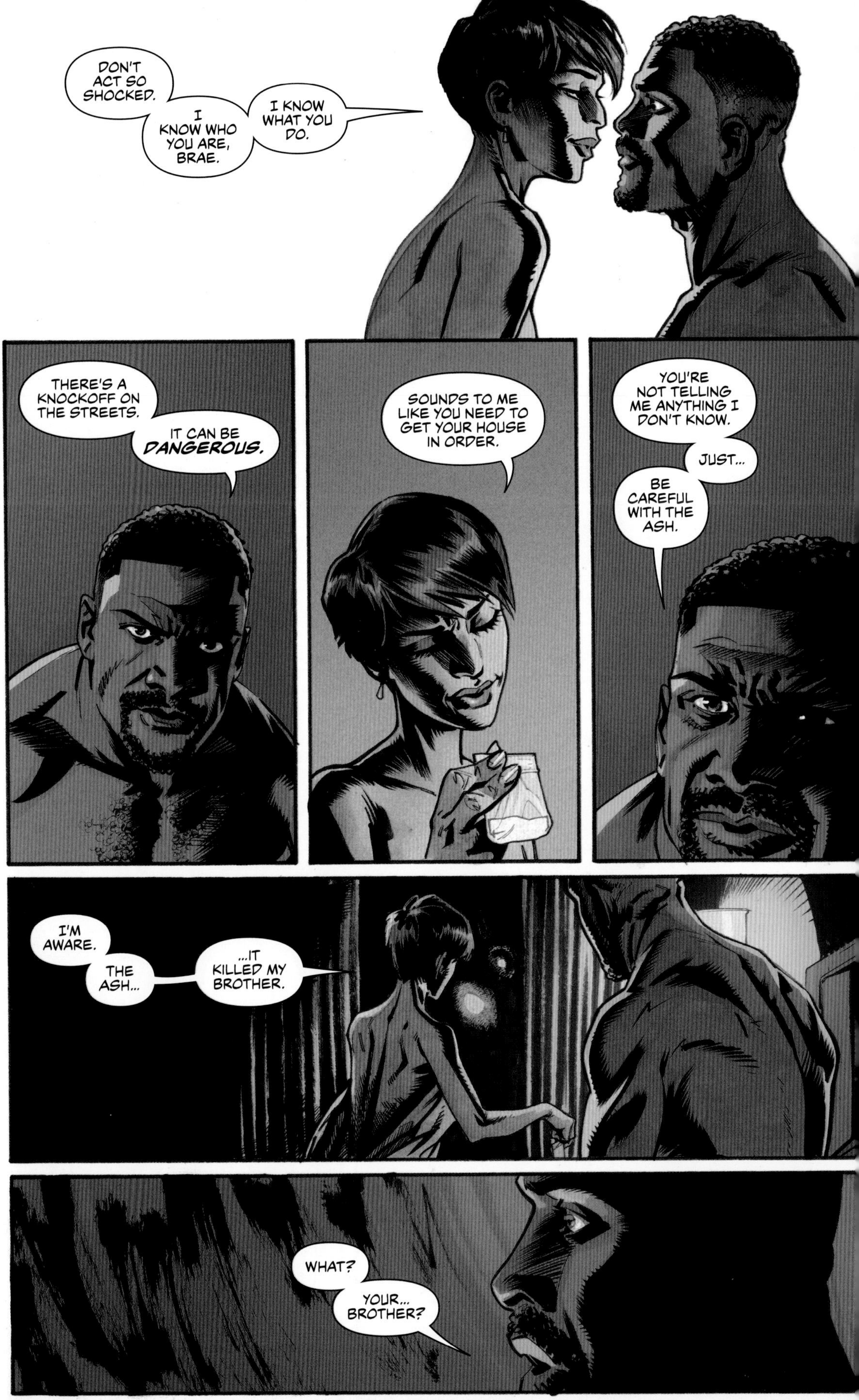
DON'T ACT SO SHOCKED.
I KNOW WHO YOU ARE, BRAE.
I KNOW WHAT YOU DO.
THERE'S A KNOCKOFF ON THE STREETS.
IT CAN BE *DANGEROUS.*
SOUNDS TO ME LIKE YOU NEED TO GET YOUR HOUSE IN ORDER.
YOU'RE NOT TELLING ME ANYTHING I DON'T KNOW.
JUST...
BE CAREFUL WITH THE ASH.
I'M AWARE.
THE ASH...
...IT KILLED MY BROTHER.
WHAT?
YOUR... BROTHER?

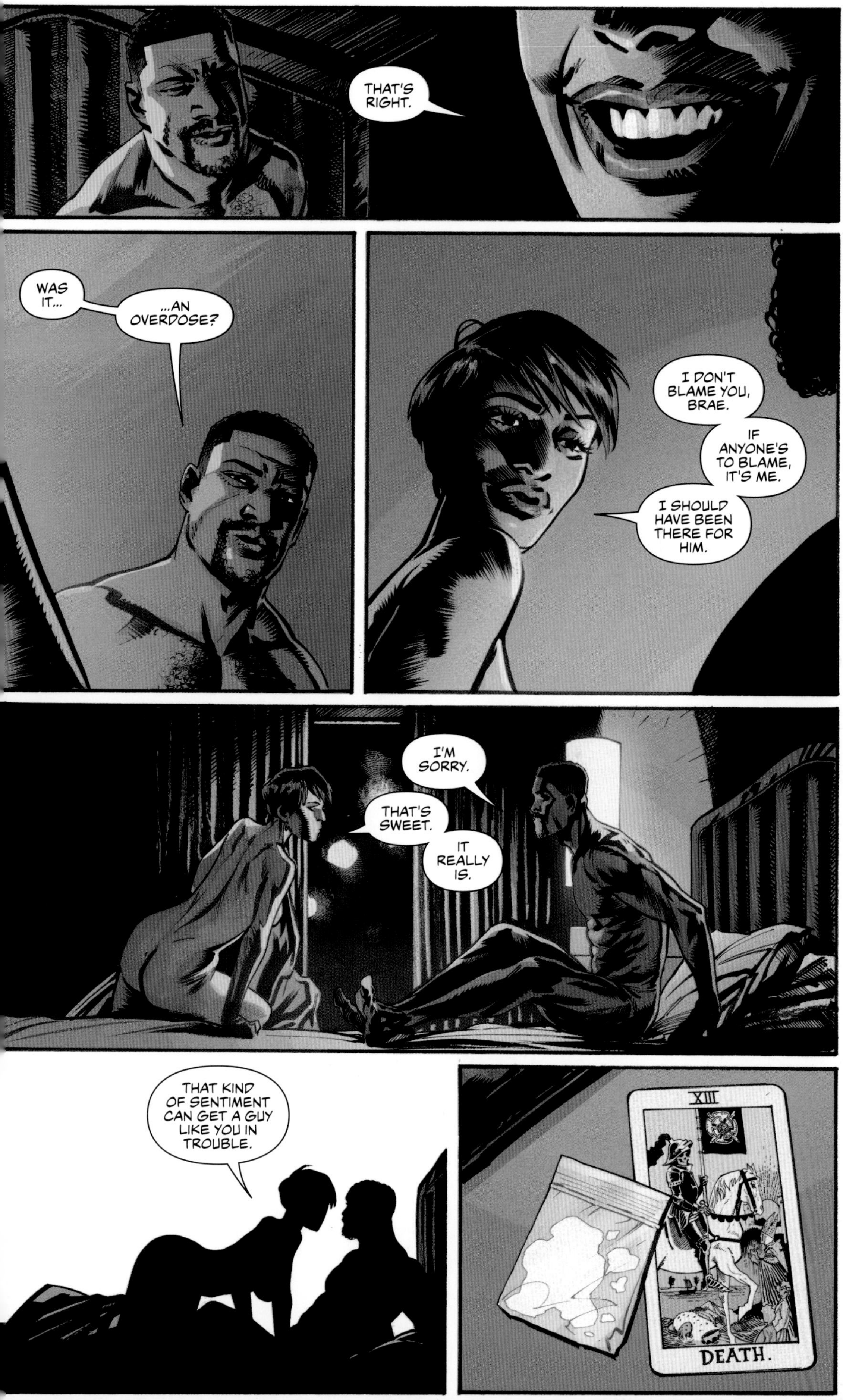
THAT'S RIGHT.
WAS IT...
...AN OVERDOSE?
I DON'T BLAME YOU, BRAE.
IF ANYONE'S TO BLAME, IT'S ME.
I SHOULD HAVE BEEN THERE FOR HIM.
I'M SORRY.
THAT'S SWEET.
IT REALLY IS.
THAT KIND OF SENTIMENT CAN GET A GUY LIKE YOU IN TROUBLE.
XIII
DEATH.

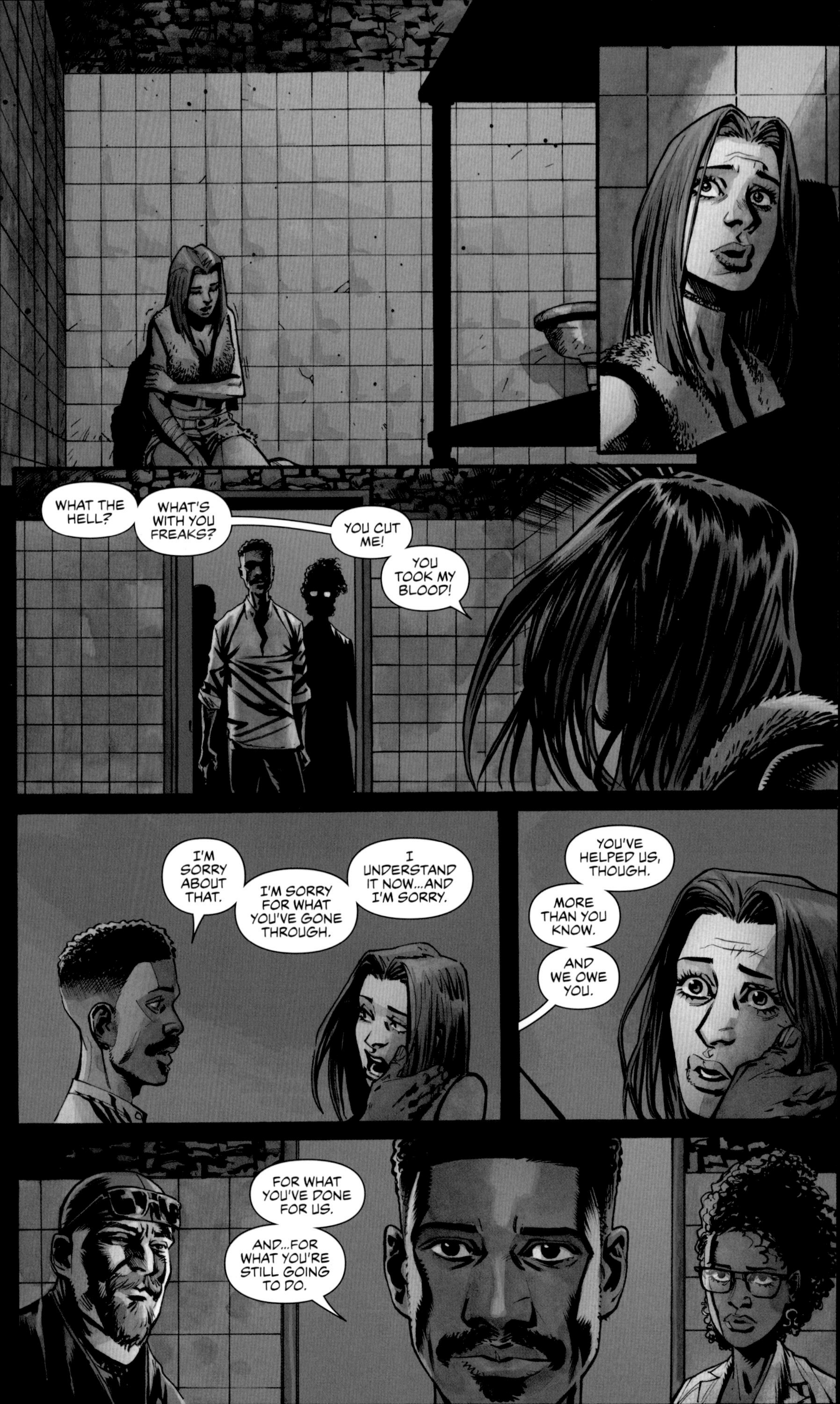
WHAT THE HELL?
WHAT'S WITH YOU FREAKS?
YOU CUT ME!
YOU TOOK MY BLOOD!
I'M SORRY ABOUT THAT.
I'M SORRY FOR WHAT YOU'VE GONE THROUGH.
I UNDERSTAND IT NOW...AND I'M SORRY.
YOU'VE HELPED US, THOUGH.
MORE THAN YOU KNOW.
AND WE OWE YOU.
FOR WHAT YOU'VE DONE FOR US.
AND...FOR WHAT YOU'RE STILL GOING TO DO.

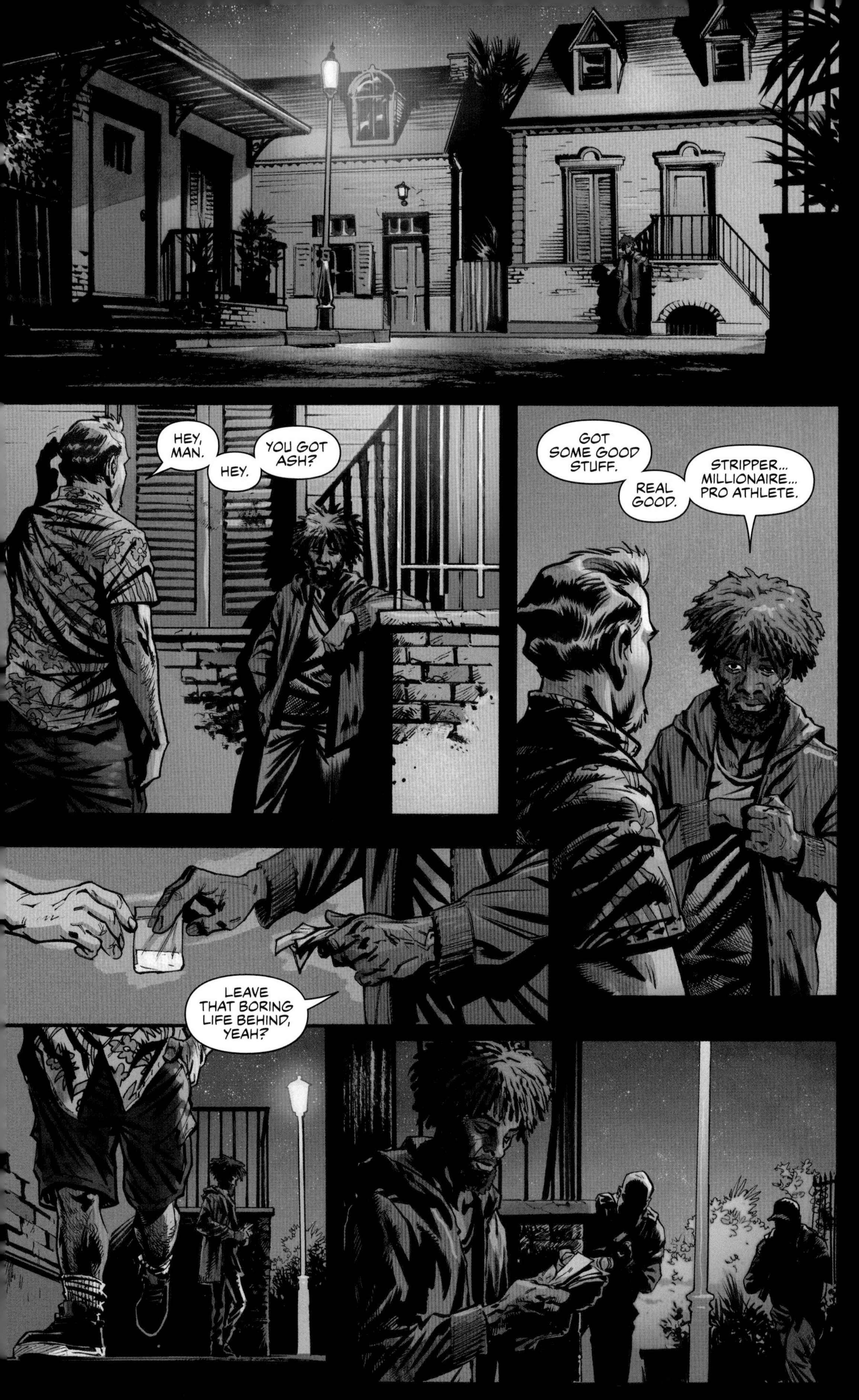
HEY, MAN.
HEY.
YOU GOT ASH?
GOT SOME GOOD STUFF.
REAL GOOD.
STRIPPER... MILLIONAIRE... PRO ATHLETE.
LEAVE THAT BORING LIFE BEHIND, YEAH?

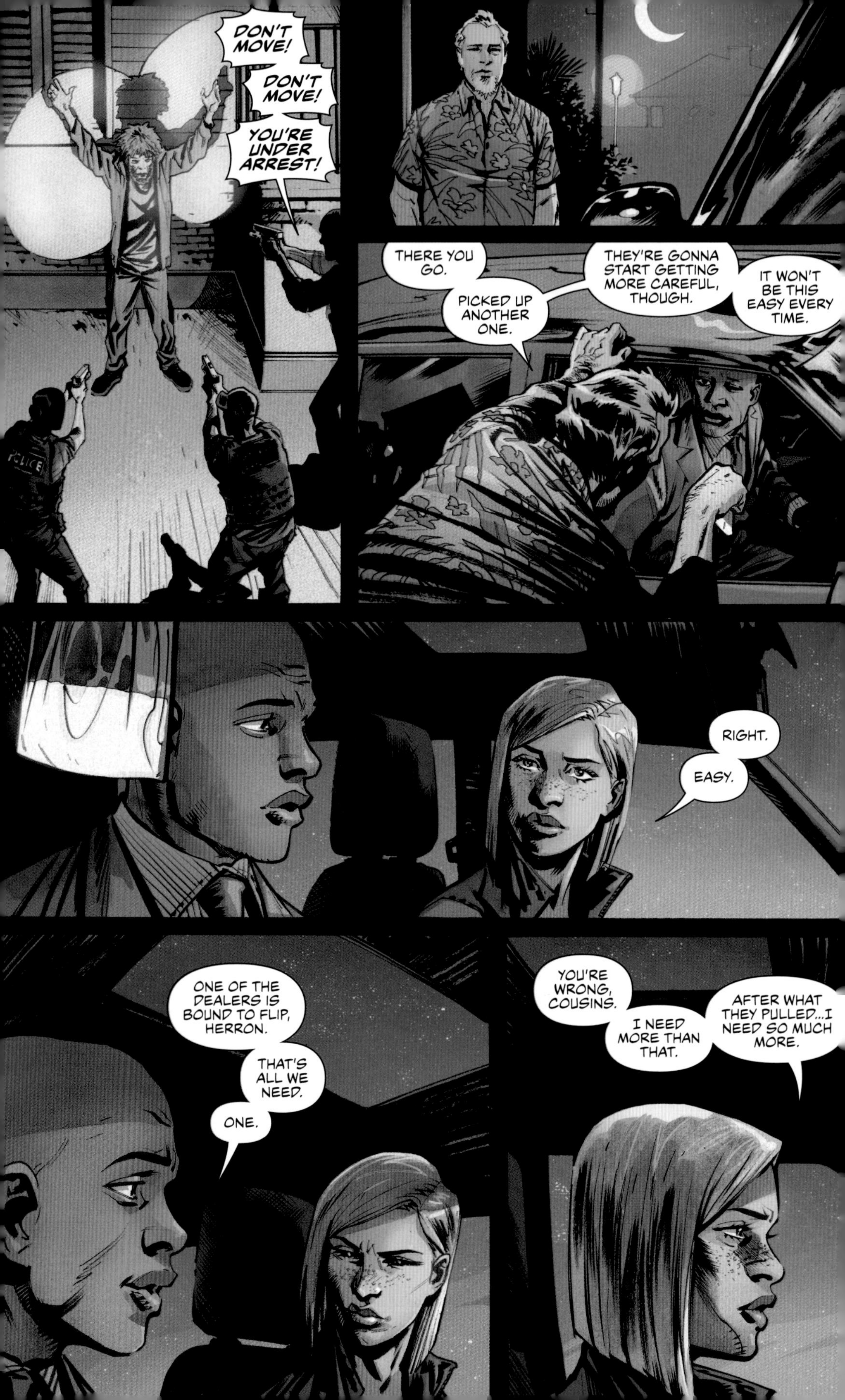
DON'T MOVE!
DON'T MOVE!
YOU'RE UNDER ARREST!
POLICE
THERE YOU GO.
PICKED UP ANOTHER ONE.
THEY'RE GONNA START GETTING MORE CAREFUL, THOUGH.
IT WON'T BE THIS EASY EVERY TIME.
RIGHT.
EASY.
ONE OF THE DEALERS IS BOUND TO FLIP, HERRON.
THAT'S ALL WE NEED.
ONE.
YOU'RE WRONG, COUSINS.
I NEED MORE THAN THAT.
AFTER WHAT THEY PULLED...I NEED SO MUCH MORE.

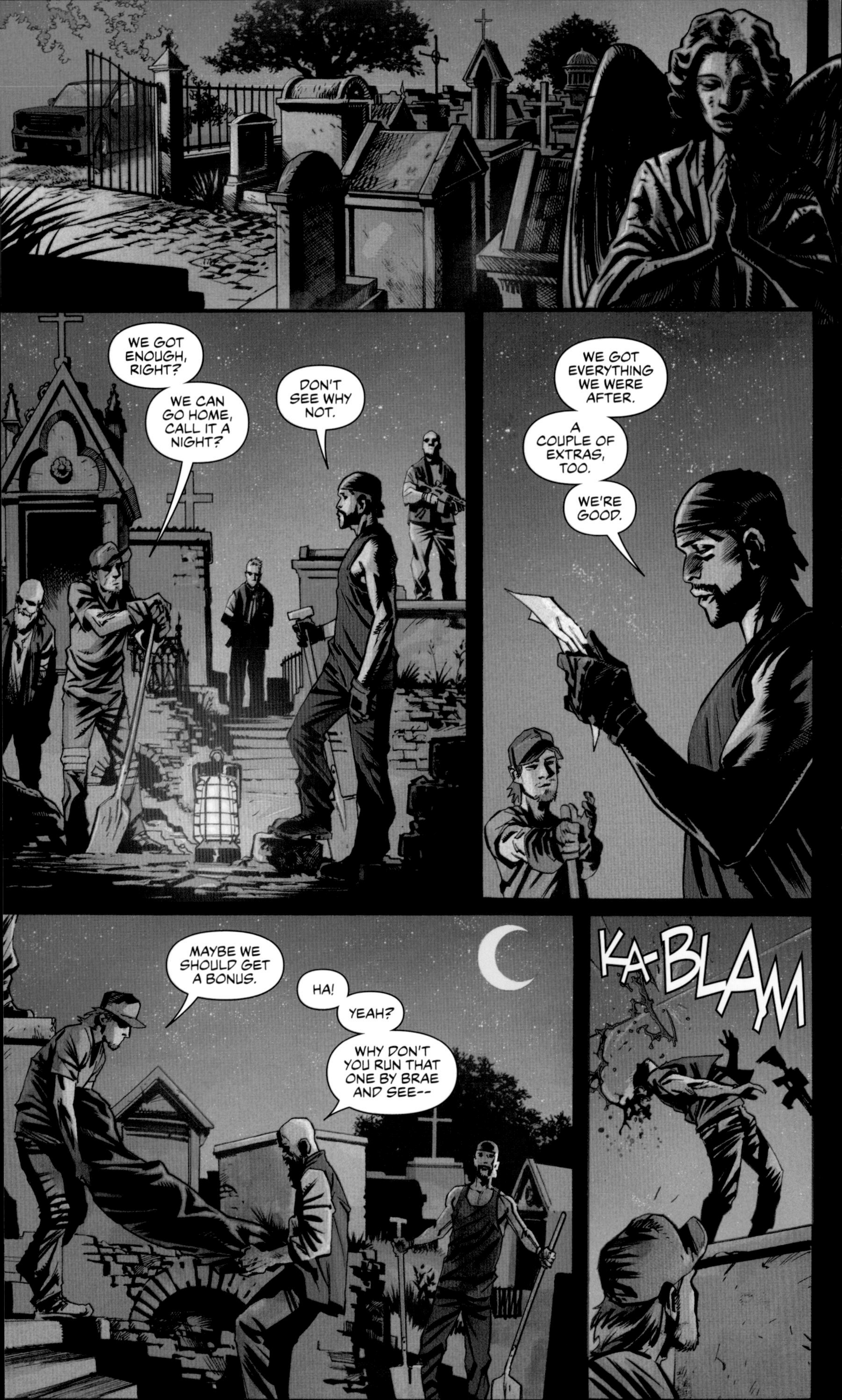
WE GOT ENOUGH, RIGHT?
WE CAN GO HOME, CALL IT A NIGHT?
DON'T SEE WHY NOT.
WE GOT EVERYTHING WE WERE AFTER.
A COUPLE OF EXTRAS, TOO.
WE'RE GOOD.
MAYBE WE SHOULD GET A BONUS.
HA!
YEAH?
WHY DON'T YOU RUN THAT ONE BY BRAE AND SEE--
KA-BLAM

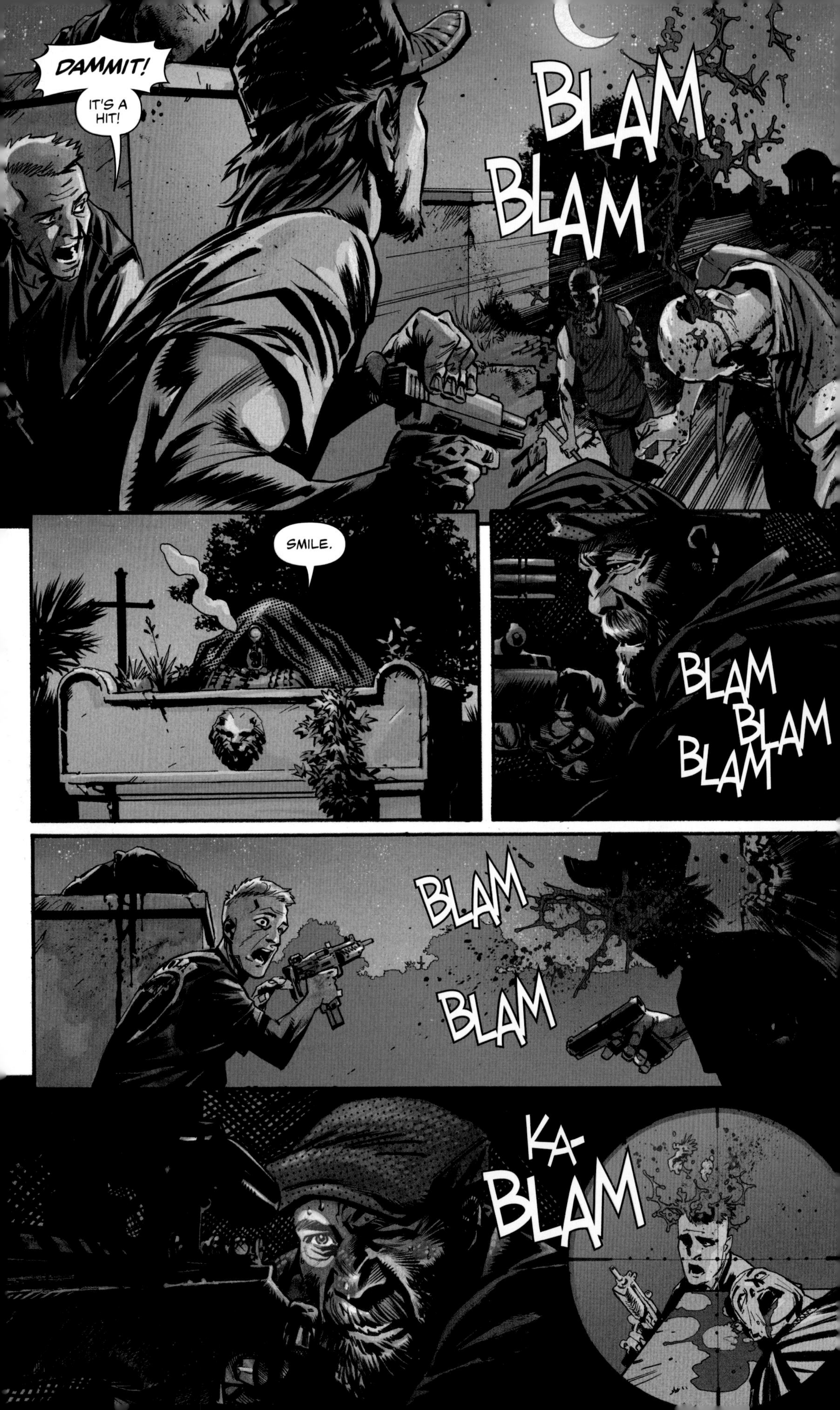
DAMMIT!
IT'S A HIT!
BLAM
BLAM
SMILE.
BLAM
BLAM
BLAM
BLAM
BLAM
KA-
BLAM

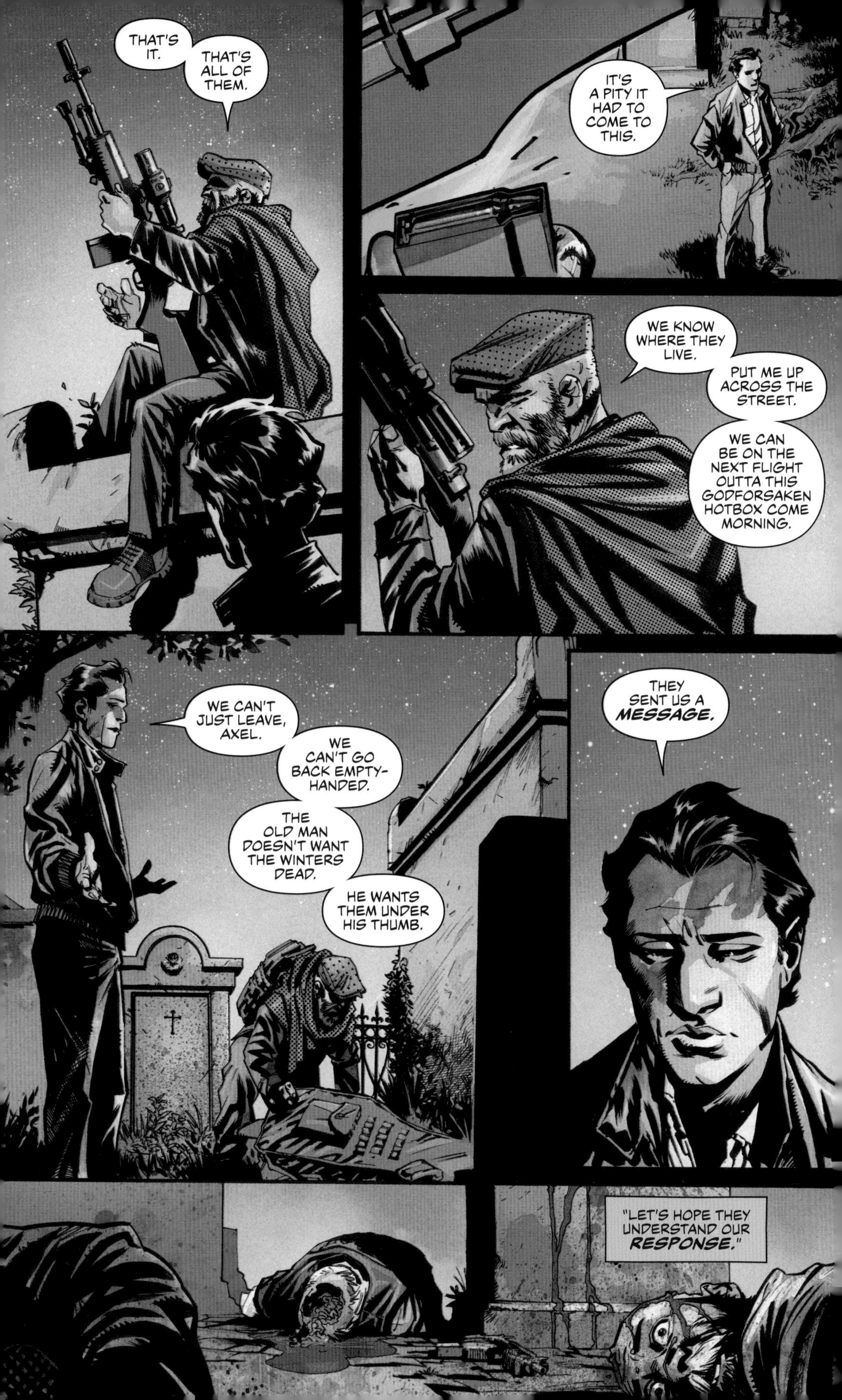
THAT'S IT.
THAT'S ALL OF THEM.
IT'S A PITY IT HAD TO COME TO THIS.
WE KNOW WHERE THEY LIVE.
PUT ME UP ACROSS THE STREET.
WE CAN BE ON THE NEXT FLIGHT OUTTA THIS GODFORSAKEN HOTBOX COME MORNING.
WE CAN'T JUST LEAVE, AXEL.
WE CAN'T GO BACK EMPTY-HANDED.
THE OLD MAN DOESN'T WANT THE WINTERS DEAD.
HE WANTS THEM UNDER HIS THUMB.
THEY SENT US A *MESSAGE.*
"LET'S HOPE THEY UNDERSTAND OUR *RESPONSE.*"

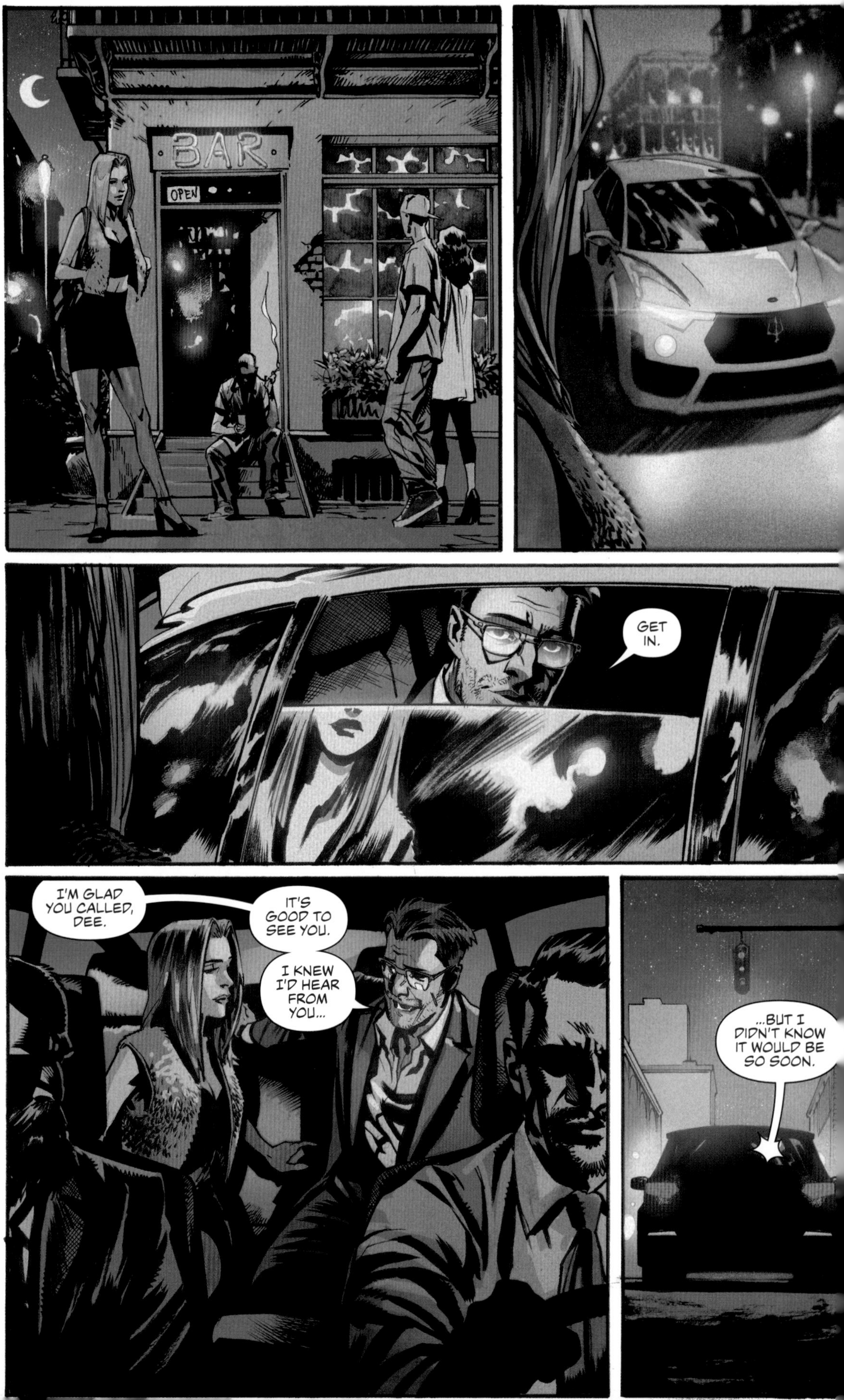
BAR
OPEN
GET IN.
I'M GLAD YOU CALLED, DEE.
IT'S GOOD TO SEE YOU.
I KNEW I'D HEAR FROM YOU...
...BUT I DIDN'T KNOW IT WOULD BE SO SOON.

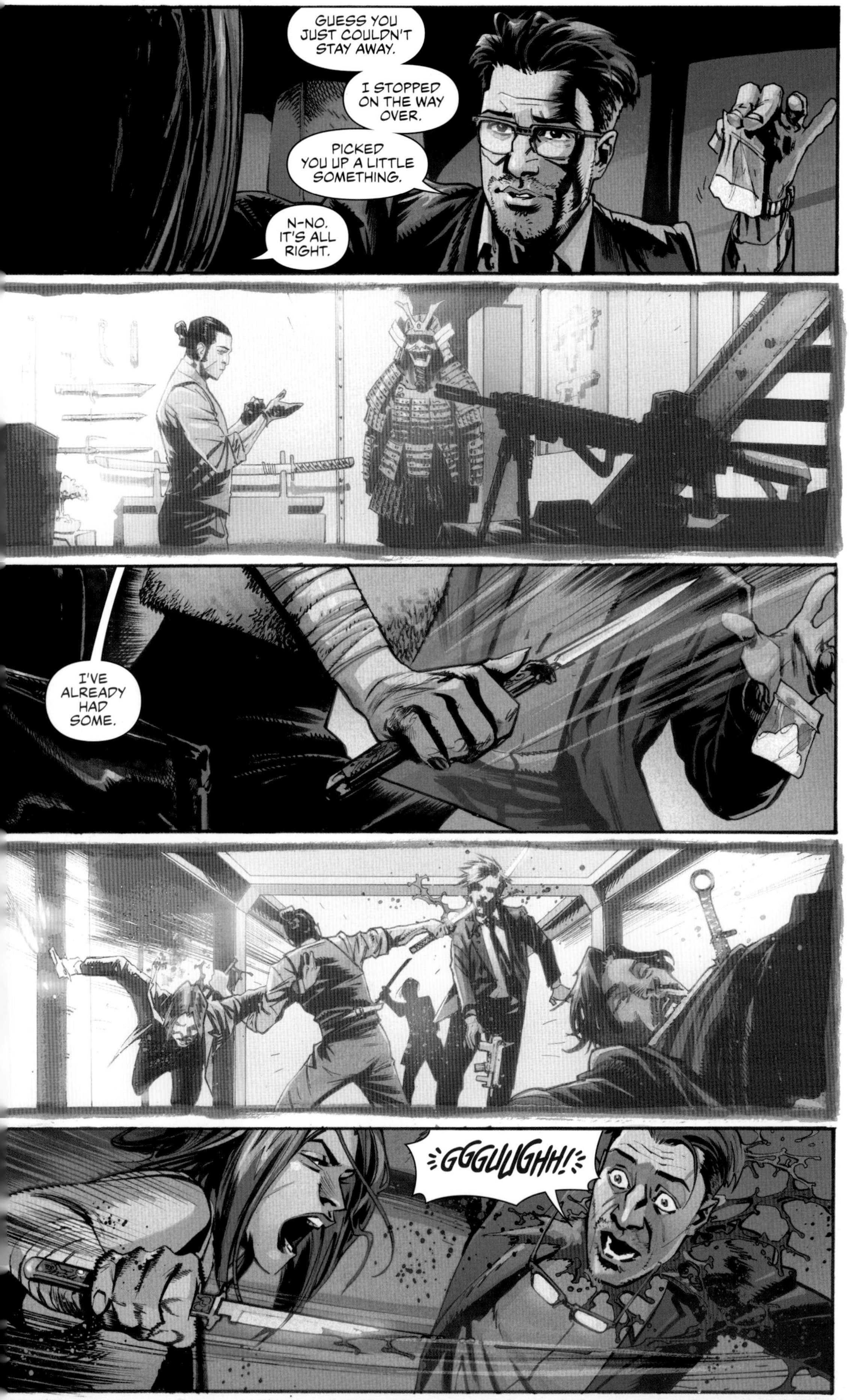
GUESS YOU JUST COULDN'T STAY AWAY.
I STOPPED ON THE WAY OVER.
PICKED YOU UP A LITTLE SOMETHING.
N-NO. IT'S ALL RIGHT.
I'VE ALREADY HAD SOME.
GGGULUGHH!

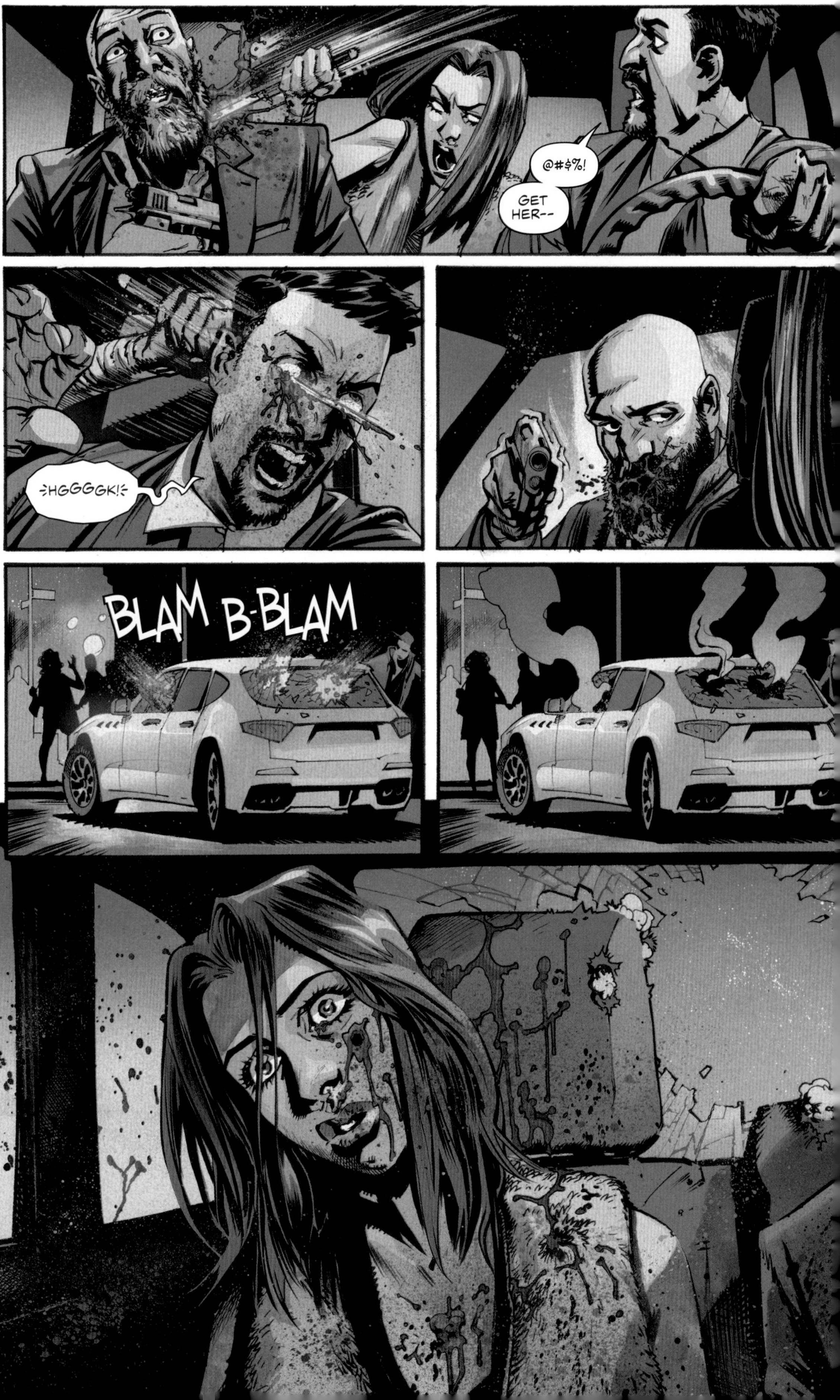
@#$%!
GET HER--
≈HGGGGK!≈
BLAM B-BLAM

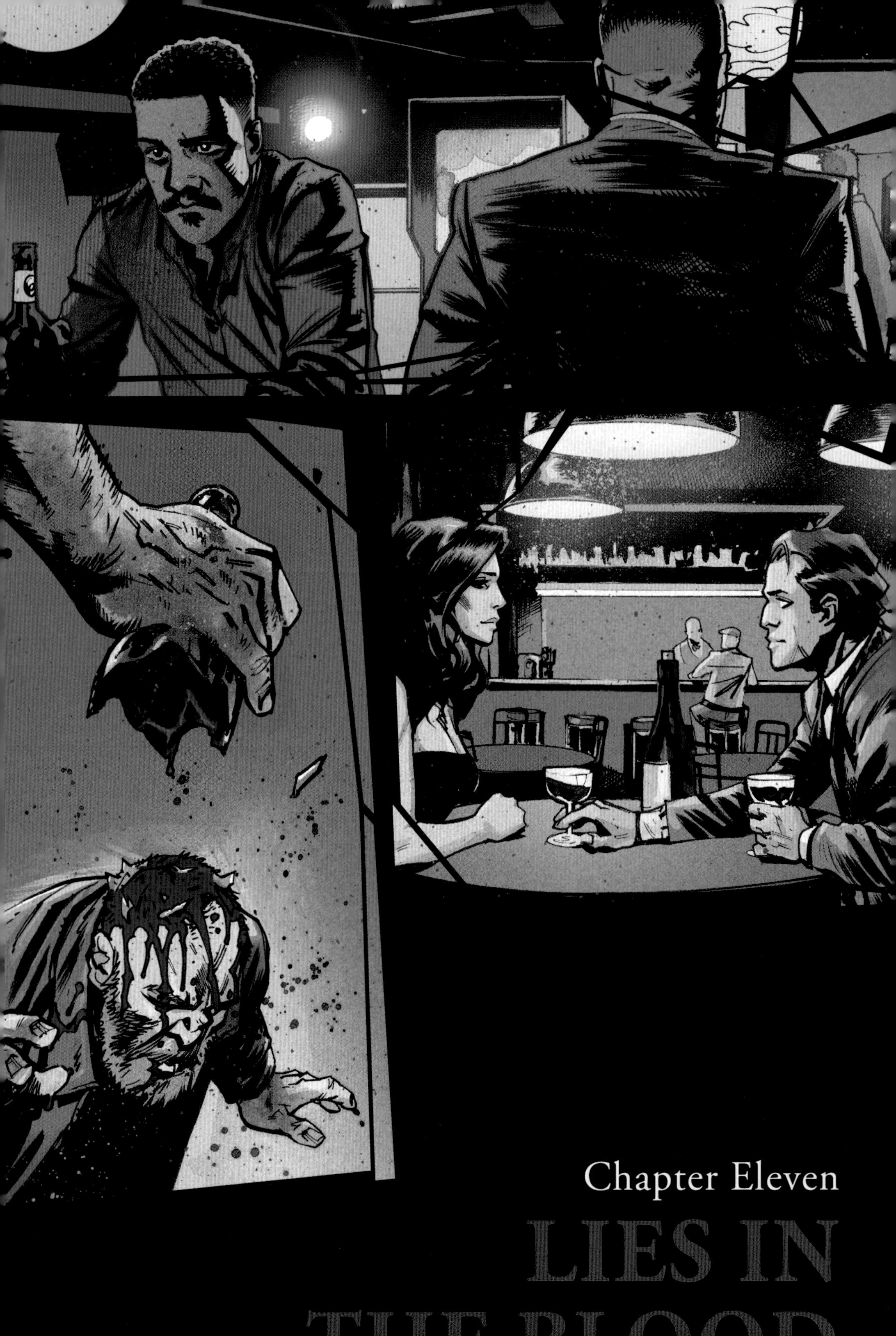

Chapter Eleven
LIES IN THE BLOOD

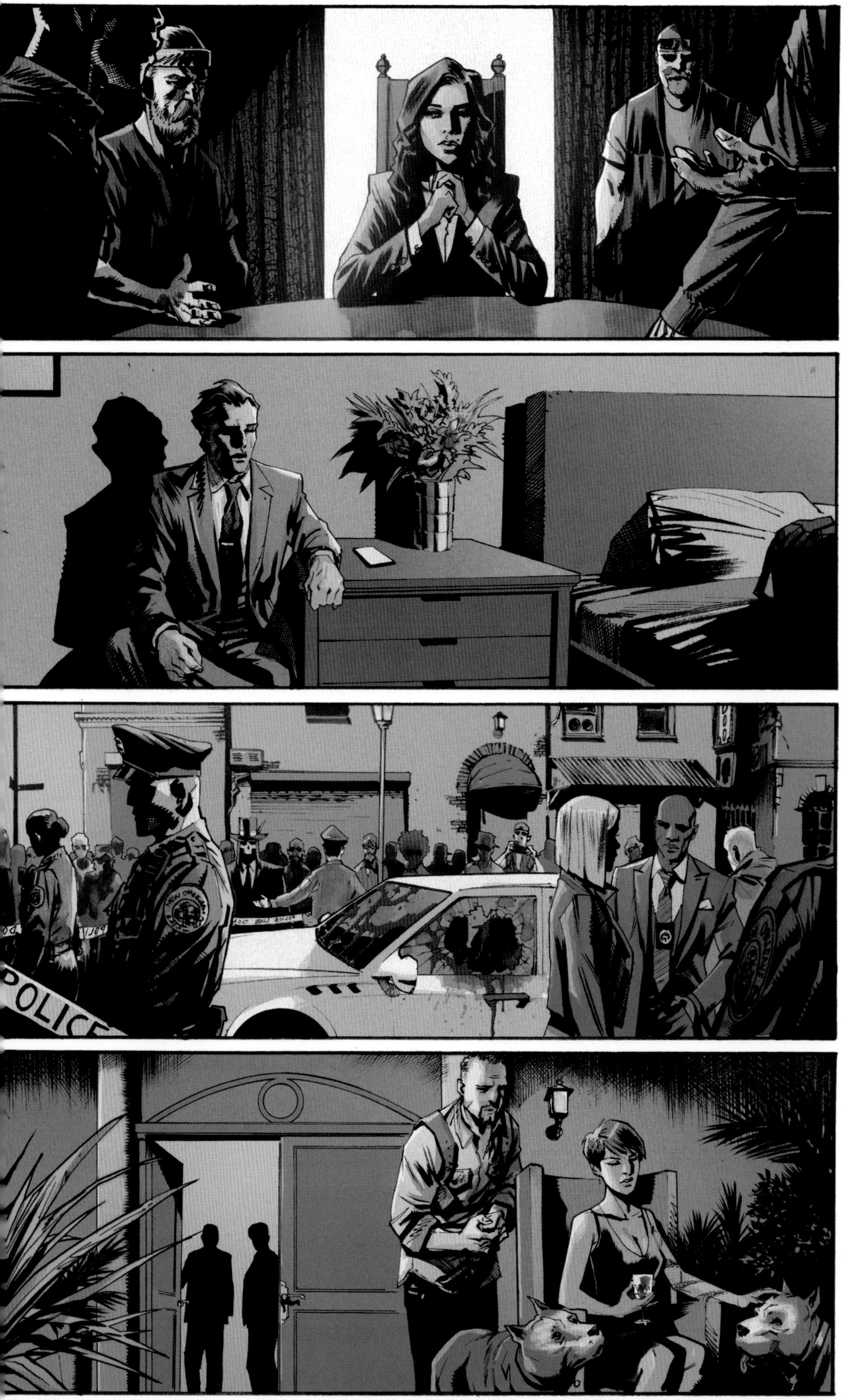

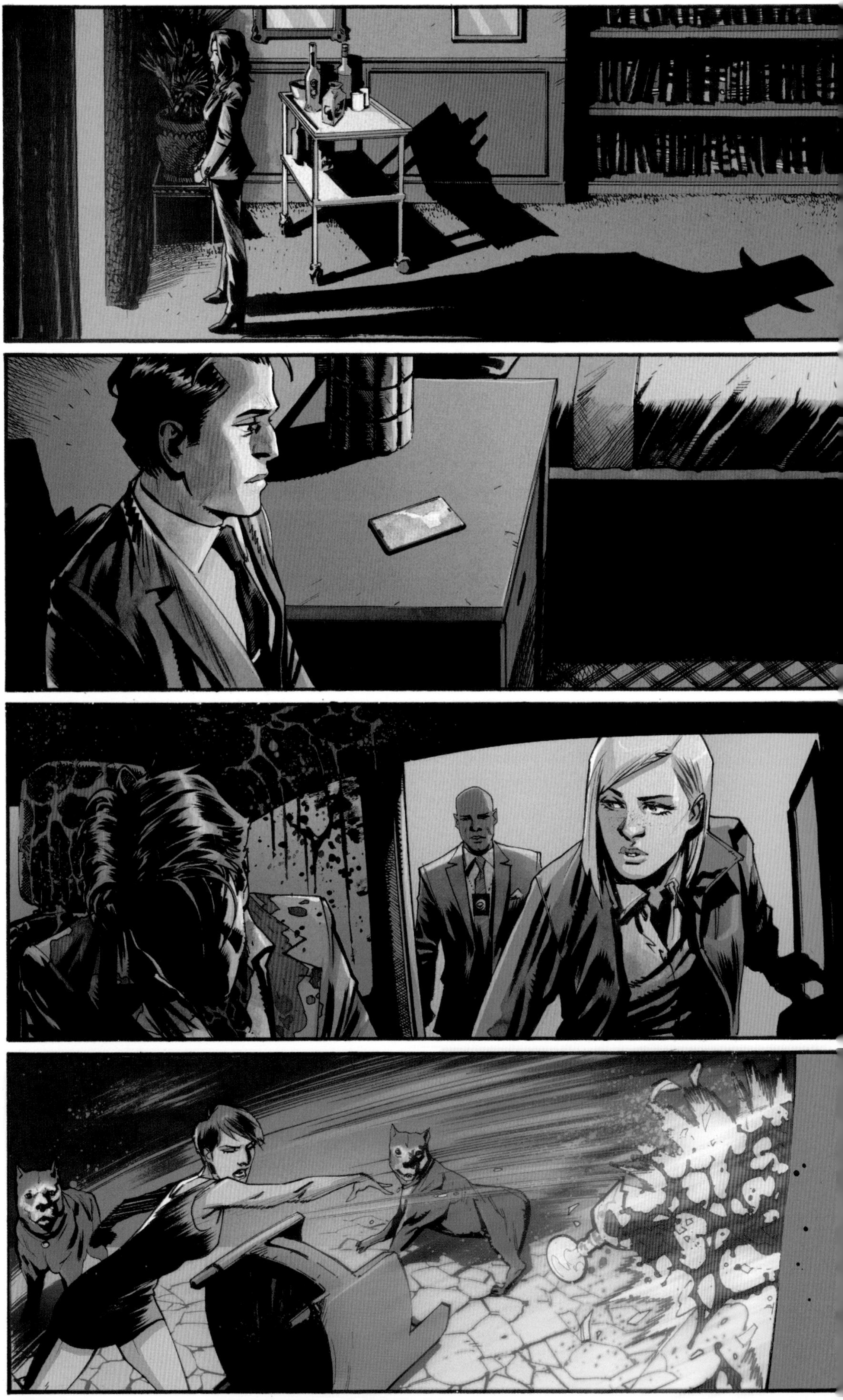

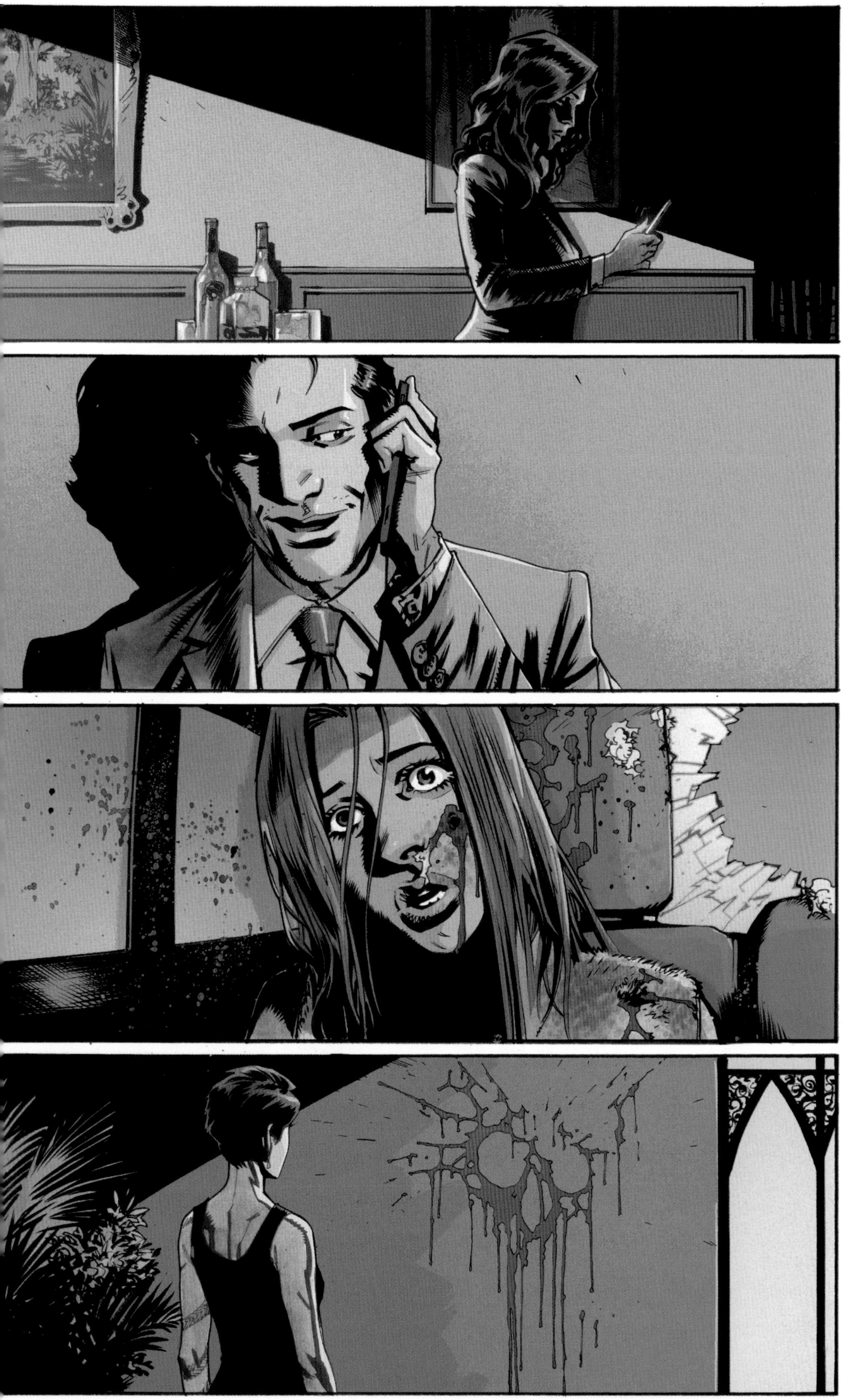

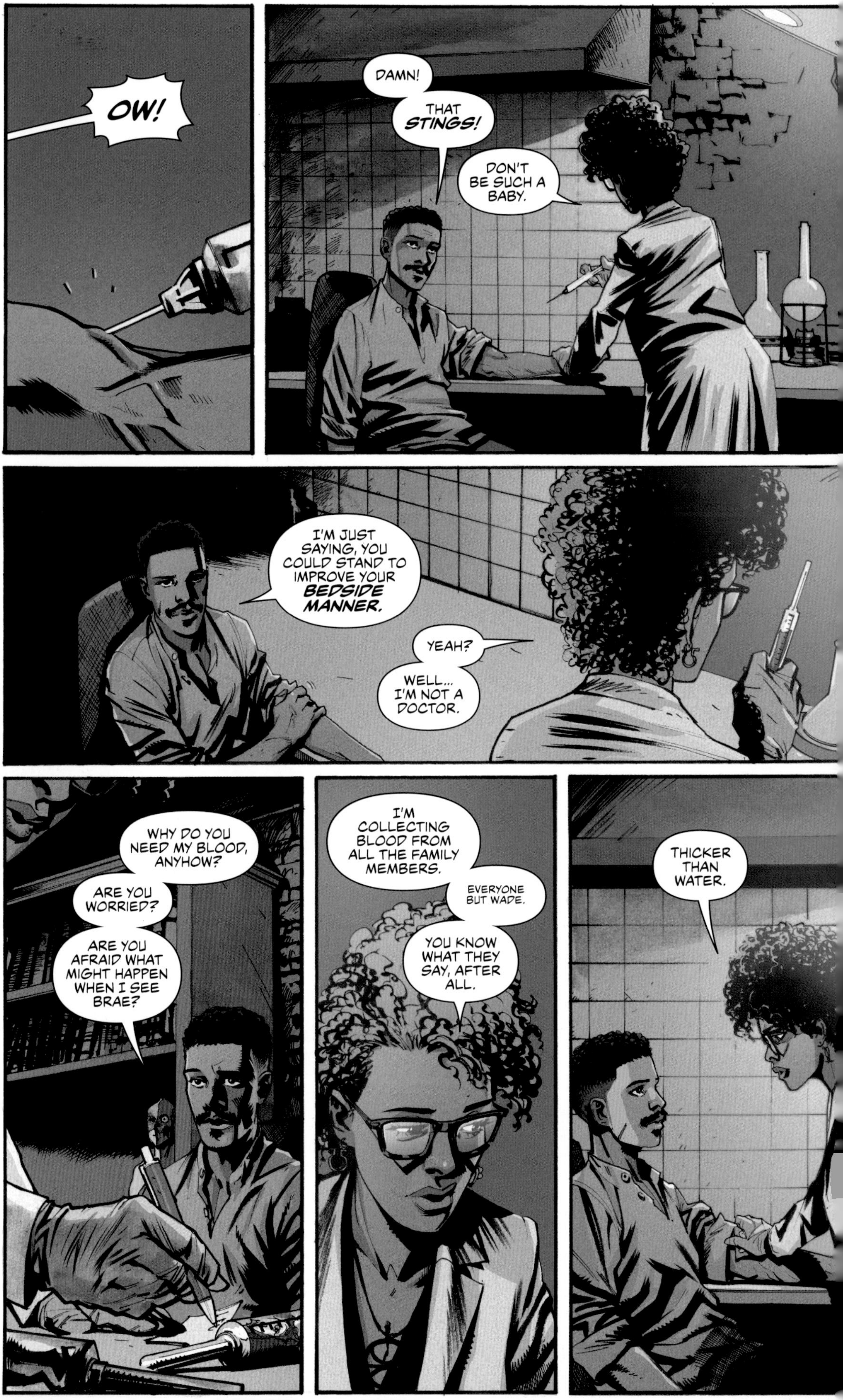
OW!
DAMN!
THAT STINGS!
DON'T BE SUCH A BABY.
I'M JUST SAYING, YOU COULD STAND TO IMPROVE YOUR BEDSIDE MANNER.
YEAH?
WELL... I'M NOT A DOCTOR.
WHY DO YOU NEED MY BLOOD, ANYHOW?
ARE YOU WORRIED?
ARE YOU AFRAID WHAT MIGHT HAPPEN WHEN I SEE BRAE?
I'M COLLECTING BLOOD FROM ALL THE FAMILY MEMBERS.
EVERYONE BUT WADE.
YOU KNOW WHAT THEY SAY, AFTER ALL.
THICKER THAN WATER.

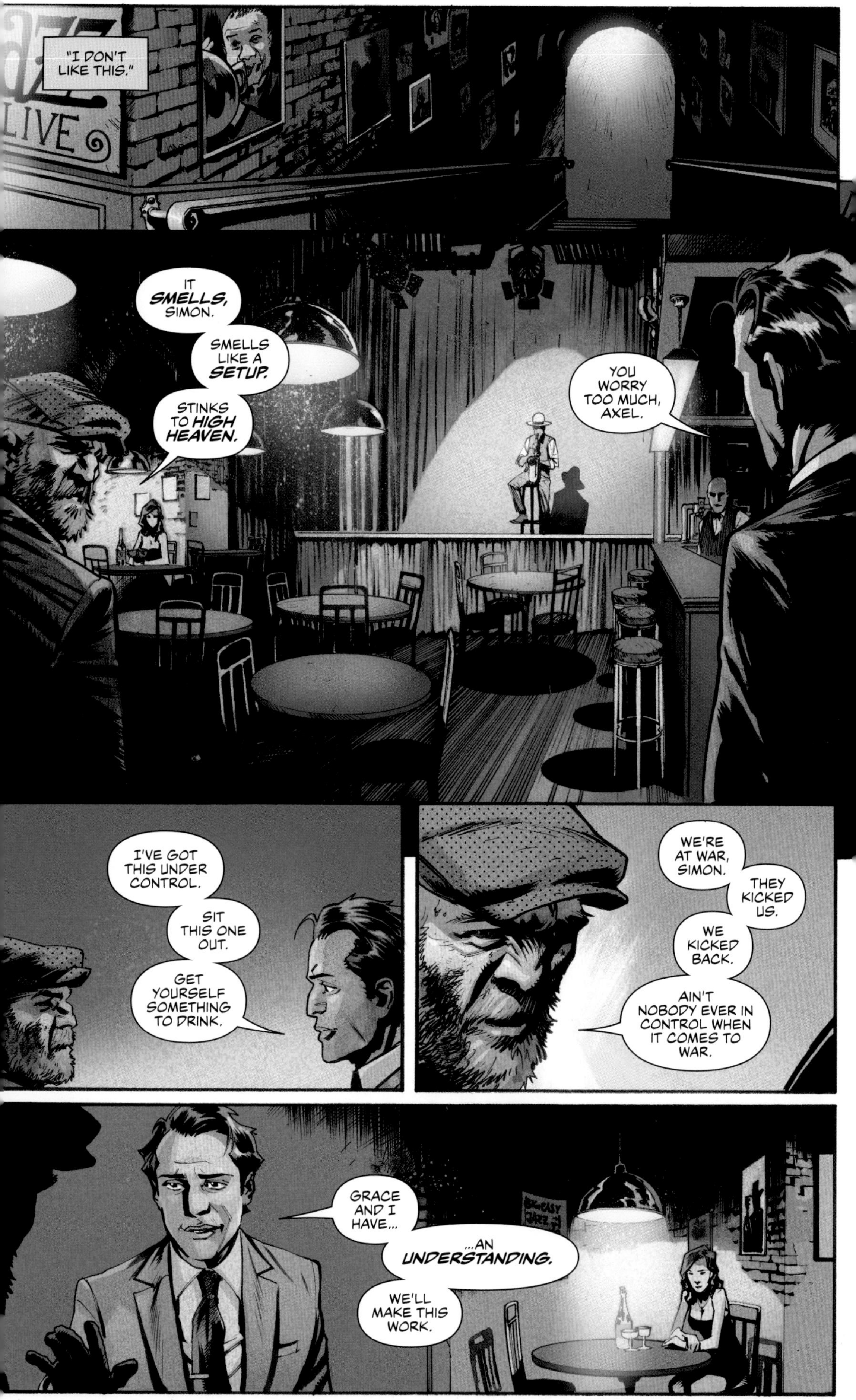

"I DON'T LIKE THIS."
LIVE
IT SMELLS, SIMON.
SMELLS LIKE A SETUP.
STINKS TO HIGH HEAVEN.
YOU WORRY TOO MUCH, AXEL.
I'VE GOT THIS UNDER CONTROL.
SIT THIS ONE OUT.
GET YOURSELF SOMETHING TO DRINK.
WE'RE AT WAR, SIMON.
THEY KICKED US.
WE KICKED BACK.
AIN'T NOBODY EVER IN CONTROL WHEN IT COMES TO WAR.
GRACE AND I HAVE...
...AN UNDERSTANDING.
WE'LL MAKE THIS WORK.

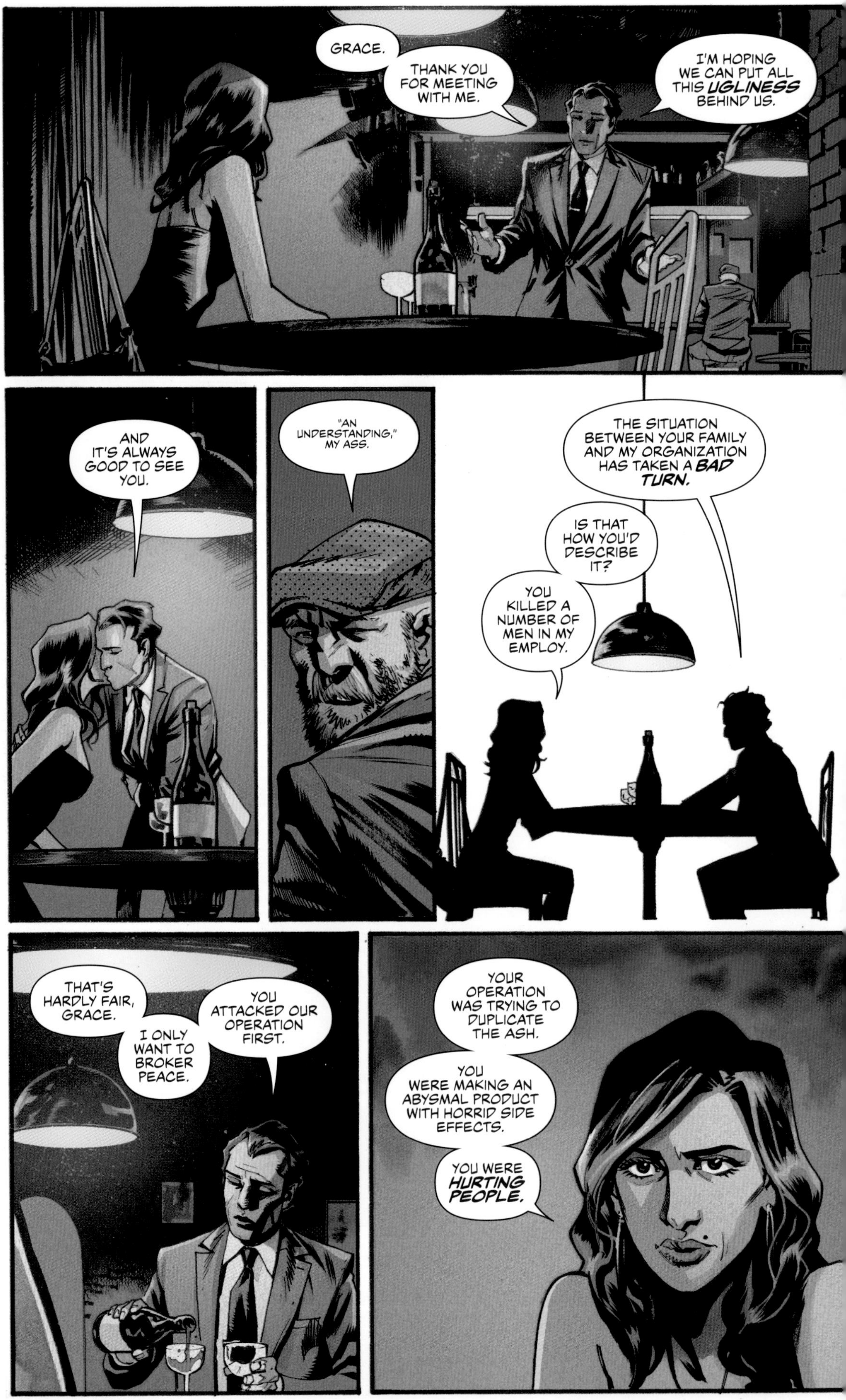

GRACE.
THANK YOU FOR MEETING WITH ME.
I'M HOPING WE CAN PUT ALL THIS *UGLINESS* BEHIND US.
AND IT'S ALWAYS GOOD TO SEE YOU.
"AN UNDERSTANDING," MY ASS.
THE SITUATION BETWEEN YOUR FAMILY AND MY ORGANIZATION HAS TAKEN A *BAD TURN.*
IS THAT HOW YOU'D DESCRIBE IT?
YOU KILLED A NUMBER OF MEN IN MY EMPLOY.
THAT'S HARDLY FAIR, GRACE.
I ONLY WANT TO BROKER PEACE.
YOU ATTACKED OUR OPERATION FIRST.
YOUR OPERATION WAS TRYING TO DUPLICATE THE ASH.
YOU WERE MAKING AN ABYSMAL PRODUCT WITH HORRID SIDE EFFECTS.
YOU WERE *HURTING PEOPLE.*

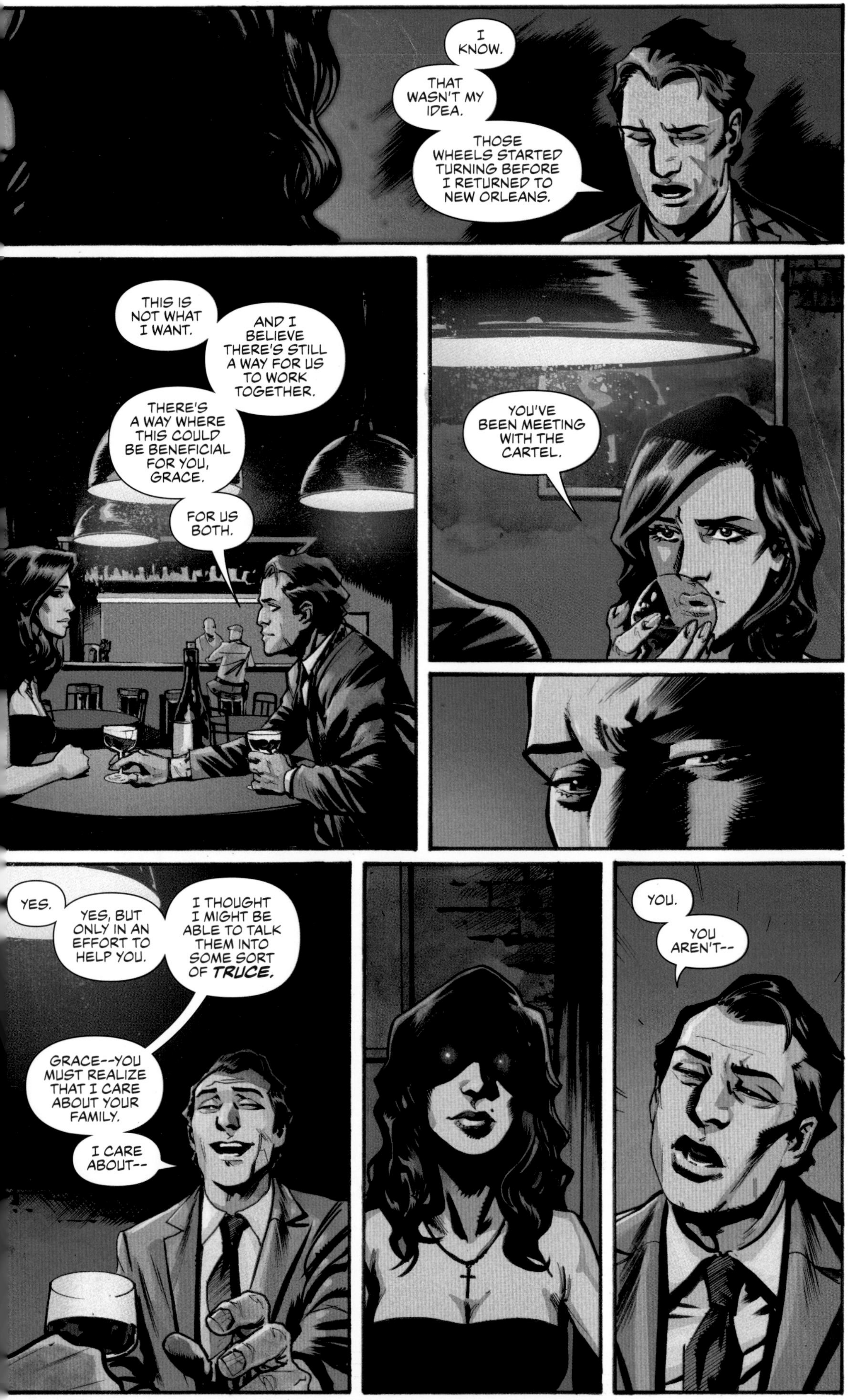
I KNOW.
THAT WASN'T MY IDEA.
THOSE WHEELS STARTED TURNING BEFORE I RETURNED TO NEW ORLEANS.
THIS IS NOT WHAT I WANT.
AND I BELIEVE THERE'S STILL A WAY FOR US TO WORK TOGETHER.
THERE'S A WAY WHERE THIS COULD BE BENEFICIAL FOR YOU, GRACE.
FOR US BOTH.
YOU'VE BEEN MEETING WITH THE CARTEL.
YES.
YES, BUT ONLY IN AN EFFORT TO HELP YOU.
I THOUGHT I MIGHT BE ABLE TO TALK THEM INTO SOME SORT OF TRUCE.
GRACE--YOU MUST REALIZE THAT I CARE ABOUT YOUR FAMILY.
I CARE ABOUT--
YOU.
YOU AREN'T--

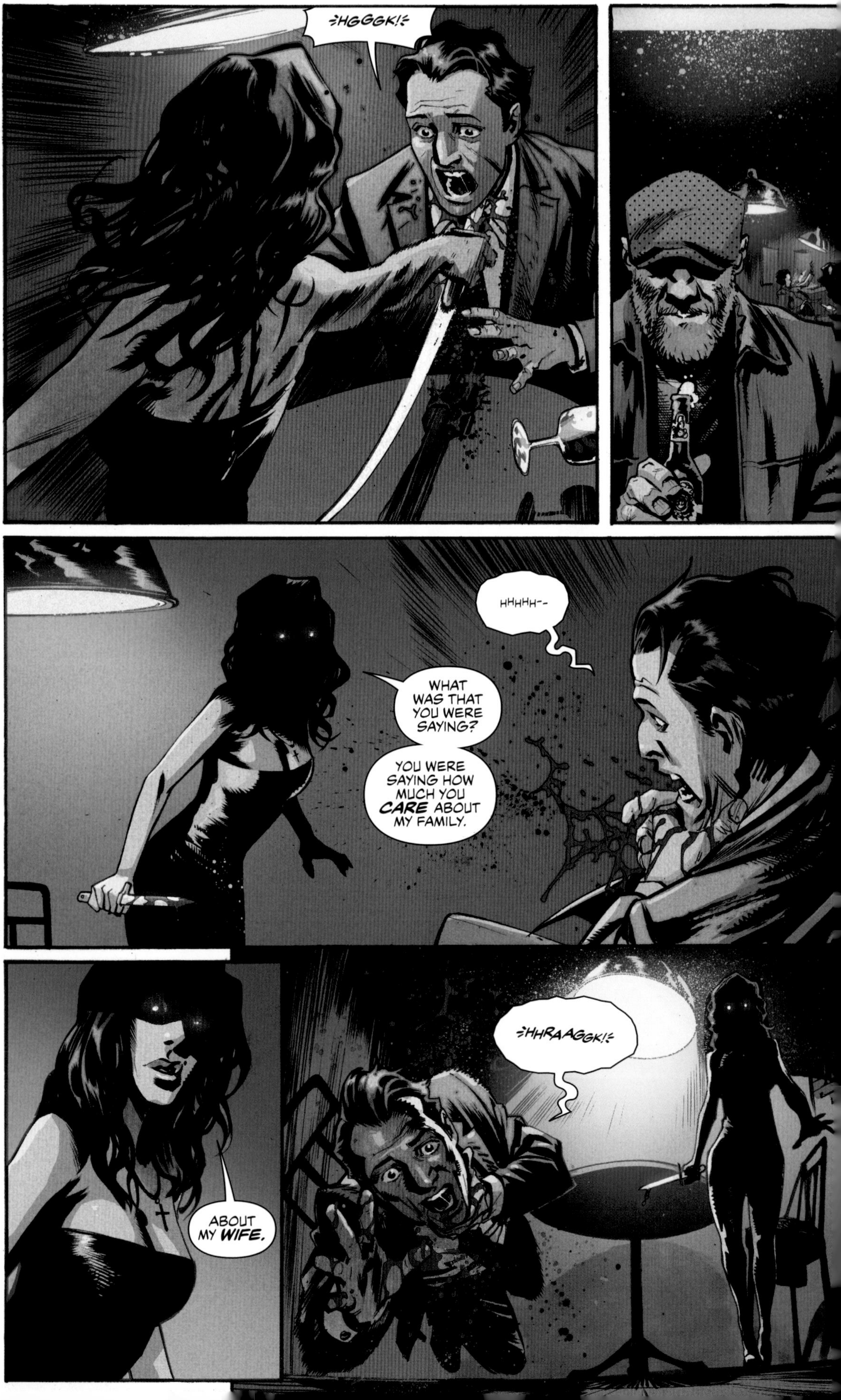

HGGGK!
HHHHH-
WHAT WAS THAT YOU WERE SAYING?
YOU WERE SAYING HOW MUCH YOU CARE ABOUT MY FAMILY.
ABOUT MY WIFE.
HHRAAGGK!

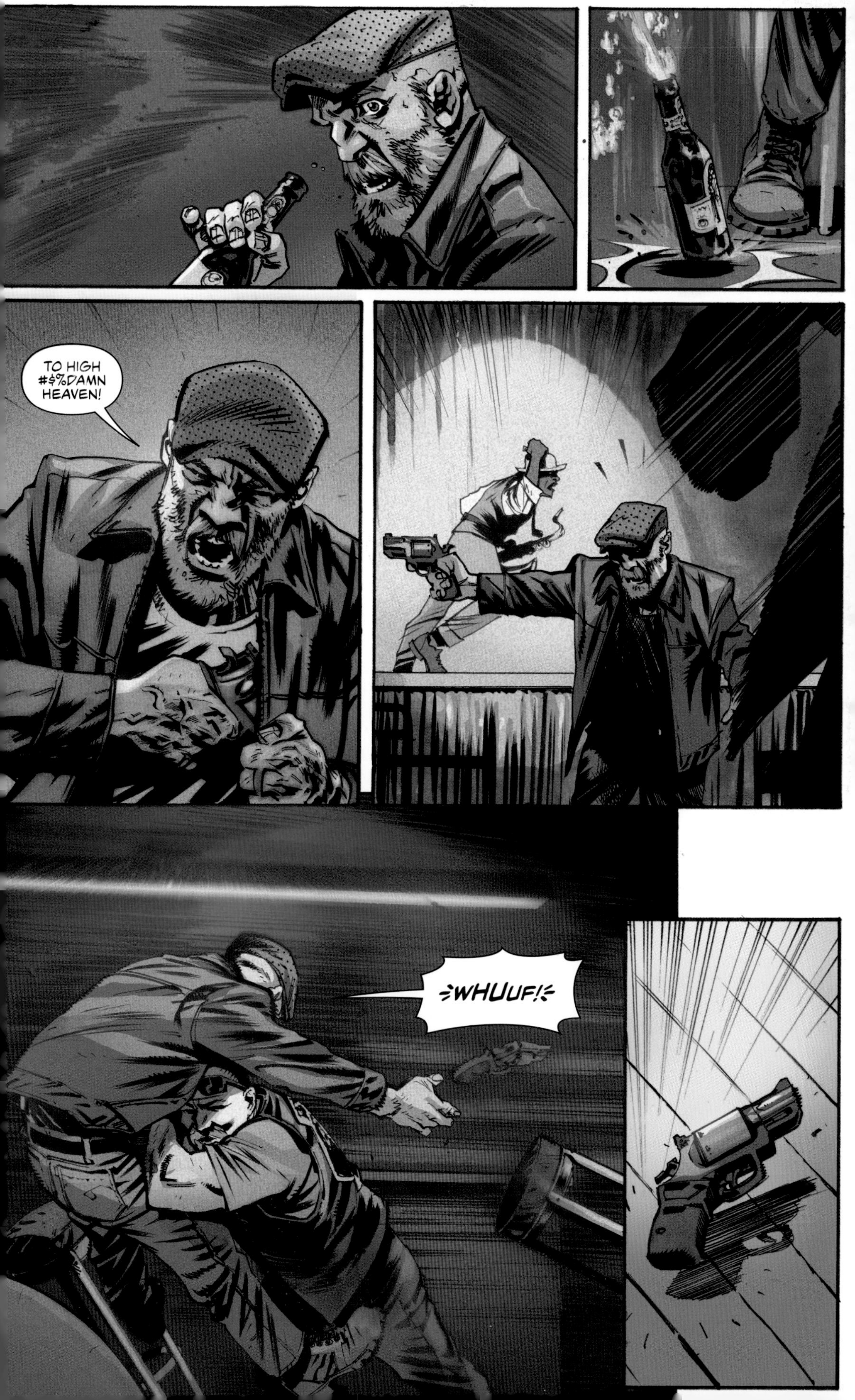
TO HIGH #$%DAMN HEAVEN!
WHUUF!

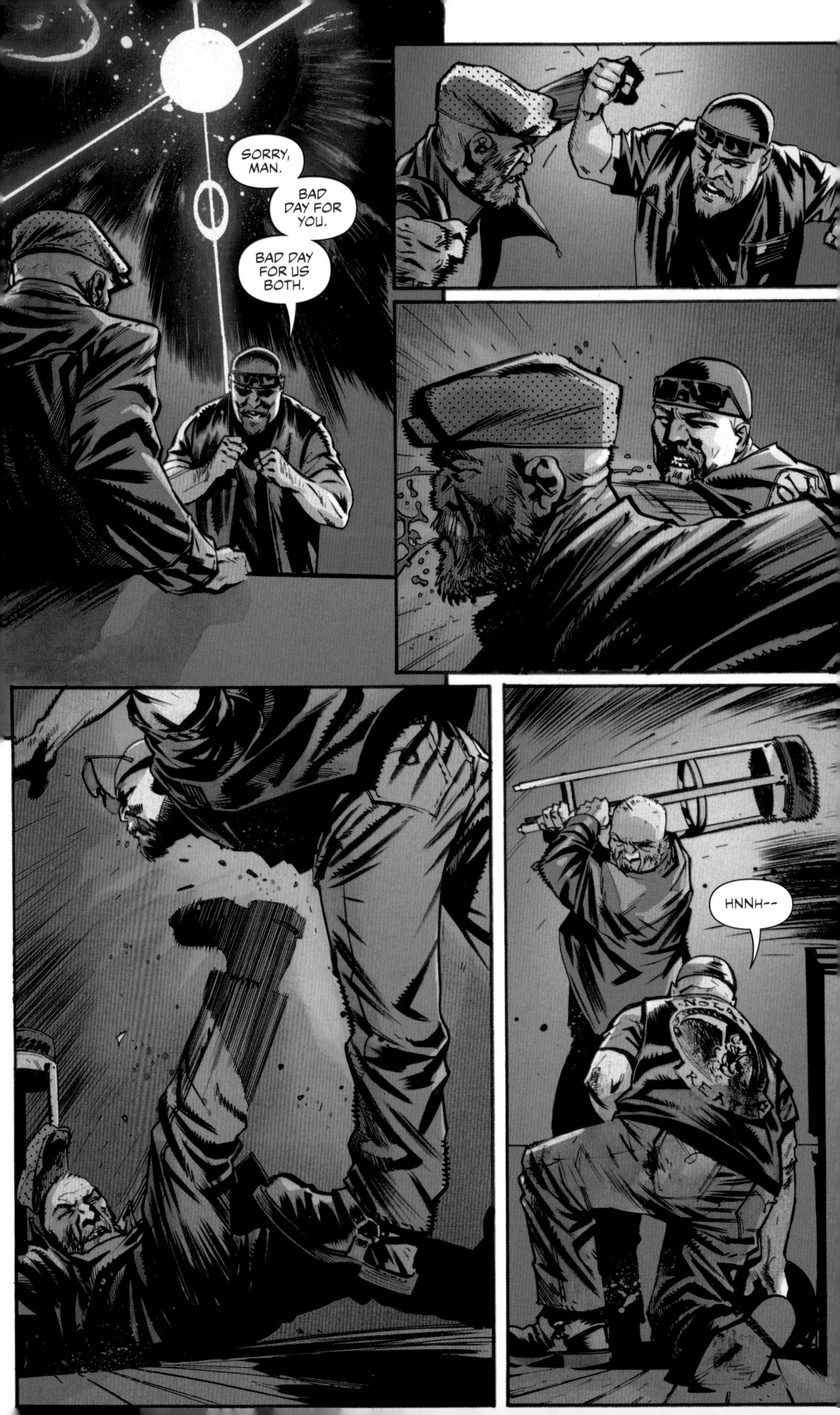
SORRY, MAN.
BAD DAY FOR YOU.
BAD DAY FOR US BOTH.
HNNH--

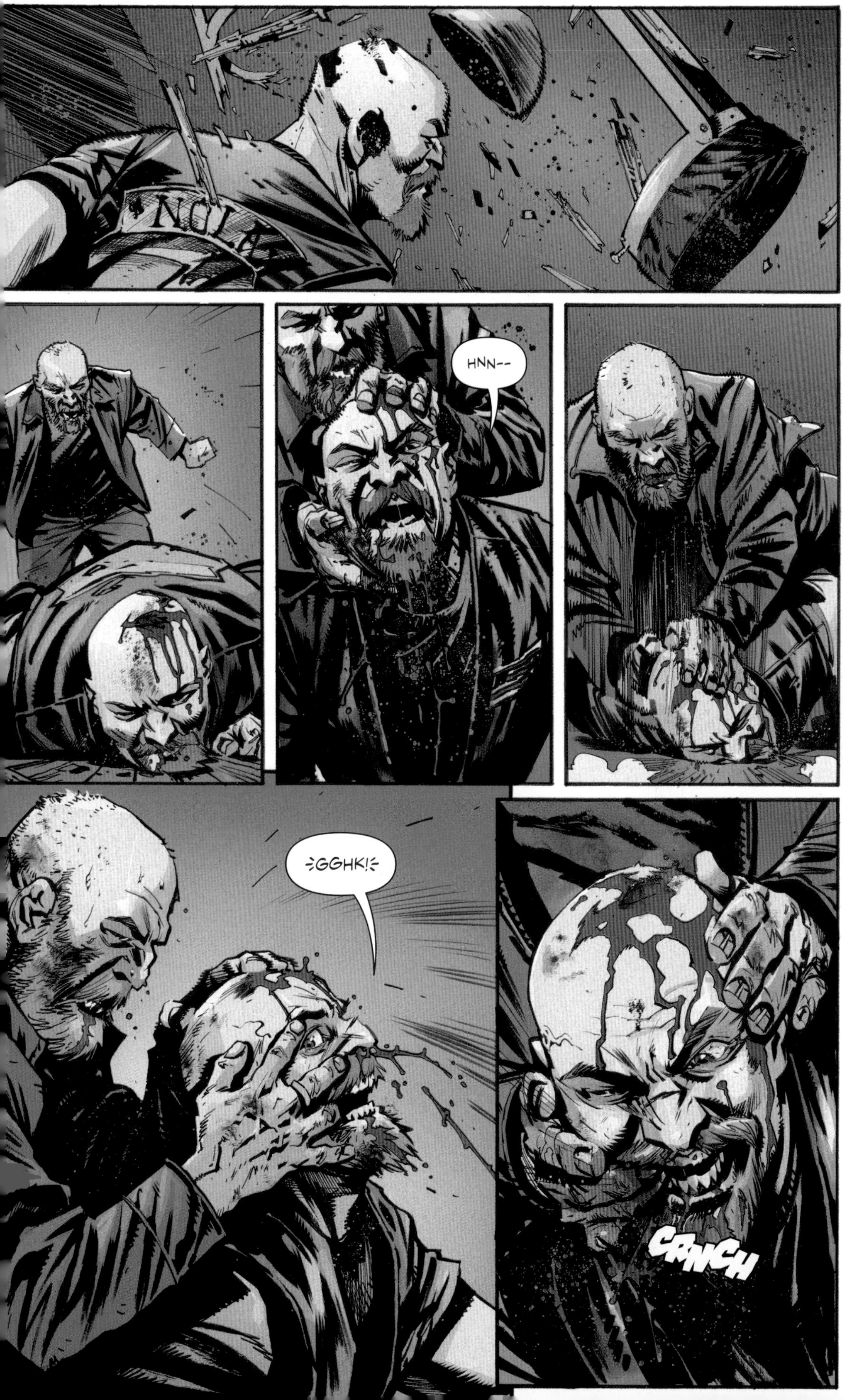
NCLA
HNN--
GGHK!
CRNCH

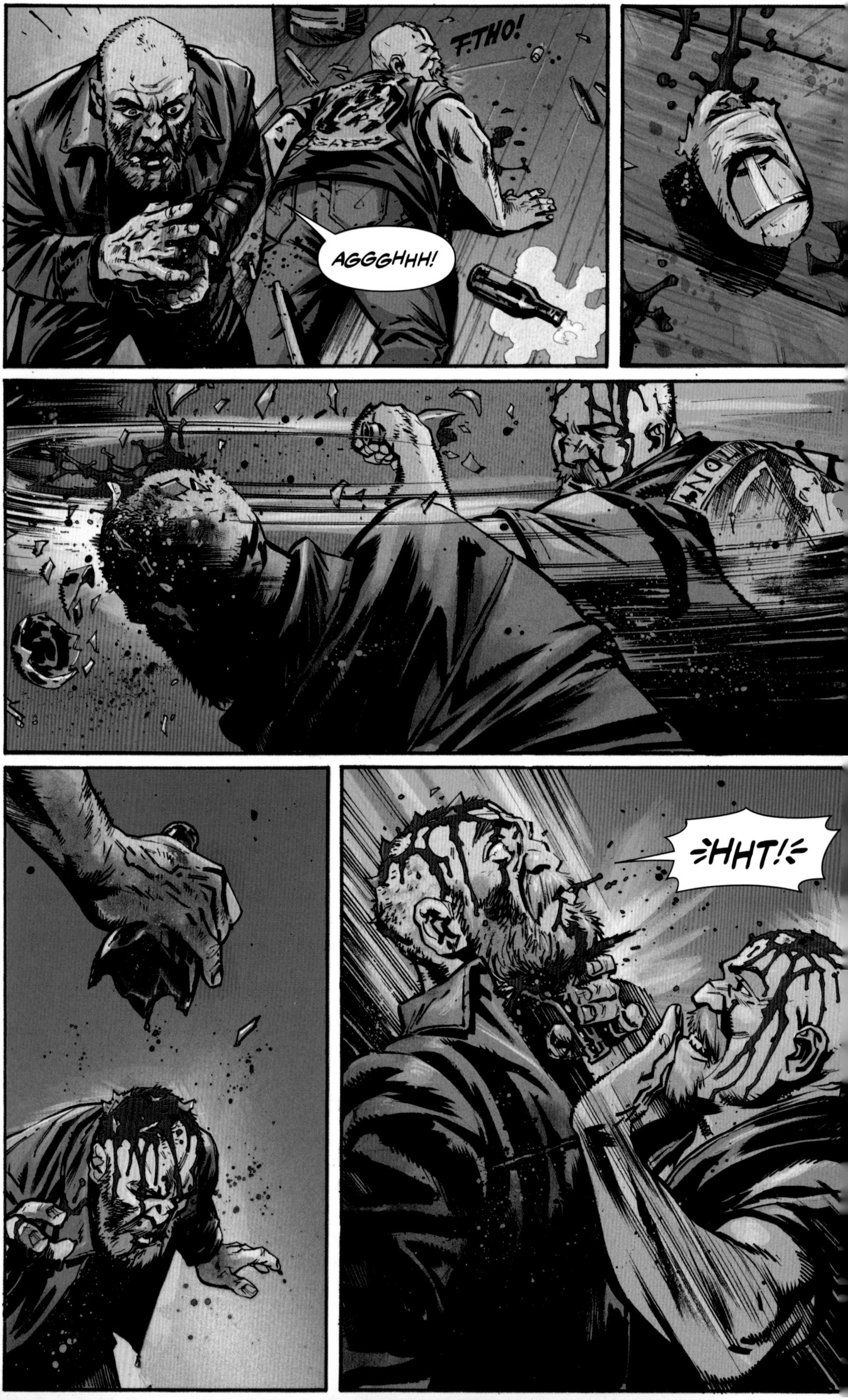
F.THO!
AGGGHHH!
HHT!

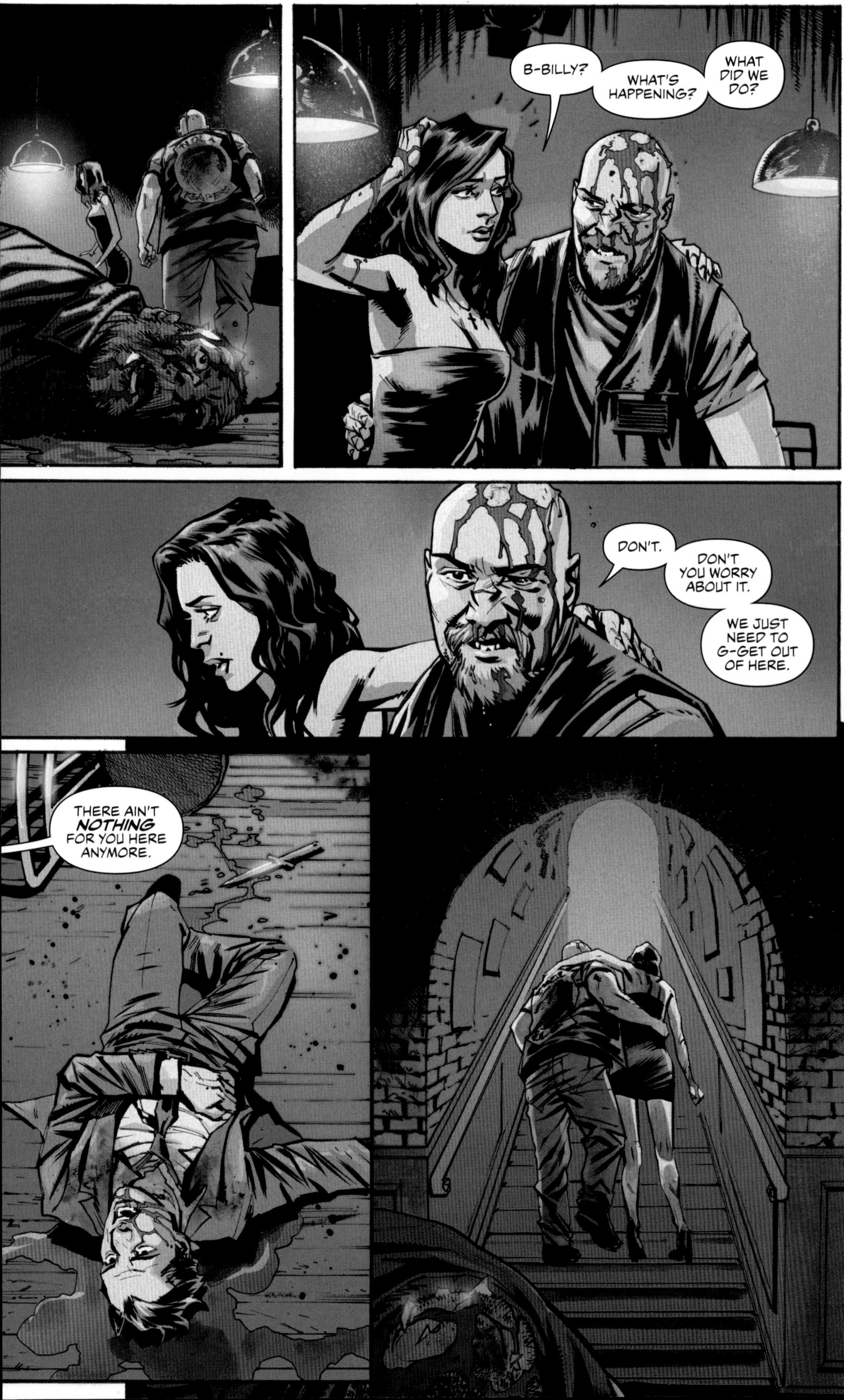
B-BILLY?
WHAT'S HAPPENING?
WHAT DID WE DO?
DON'T.
DON'T YOU WORRY ABOUT IT.
WE JUST NEED TO G-GET OUT OF HERE.
THERE AIN'T ***NOTHING*** FOR YOU HERE ANYMORE.

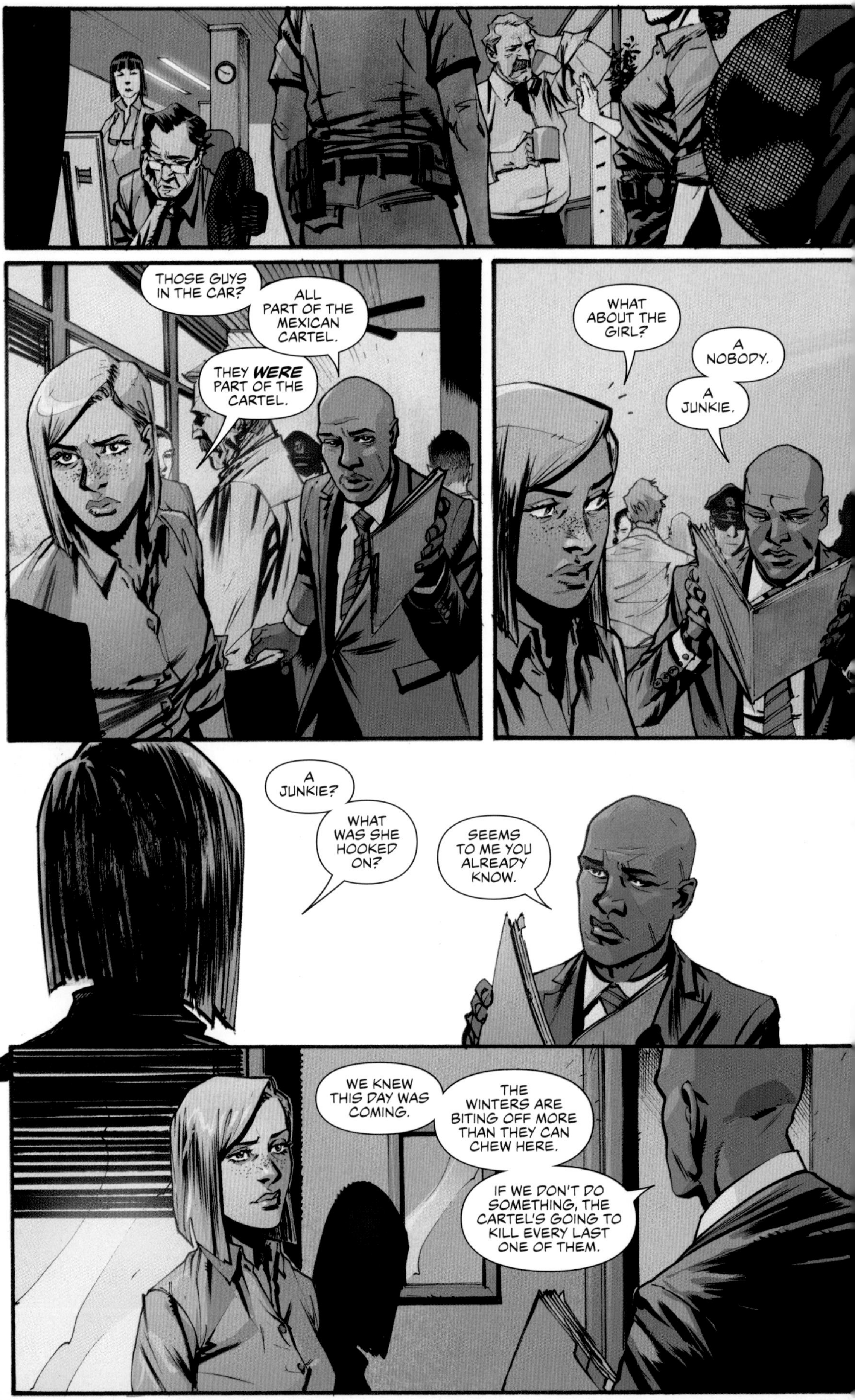
THOSE GUYS IN THE CAR?
ALL PART OF THE MEXICAN CARTEL.
THEY WERE PART OF THE CARTEL.
WHAT ABOUT THE GIRL?
A NOBODY.
A JUNKIE.
A JUNKIE?
WHAT WAS SHE HOOKED ON?
SEEMS TO ME YOU ALREADY KNOW.
WE KNEW THIS DAY WAS COMING.
THE WINTERS ARE BITING OFF MORE THAN THEY CAN CHEW HERE.
IF WE DON'T DO SOMETHING, THE CARTEL'S GOING TO KILL EVERY LAST ONE OF THEM.

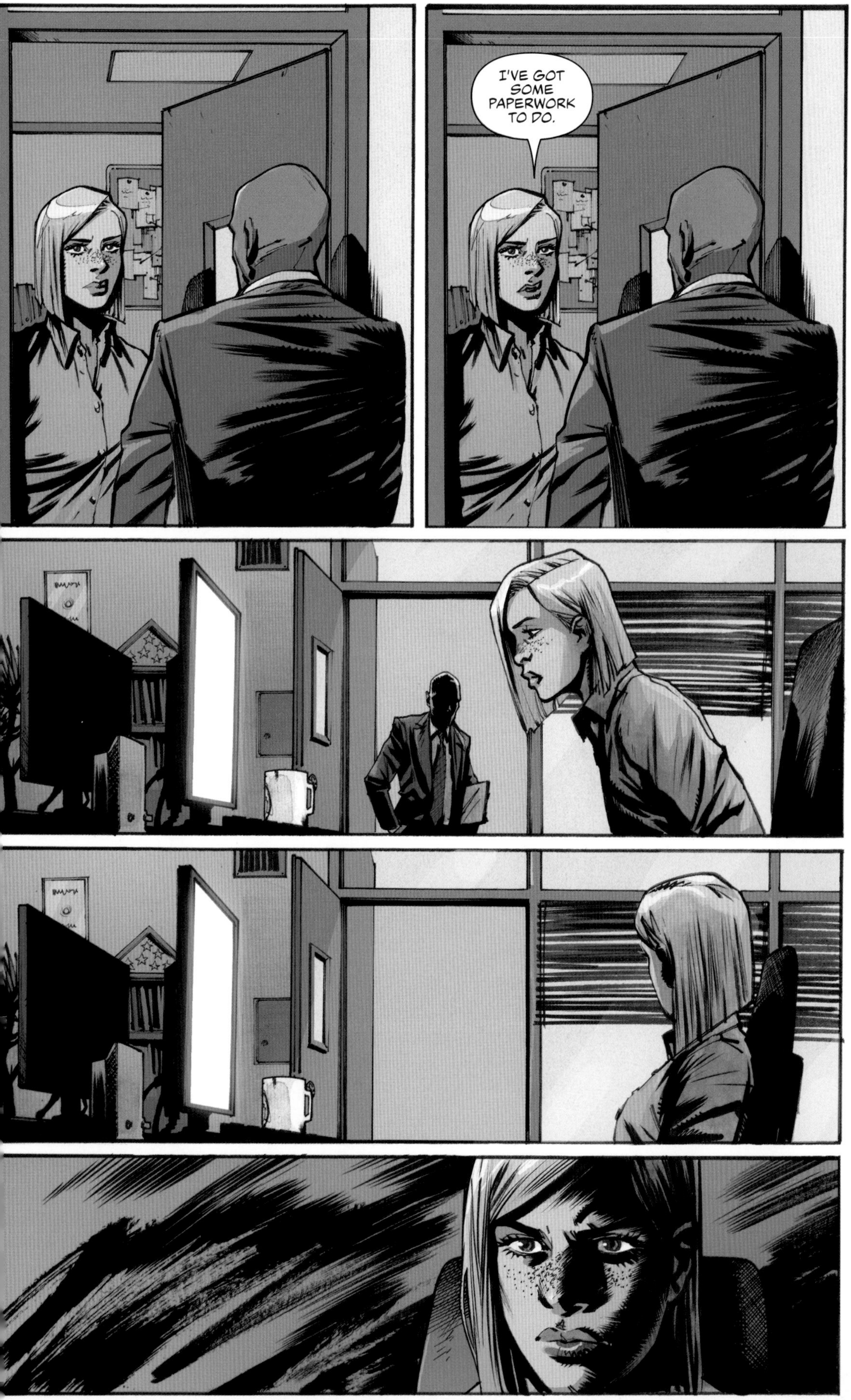
I'VE GOT SOME PAPERWORK TO DO.

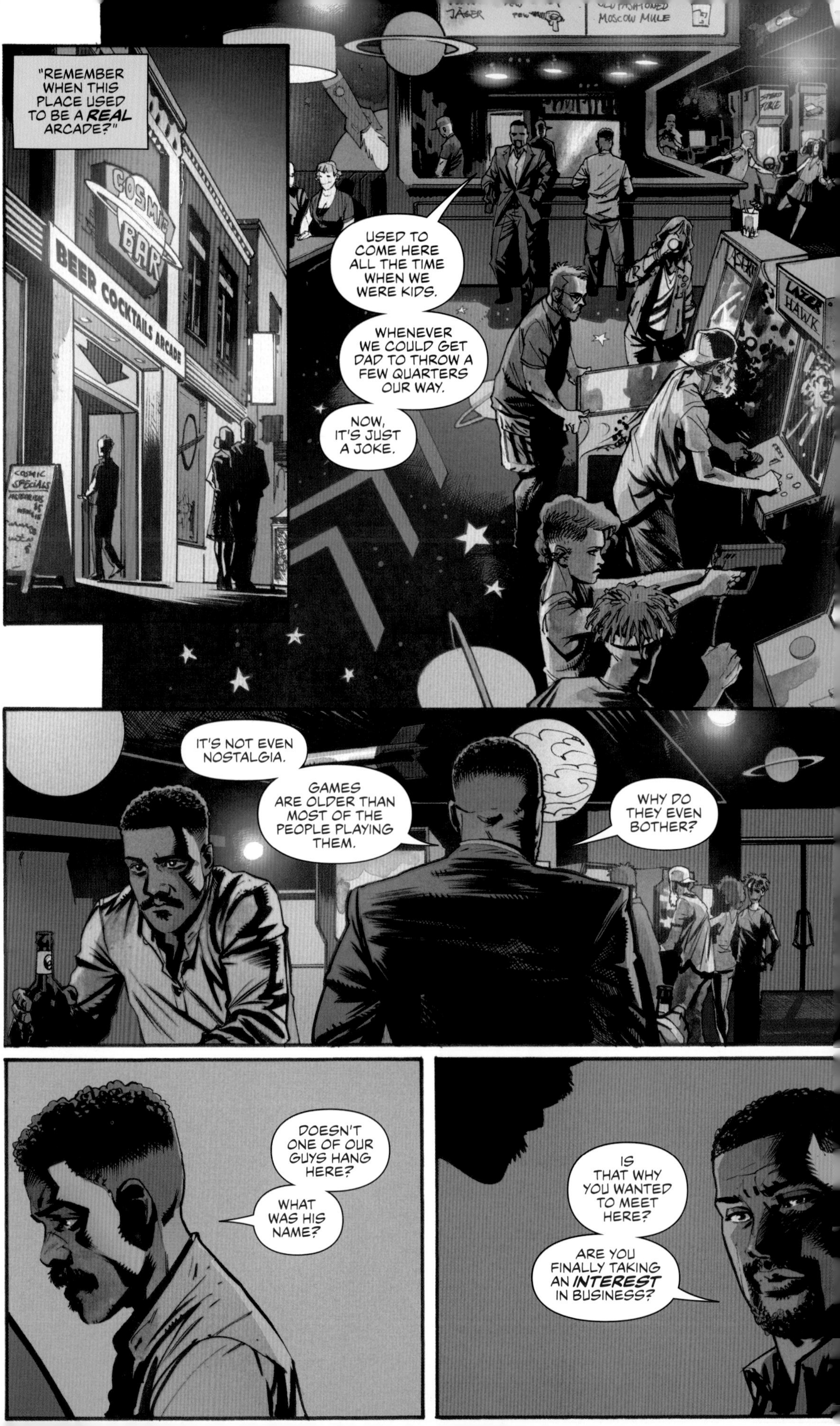

JÄGER
MOSCOW MULE
"REMEMBER WHEN THIS PLACE USED TO BE A *REAL* ARCADE?"
COSMIC BAR
BEER COCKTAILS ARCADE
USED TO COME HERE ALL THE TIME WHEN WE WERE KIDS.
WHENEVER WE COULD GET DAD TO THROW A FEW QUARTERS OUR WAY.
NOW, IT'S JUST A JOKE.
LAZER HAWK
IT'S NOT EVEN NOSTALGIA.
GAMES ARE OLDER THAN MOST OF THE PEOPLE PLAYING THEM.
WHY DO THEY EVEN BOTHER?
DOESN'T ONE OF OUR GUYS HANG HERE?
WHAT WAS HIS NAME?
IS THAT WHY YOU WANTED TO MEET HERE?
ARE YOU FINALLY TAKING AN *INTEREST* IN BUSINESS?

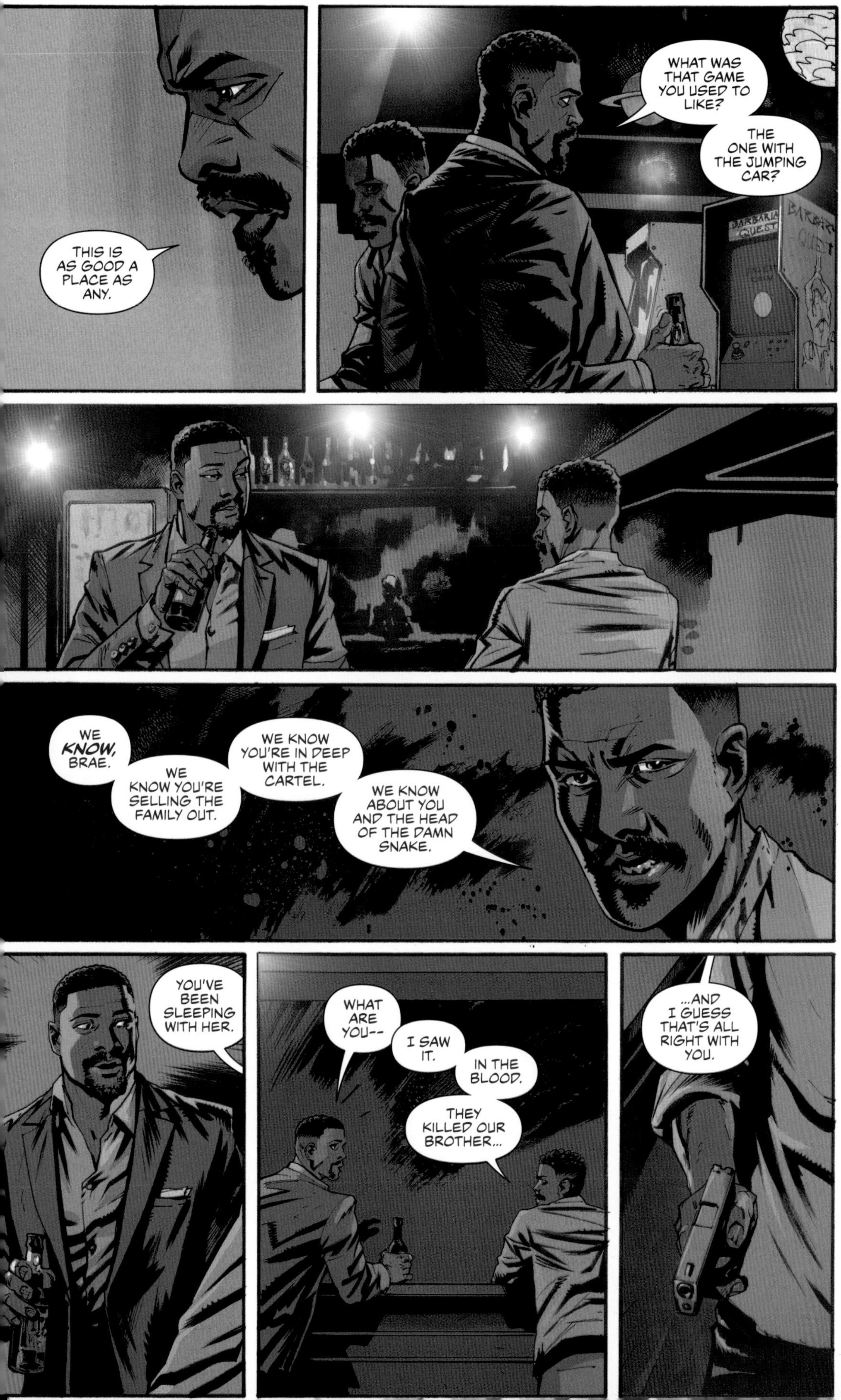
THIS IS AS GOOD A PLACE AS ANY.
WHAT WAS THAT GAME YOU USED TO LIKE?
THE ONE WITH THE JUMPING CAR?
BARBARIA QUEST
WE *KNOW,* BRAE.
WE KNOW YOU'RE SELLING THE FAMILY OUT.
WE KNOW YOU'RE IN DEEP WITH THE CARTEL.
WE KNOW ABOUT YOU AND THE HEAD OF THE DAMN SNAKE.
YOU'VE BEEN SLEEPING WITH HER.
WHAT ARE YOU--
I SAW IT.
IN THE BLOOD.
THEY KILLED OUR BROTHER...
...AND I GUESS THAT'S ALL RIGHT WITH YOU.

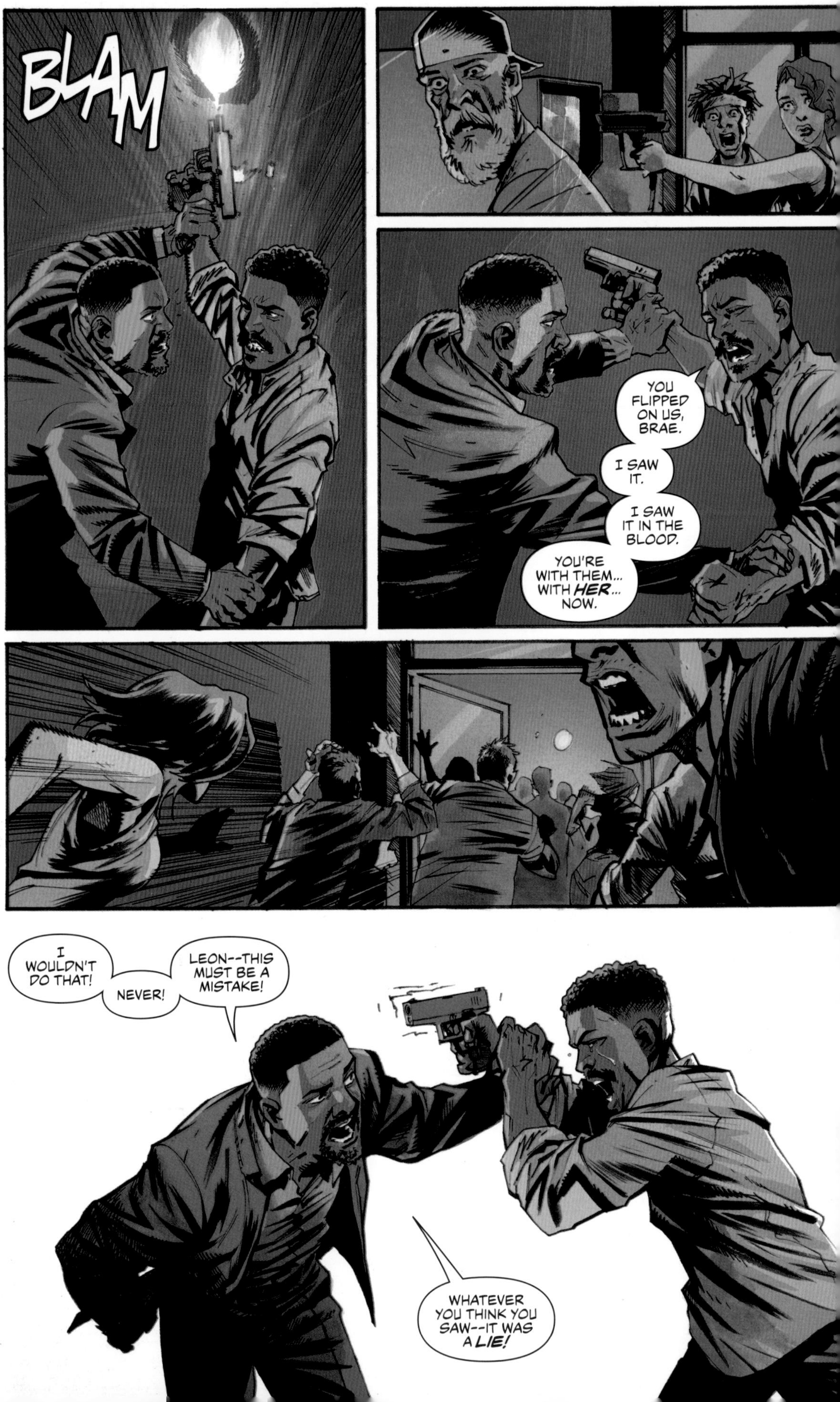
BLAM
YOU FLIPPED ON US, BRAE.
I SAW IT.
I SAW IT IN THE BLOOD.
YOU'RE WITH THEM... WITH HER... NOW.
I WOULDN'T DO THAT!
NEVER!
LEON--THIS MUST BE A MISTAKE!
WHATEVER YOU THINK YOU SAW--IT WAS A LIE!

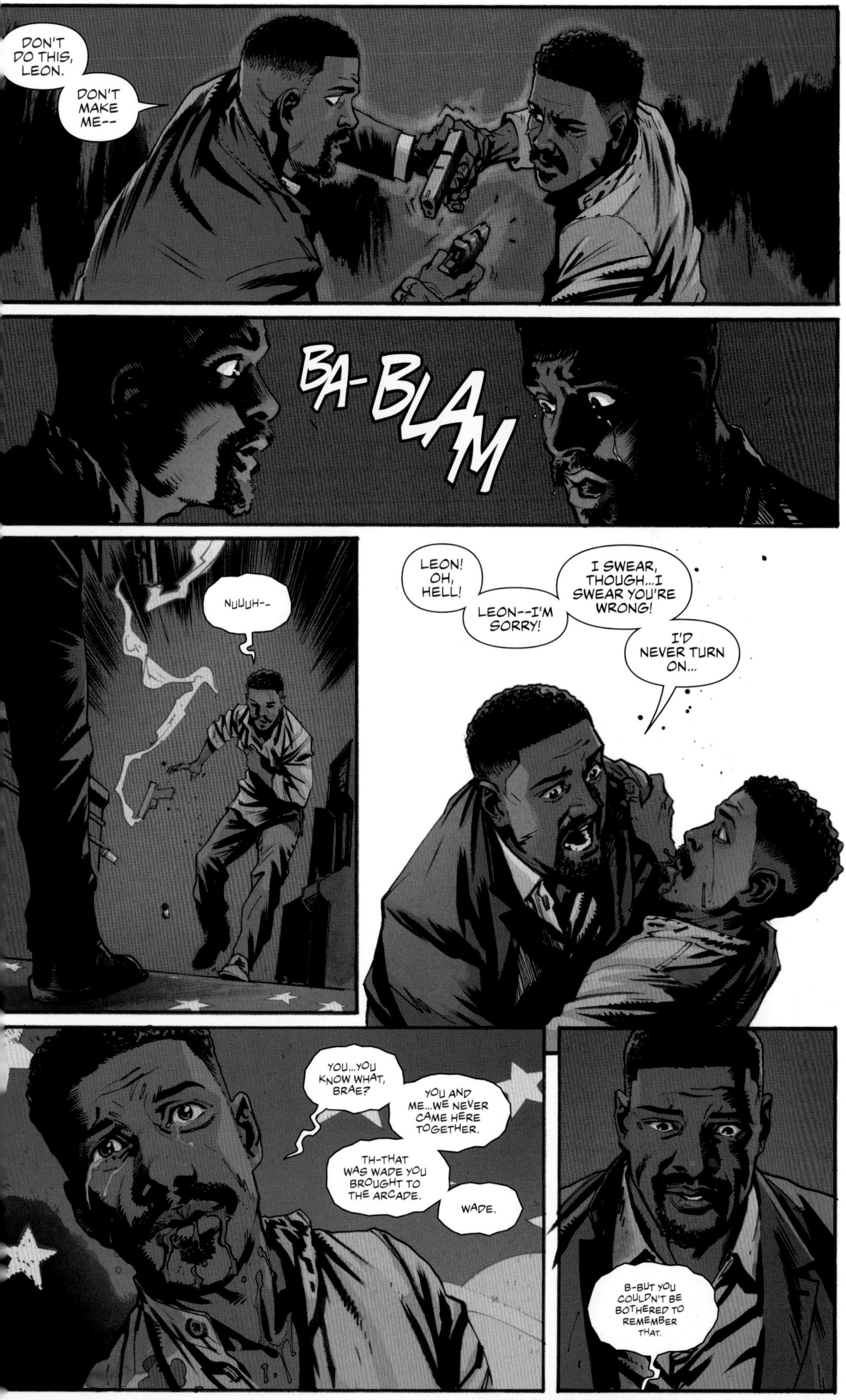
DON'T DO THIS, LEON.
DON'T MAKE ME--
BA-BLAM
NUUUH--
LEON! OH, HELL!
LEON--I'M SORRY!
I SWEAR, THOUGH...I SWEAR YOU'RE WRONG!
I'D NEVER TURN ON...
YOU...YOU KNOW WHAT, BRAE?
YOU AND ME...WE NEVER CAME HERE TOGETHER.
TH-THAT WAS WADE YOU BROUGHT TO THE ARCADE.
WADE.
B-BUT YOU COULDN'T BE BOTHERED TO REMEMBER THAT.

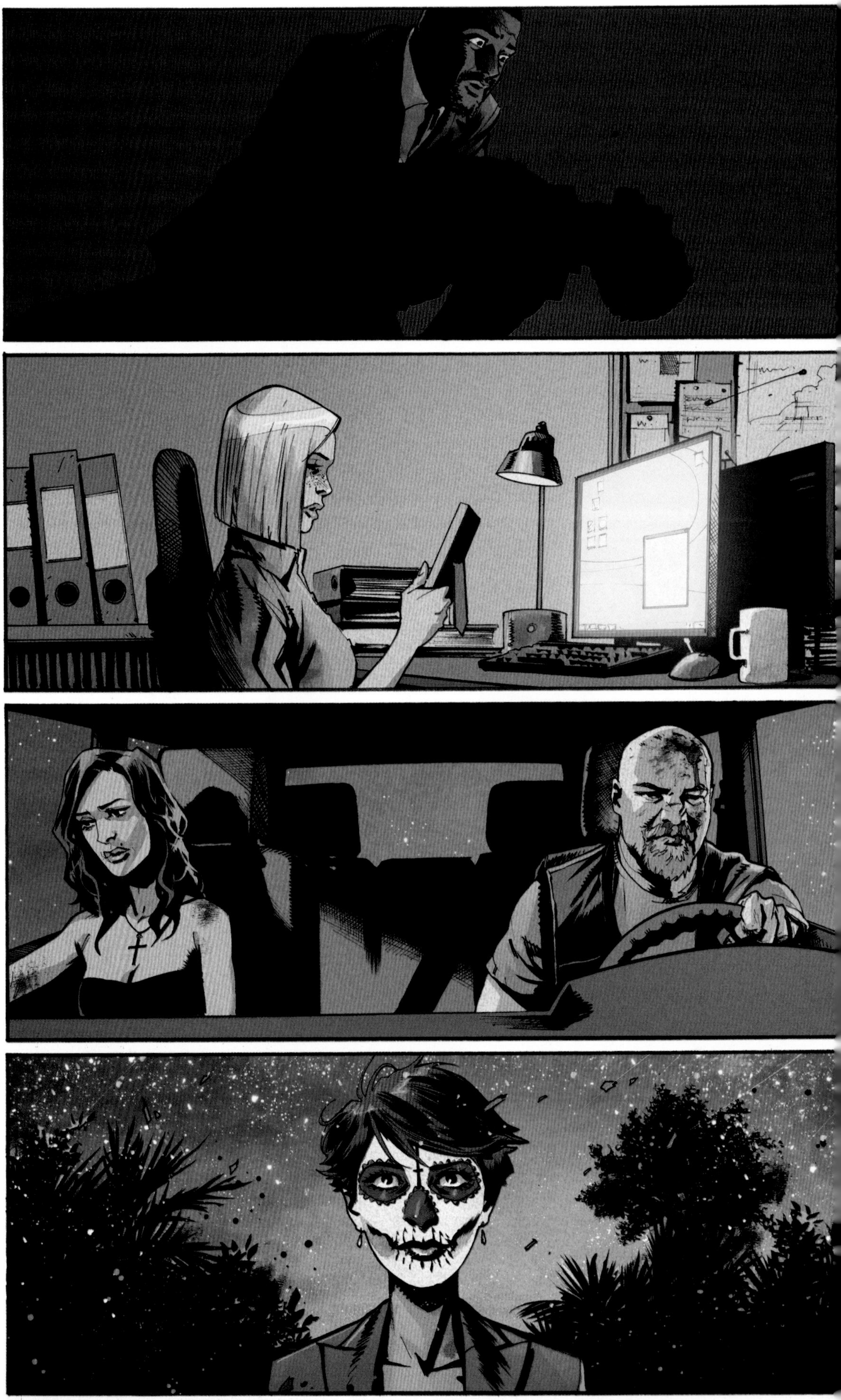

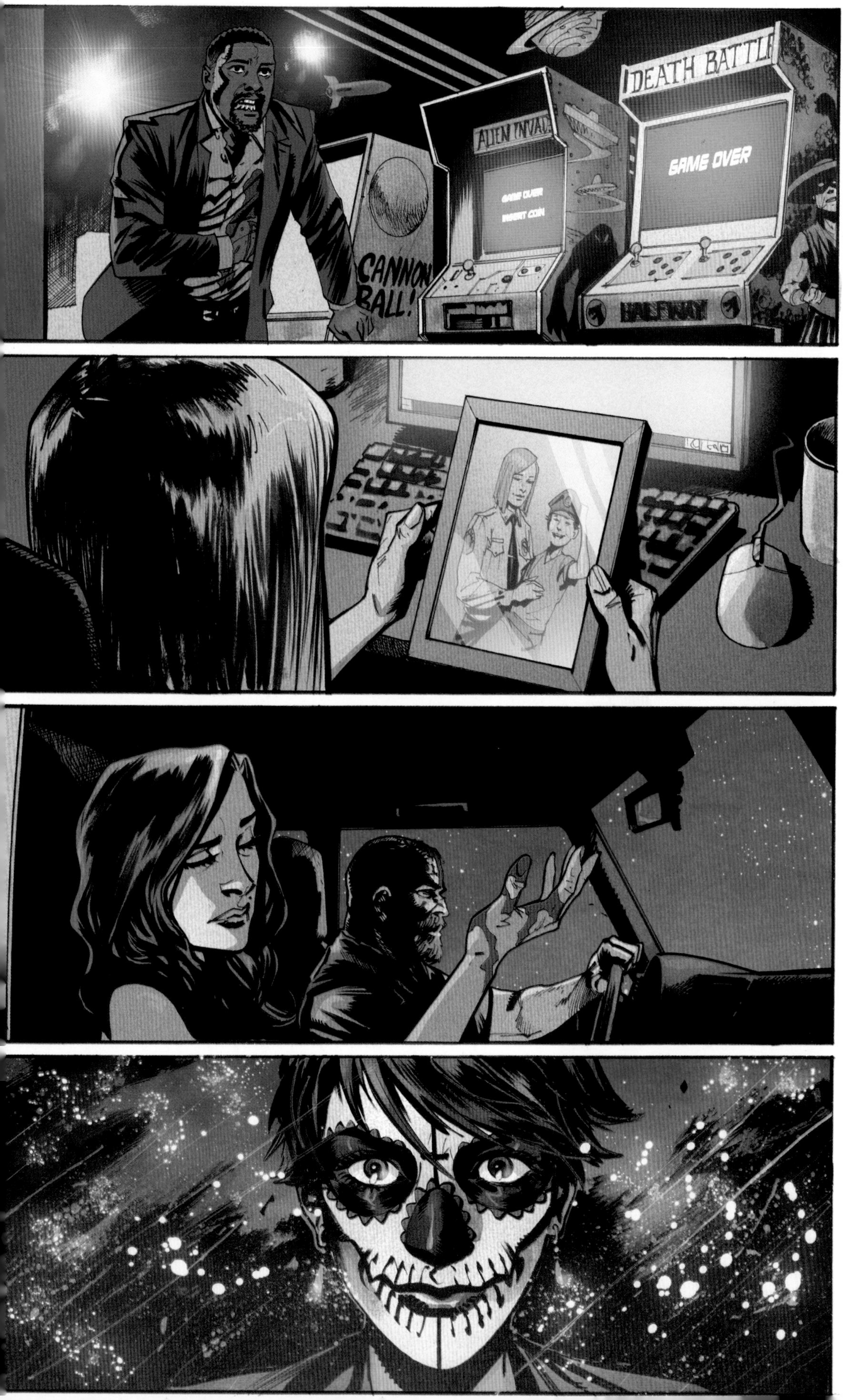
DEATH BATTL
ALIEN INVAD
GAME OVER
GAME OVER
INSERT COIN
CANNON BALL!

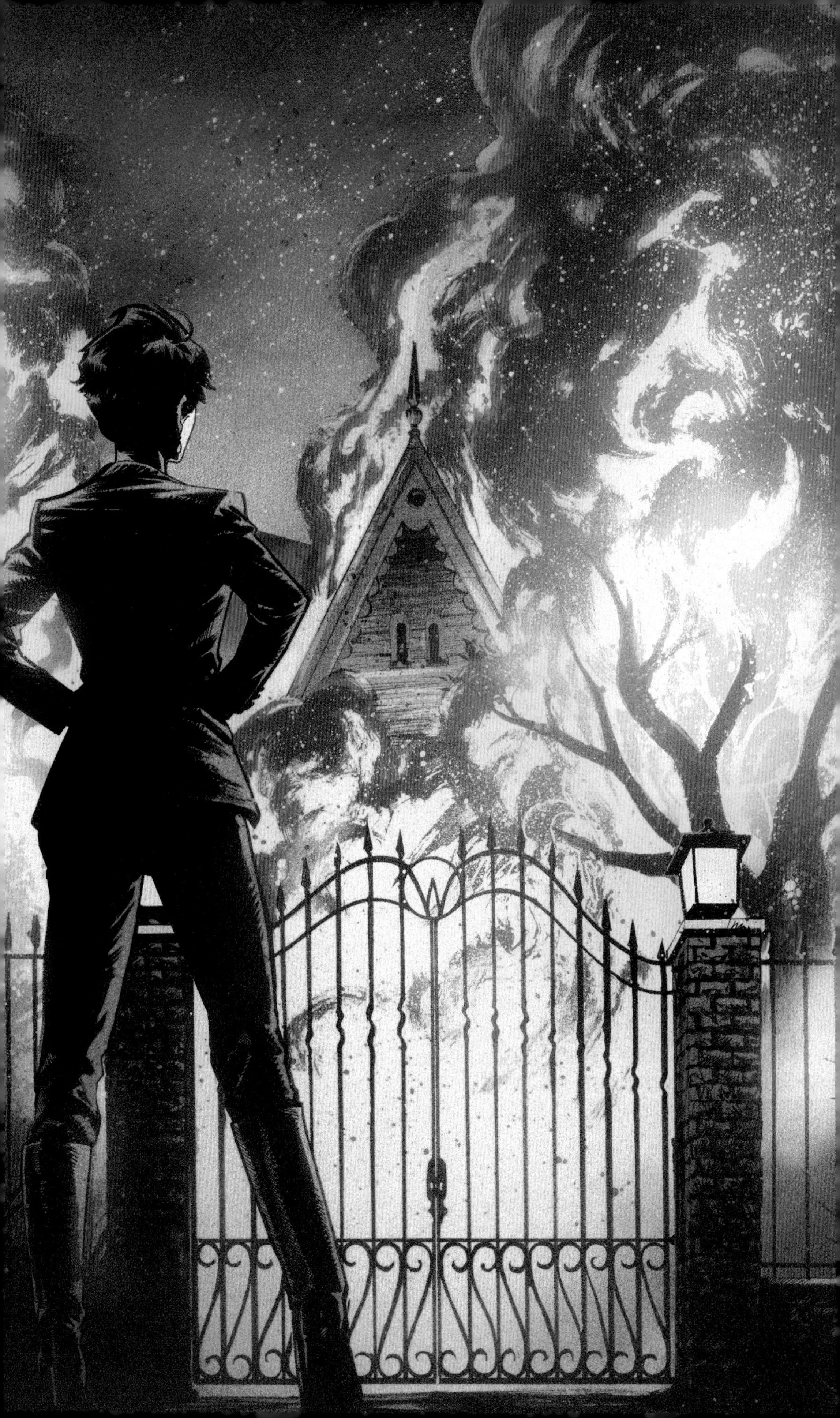

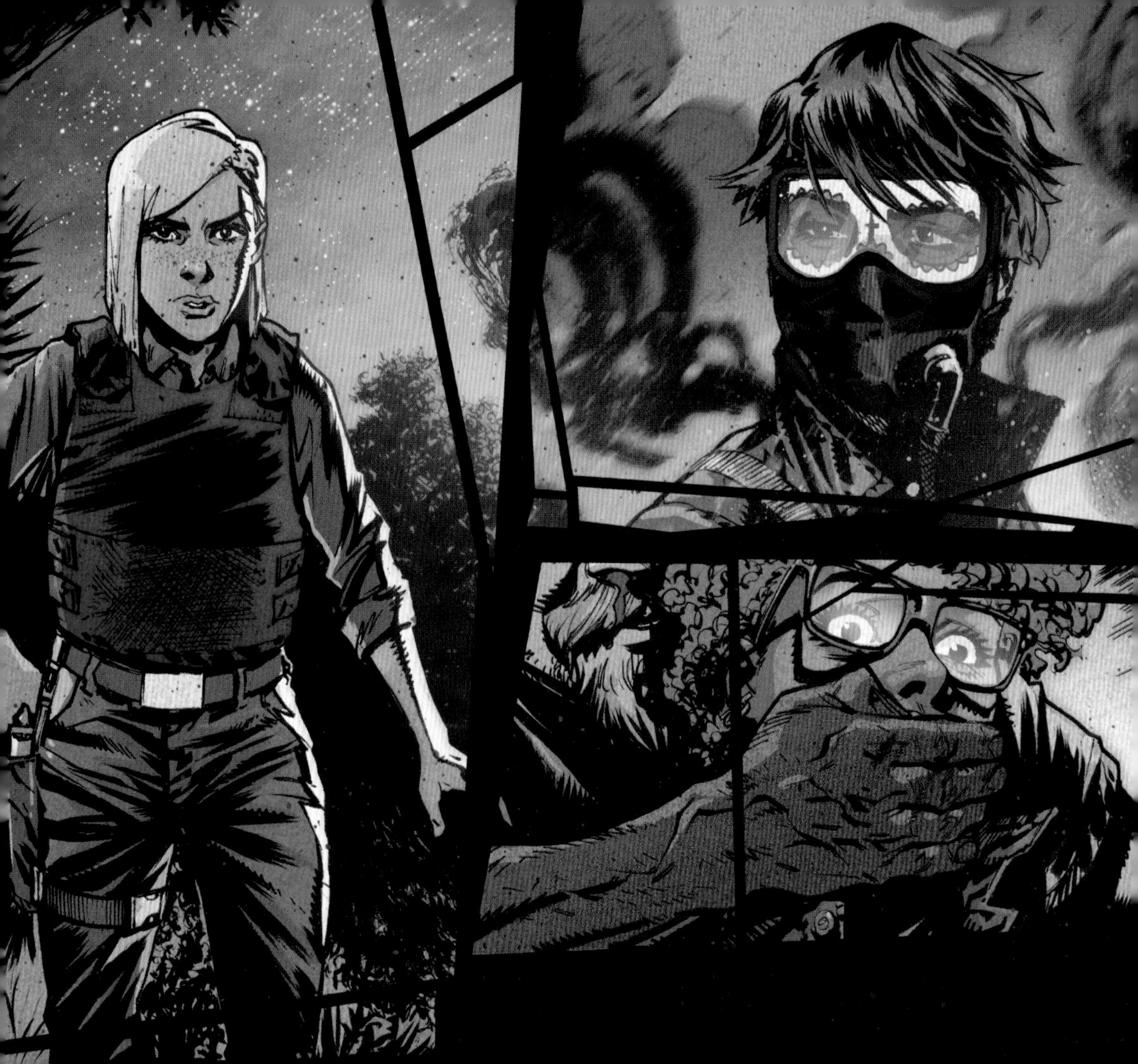

Chapter Twelve

CHASING THE LIVING

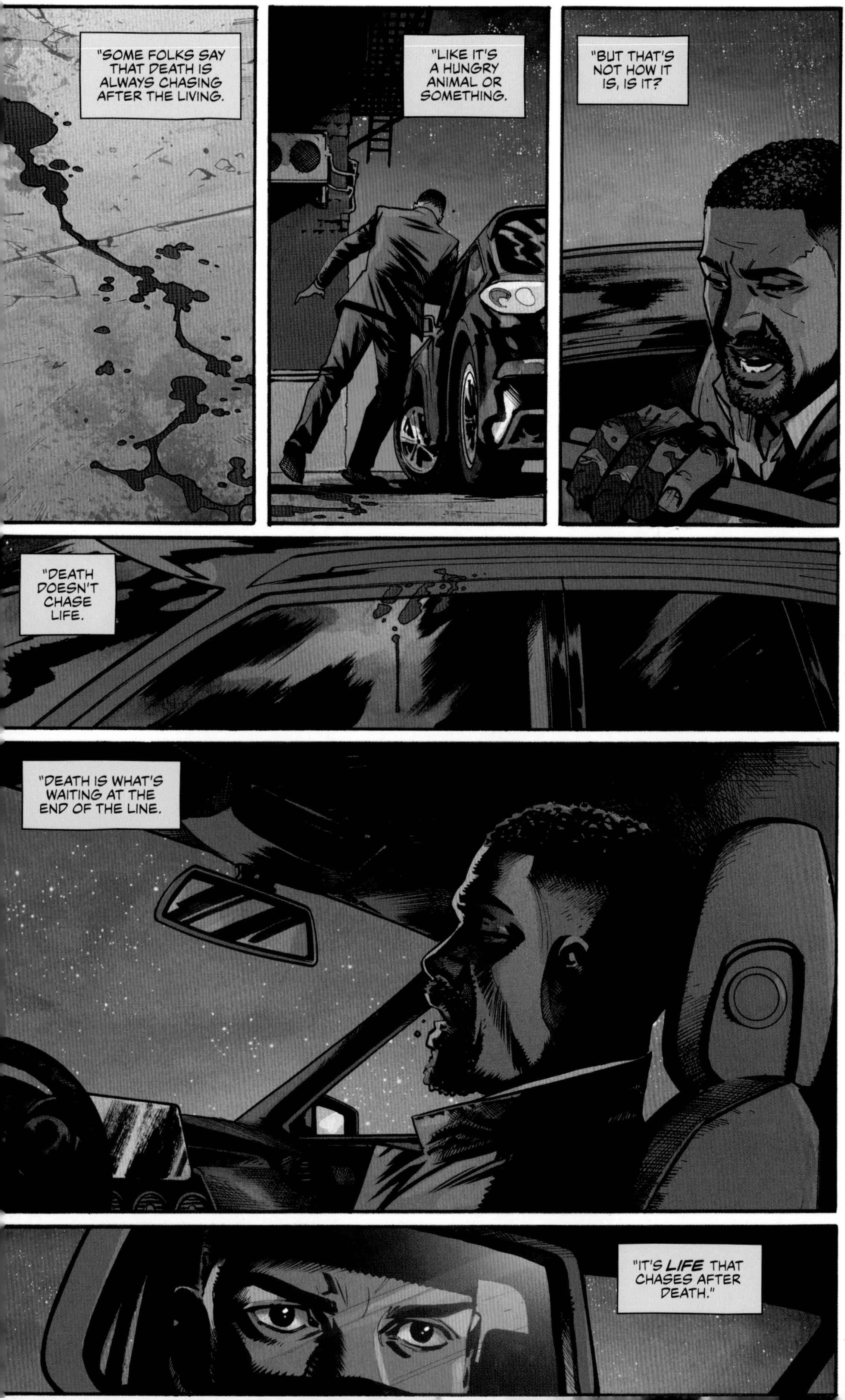
"SOME FOLKS SAY THAT DEATH IS ALWAYS CHASING AFTER THE LIVING.
"LIKE IT'S A HUNGRY ANIMAL OR SOMETHING.
"BUT THAT'S NOT HOW IT IS, IS IT?
"DEATH DOESN'T CHASE LIFE.
"DEATH IS WHAT'S WAITING AT THE END OF THE LINE.
"IT'S *LIFE* THAT CHASES AFTER DEATH."

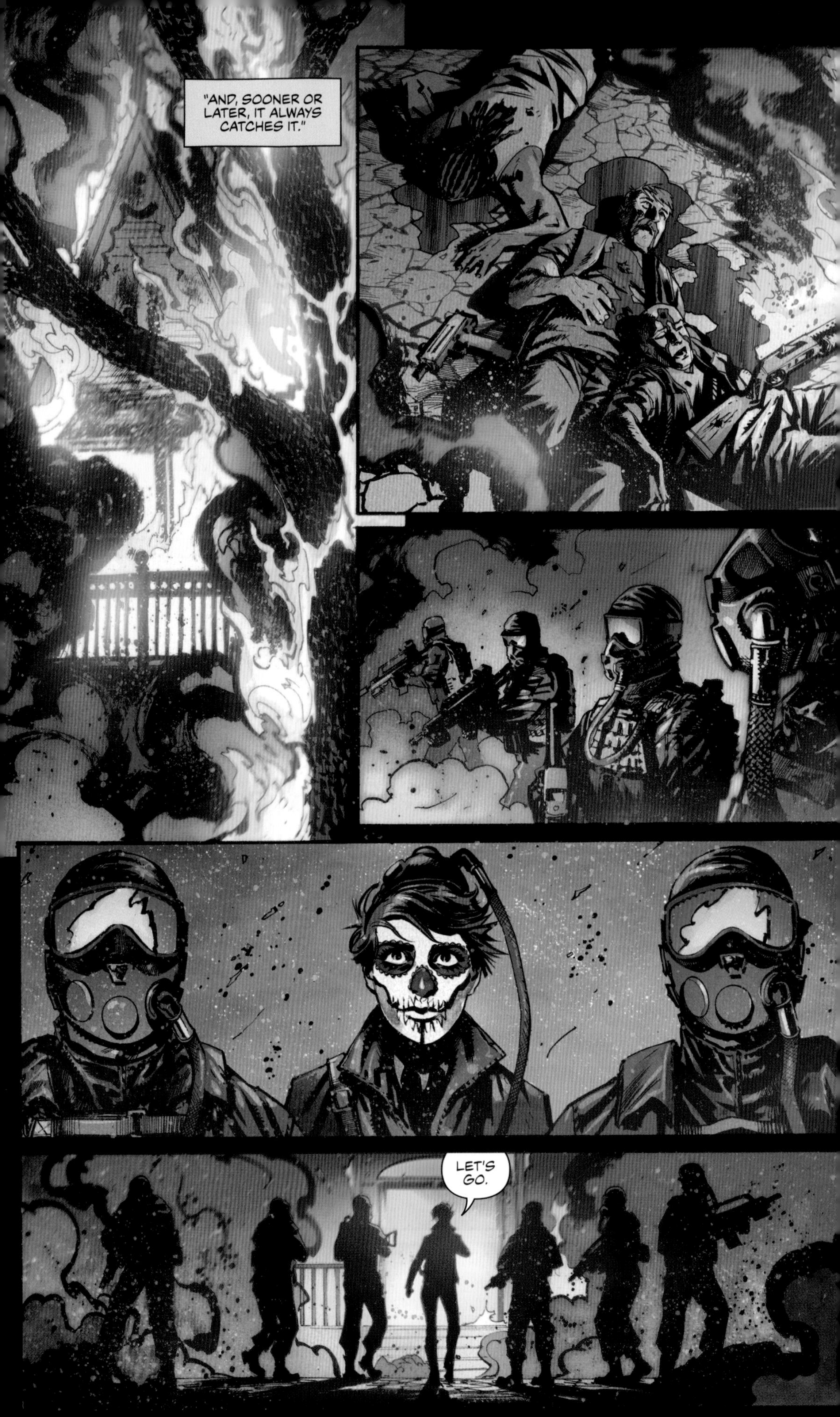
"AND, SOONER OR LATER, IT ALWAYS CATCHES IT."
LET'S GO.

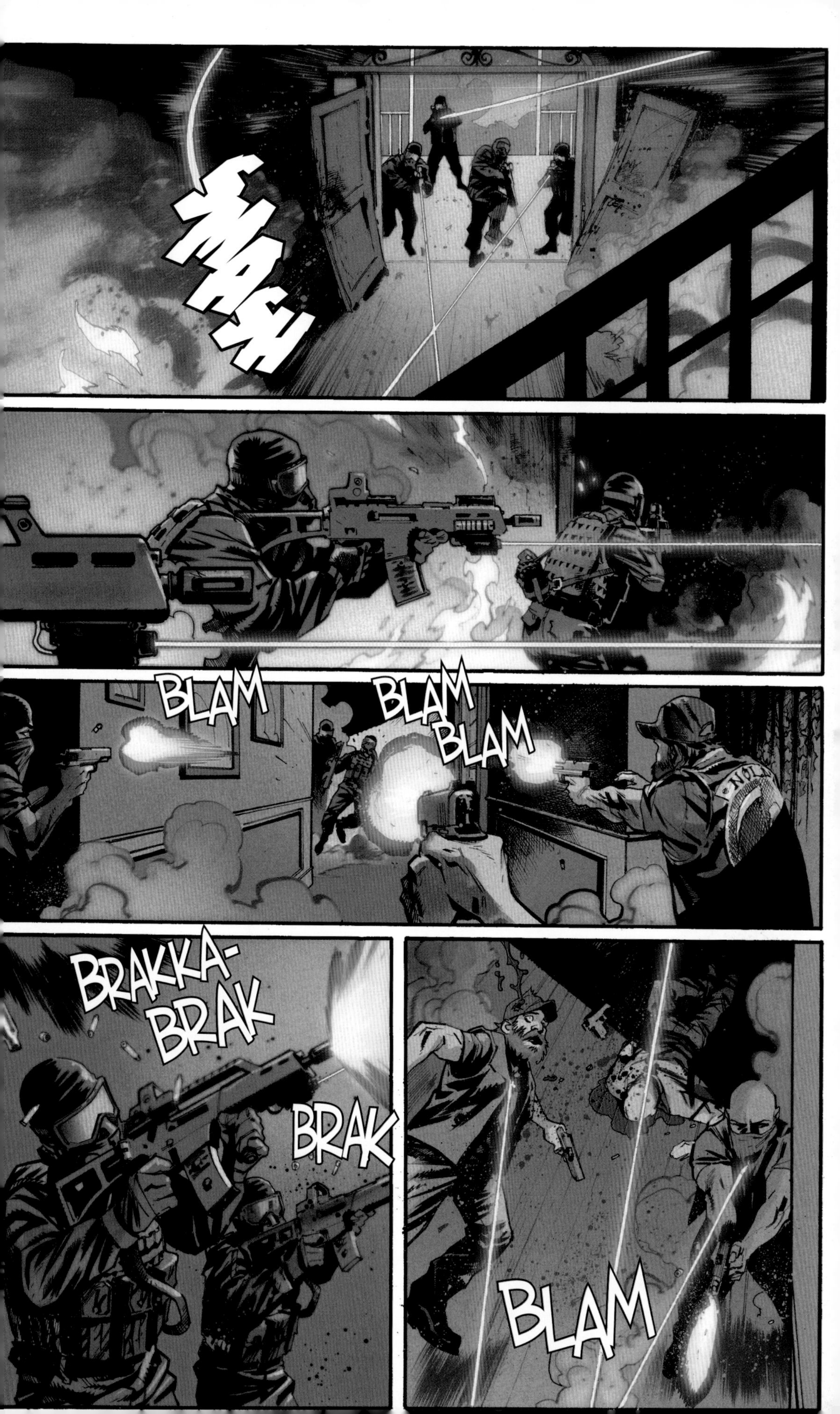
SMASH
BLAM
BLAM
BLAM
BRAKKA-
BRAK
BRAK
BLAM

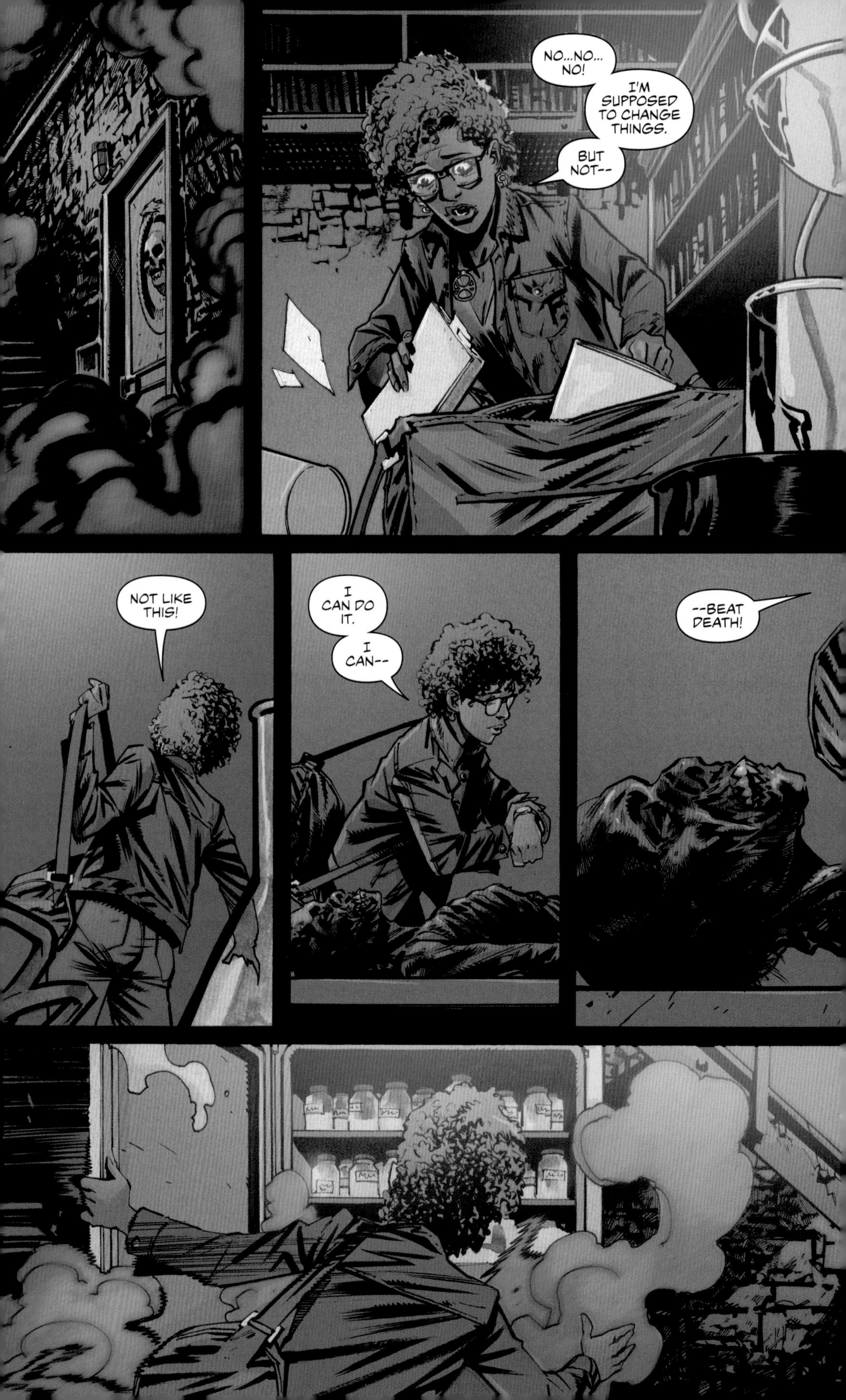
NO...NO...
NO!
I'M SUPPOSED TO CHANGE THINGS.
BUT NOT--
NOT LIKE THIS!
I CAN DO IT.
I CAN--
--BEAT DEATH!

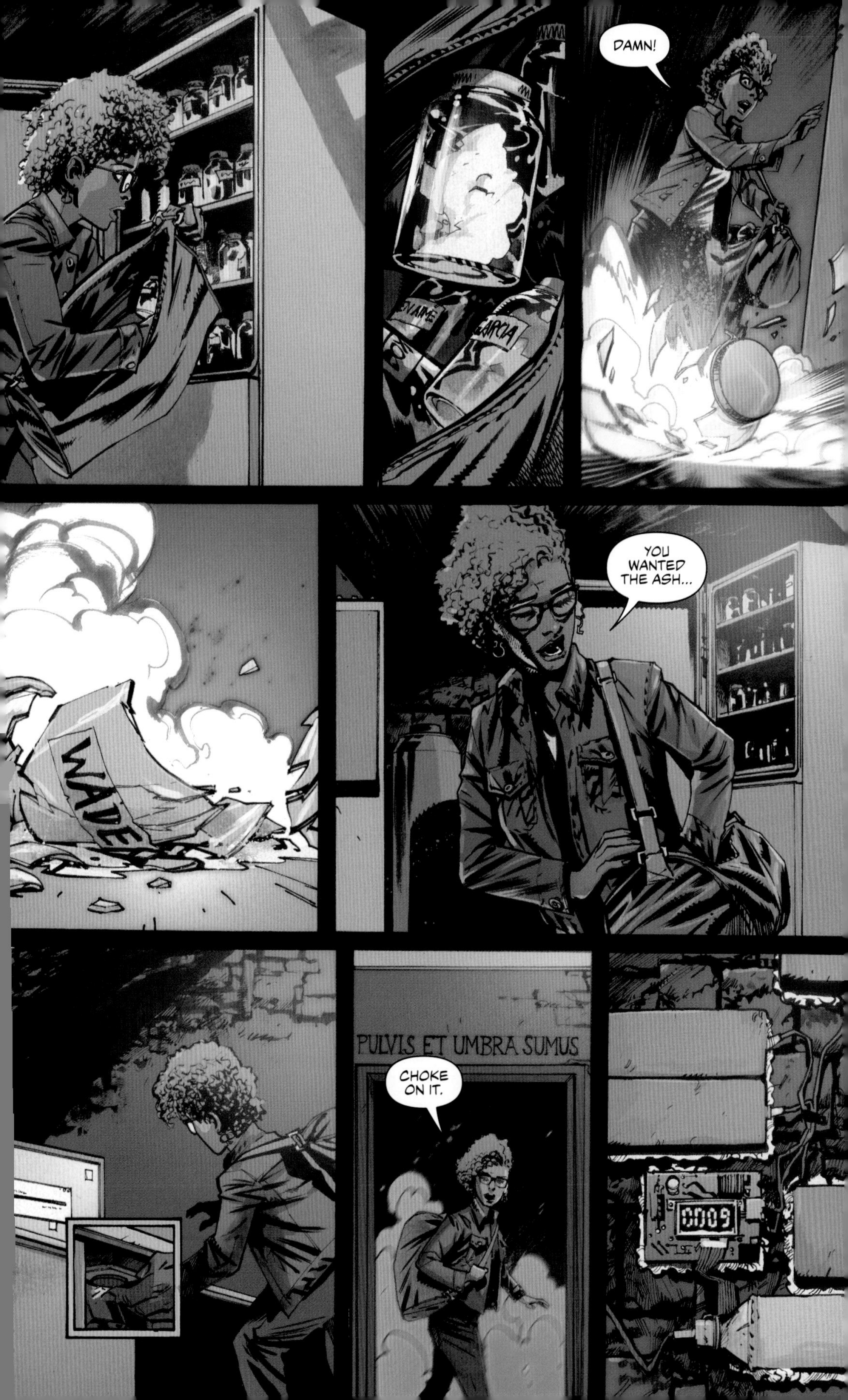

DAMN!
WADE
YOU WANTED THE ASH...
PULVIS ET UMBRA SUMUS
CHOKE ON IT.
0009

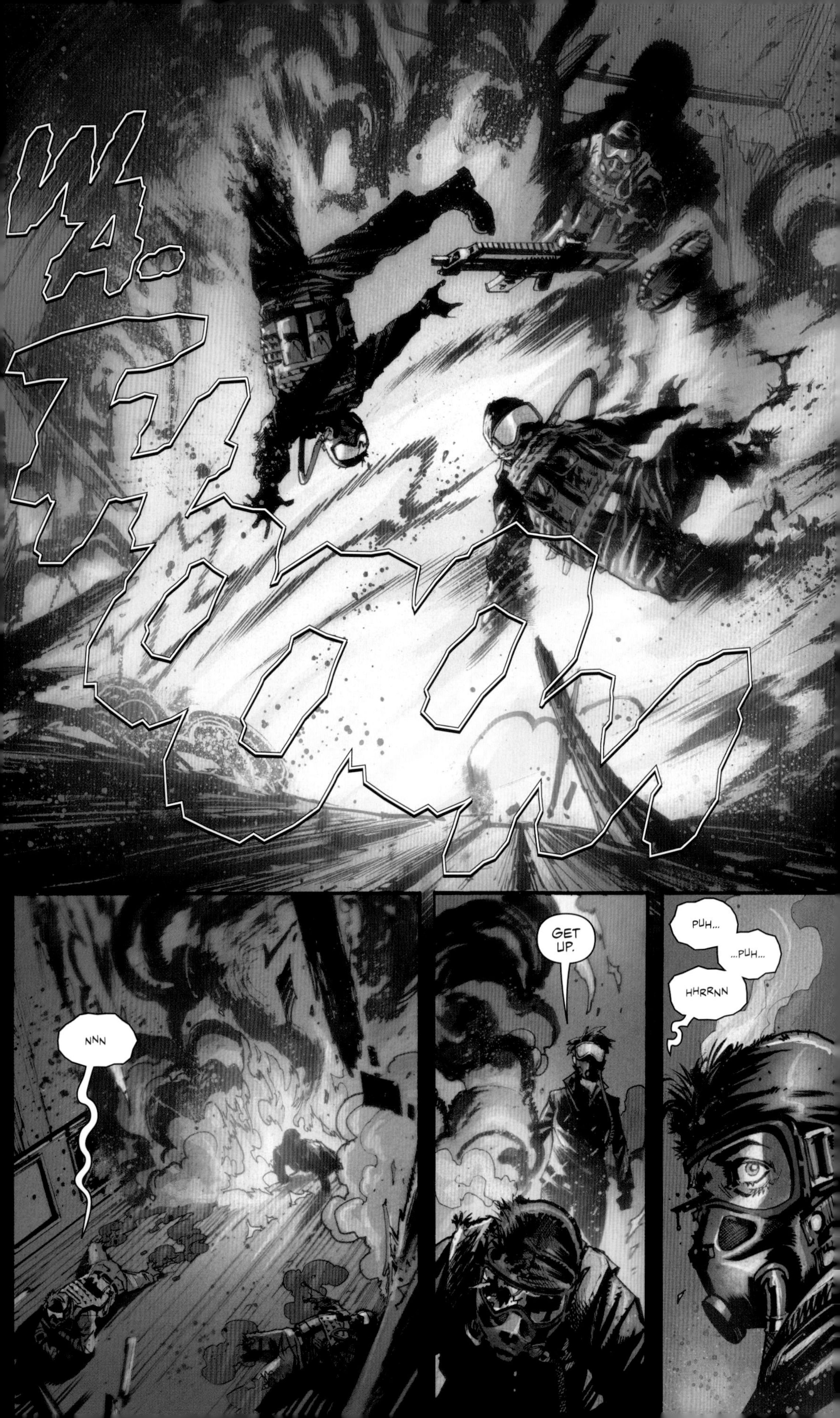
WA-THOOOM
NNN
GET UP.
PUH...
...PUH...
HHRRNN

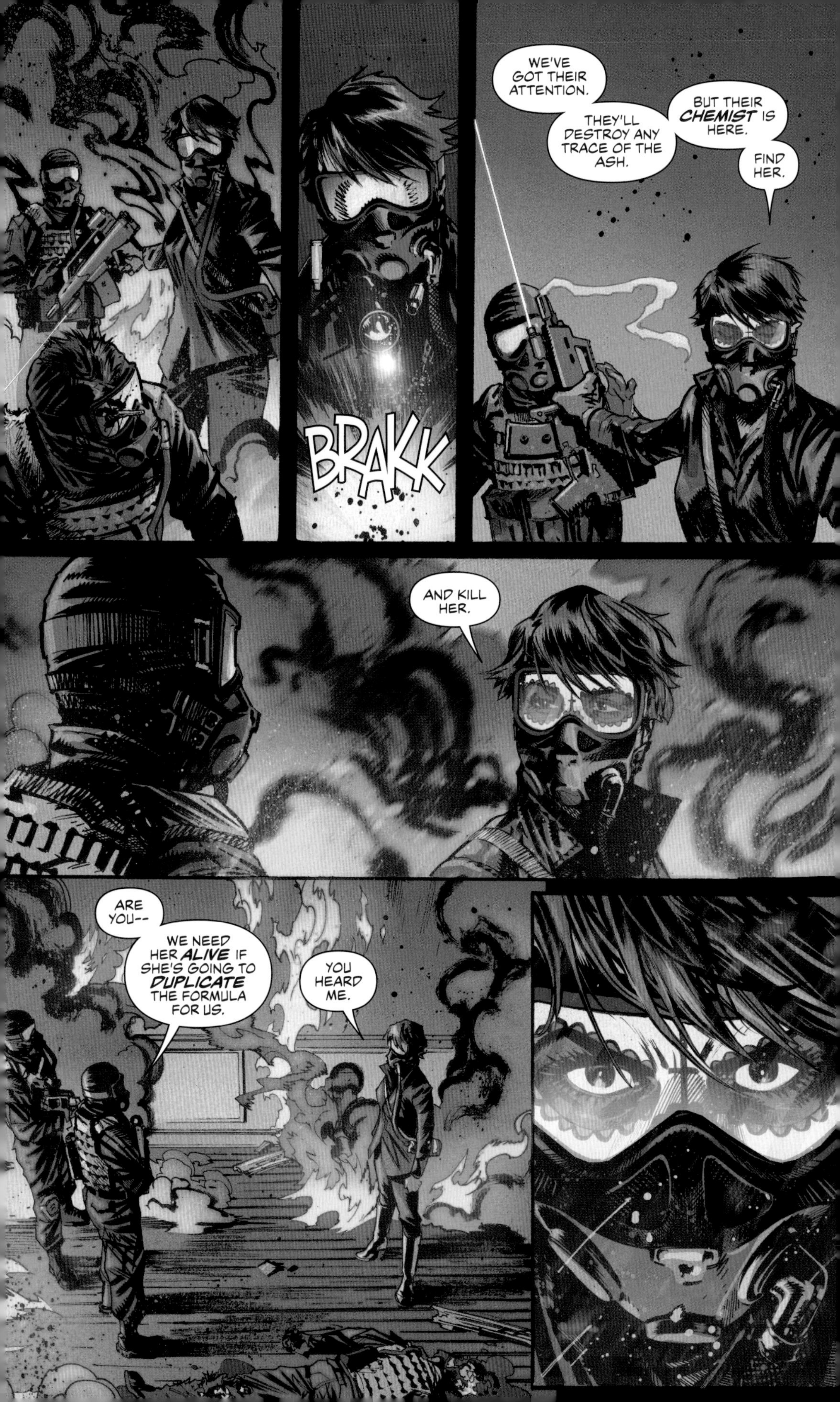
BRAKK
WE'VE GOT THEIR ATTENTION.
THEY'LL DESTROY ANY TRACE OF THE ASH.
BUT THEIR CHEMIST IS HERE.
FIND HER.
AND KILL HER.
ARE YOU--
WE NEED HER ALIVE IF SHE'S GOING TO DUPLICATE THE FORMULA FOR US.
YOU HEARD ME.

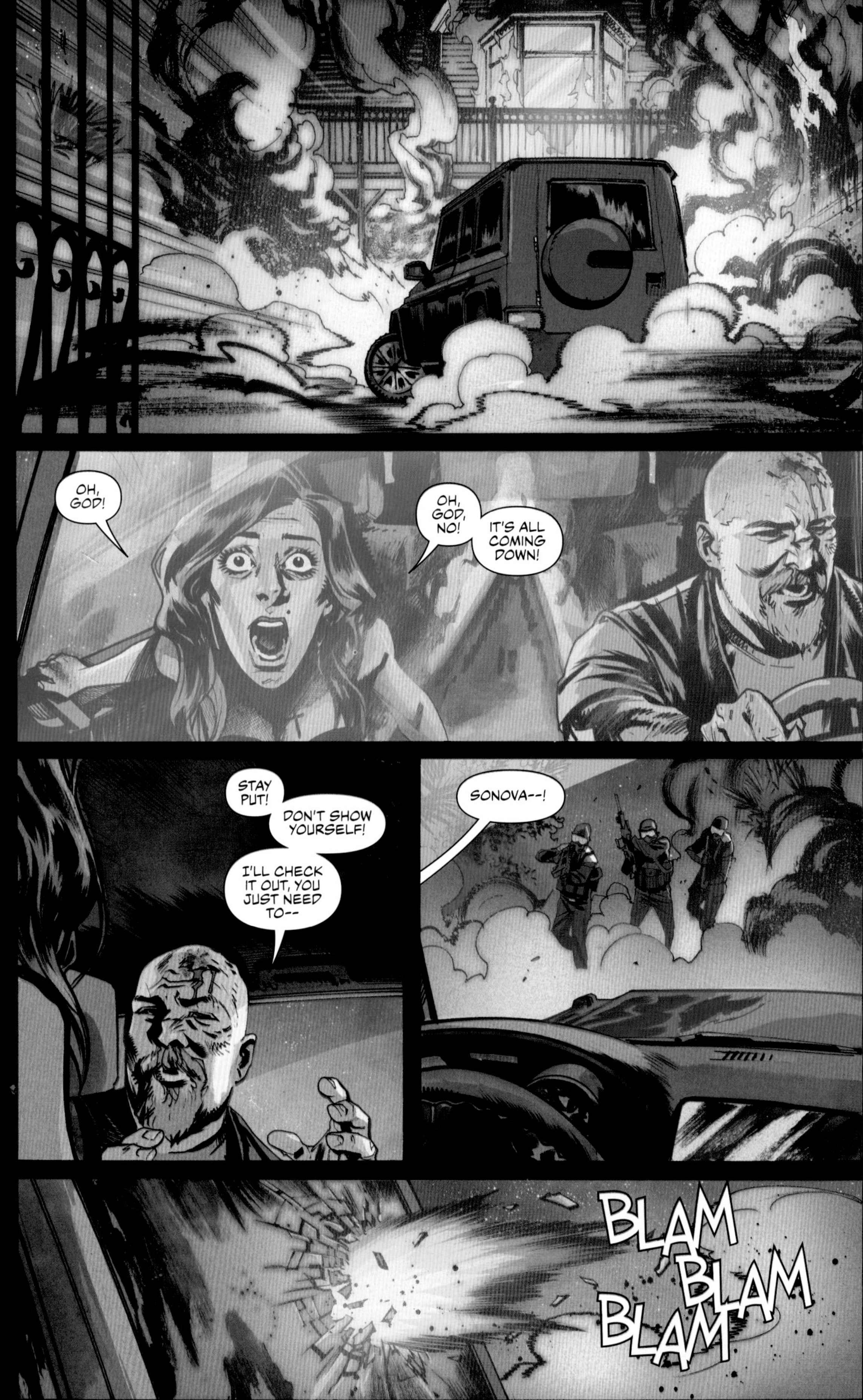
OH, GOD!
OH, GOD, NO!
IT'S ALL COMING DOWN!
STAY PUT!
DON'T SHOW YOURSELF!
I'LL CHECK IT OUT, YOU JUST NEED TO--
SONOVA--!
BLAM BLAM BLAM

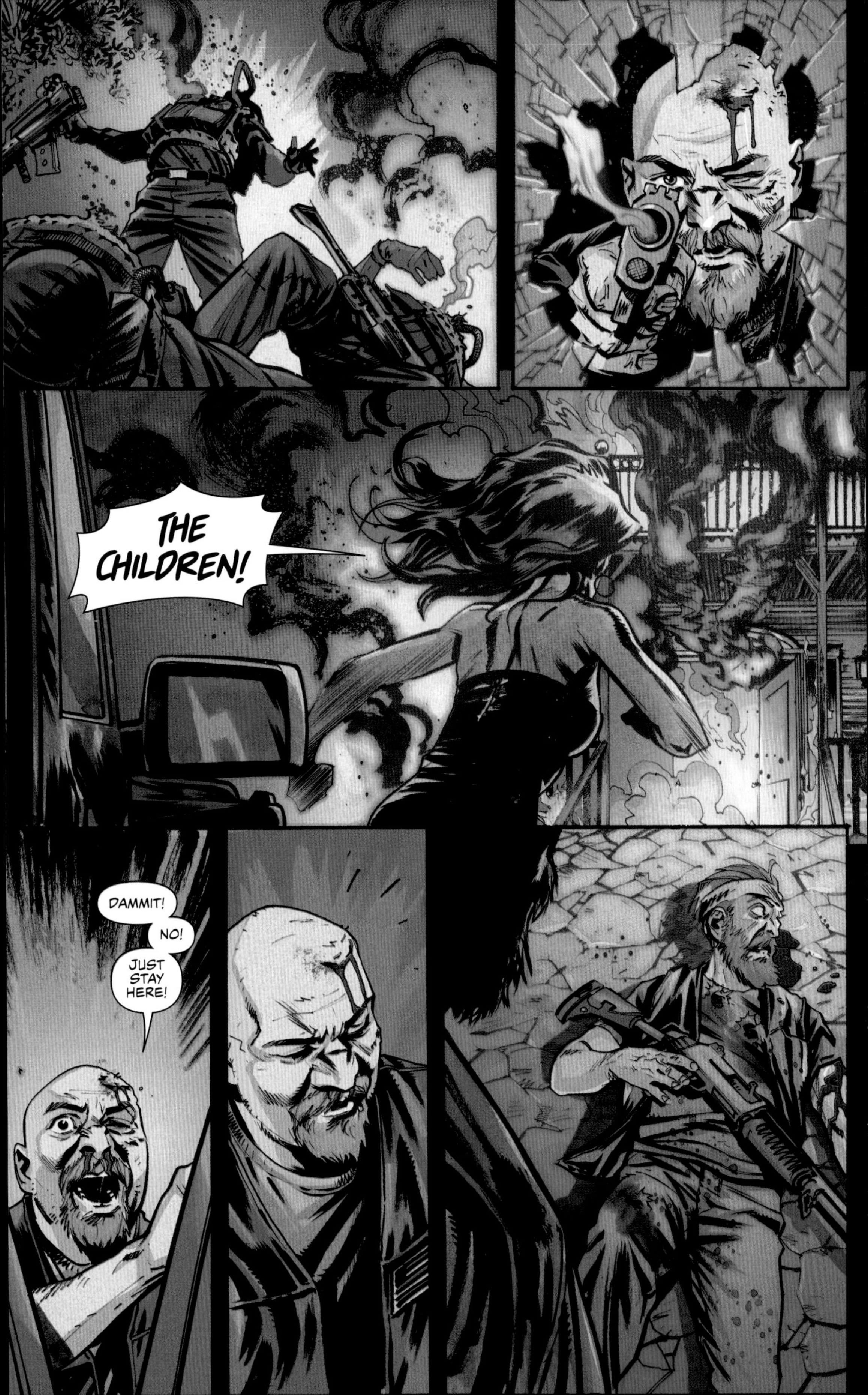
THE CHILDREN!
DAMMIT!
NO!
JUST STAY HERE!

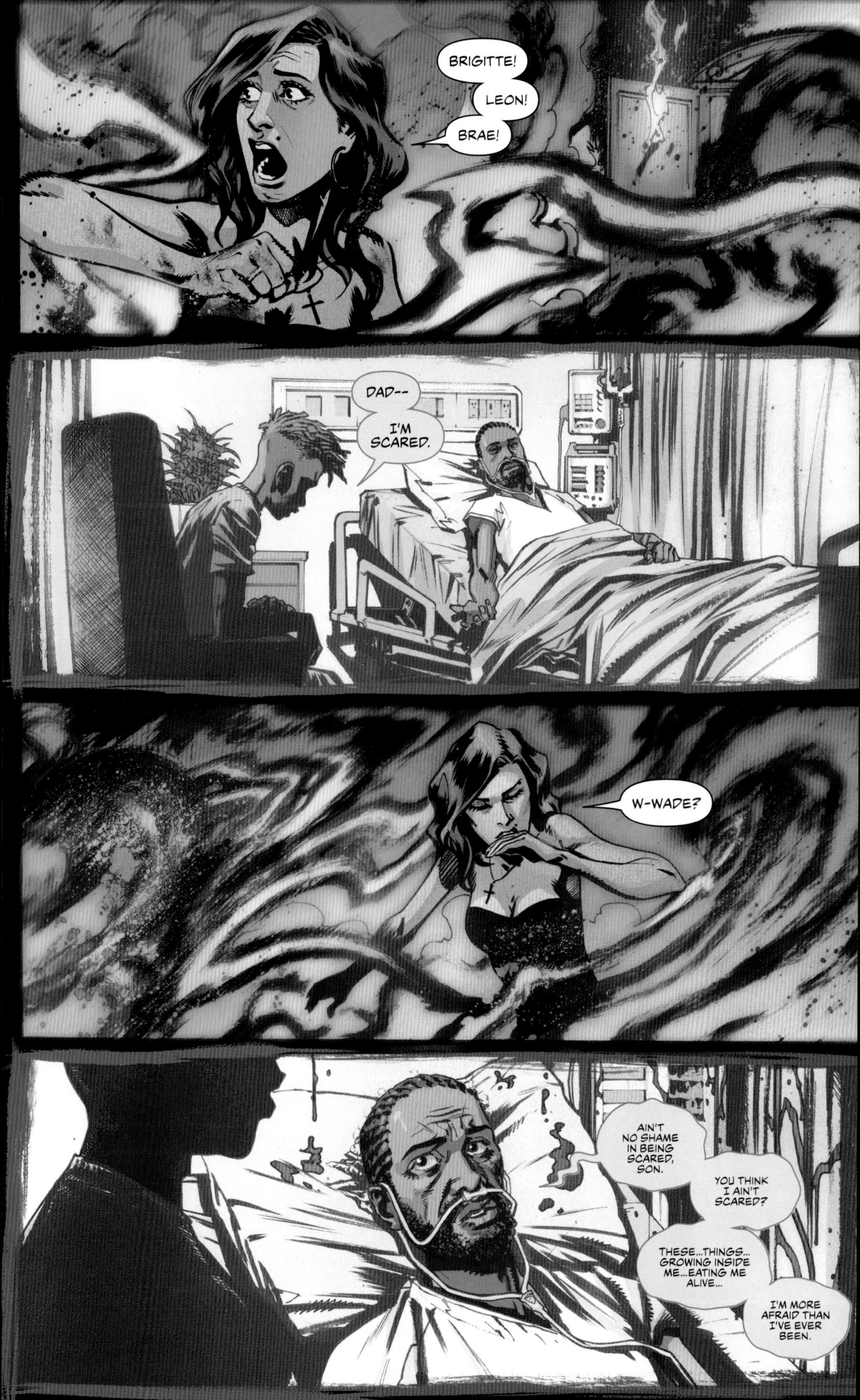
BRIGITTE!
LEON!
BRAE!
DAD--
I'M SCARED.
W-WADE?
AIN'T NO SHAME IN BEING SCARED, SON.
YOU THINK I AIN'T SCARED?
THESE...THINGS... GROWING INSIDE ME...EATING ME ALIVE...
I'M MORE AFRAID THAN I'VE EVER BEEN.

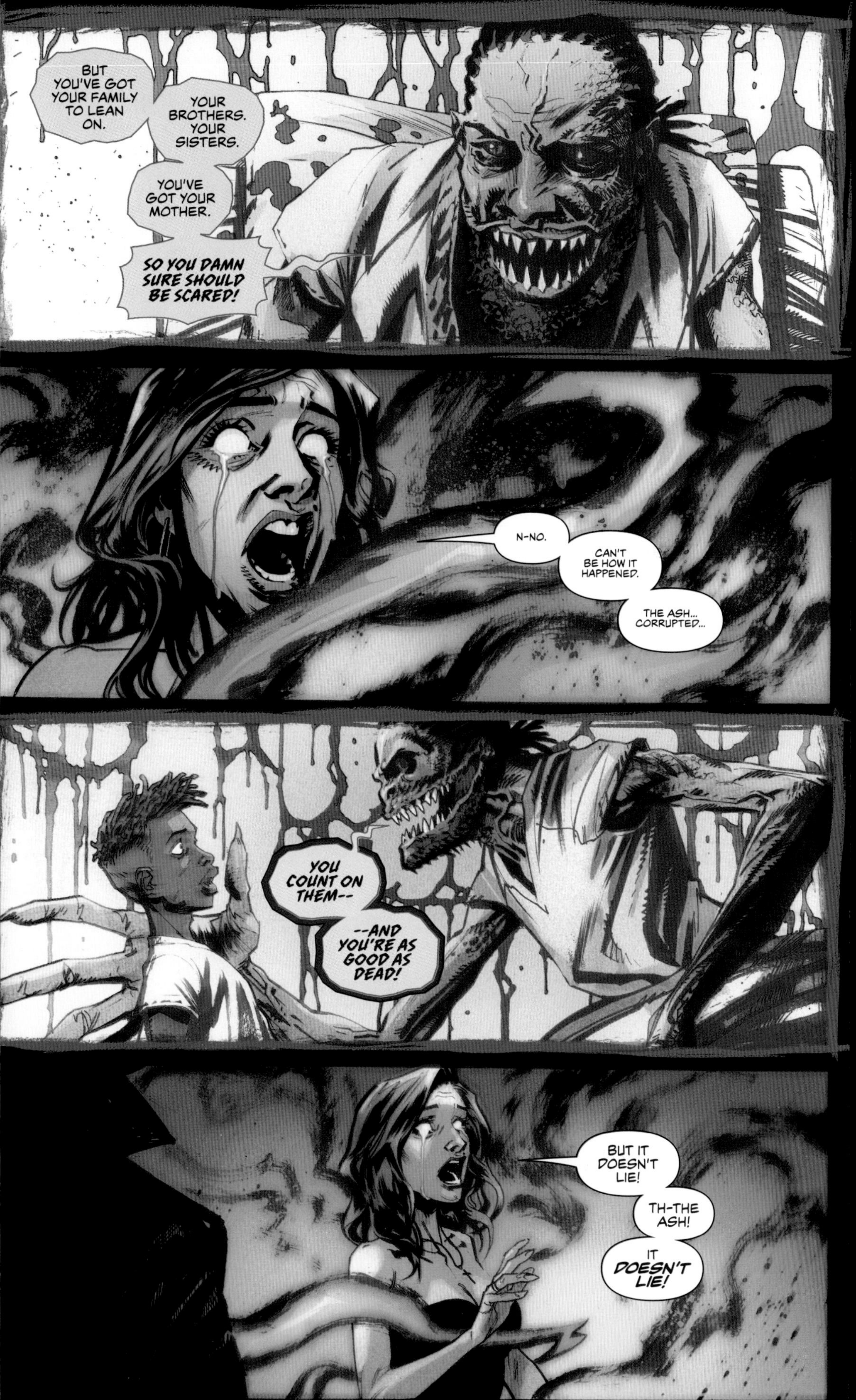

BUT YOU'VE GOT YOUR FAMILY TO LEAN ON.
YOUR BROTHERS. YOUR SISTERS.
YOU'VE GOT YOUR MOTHER.
SO YOU DAMN SURE SHOULD BE SCARED!
N-NO.
CAN'T BE HOW IT HAPPENED.
THE ASH... CORRUPTED...
YOU COUNT ON THEM--
--AND YOU'RE AS GOOD AS DEAD!
BUT IT DOESN'T LIE!
TH-THE ASH!
IT DOESN'T LIE!

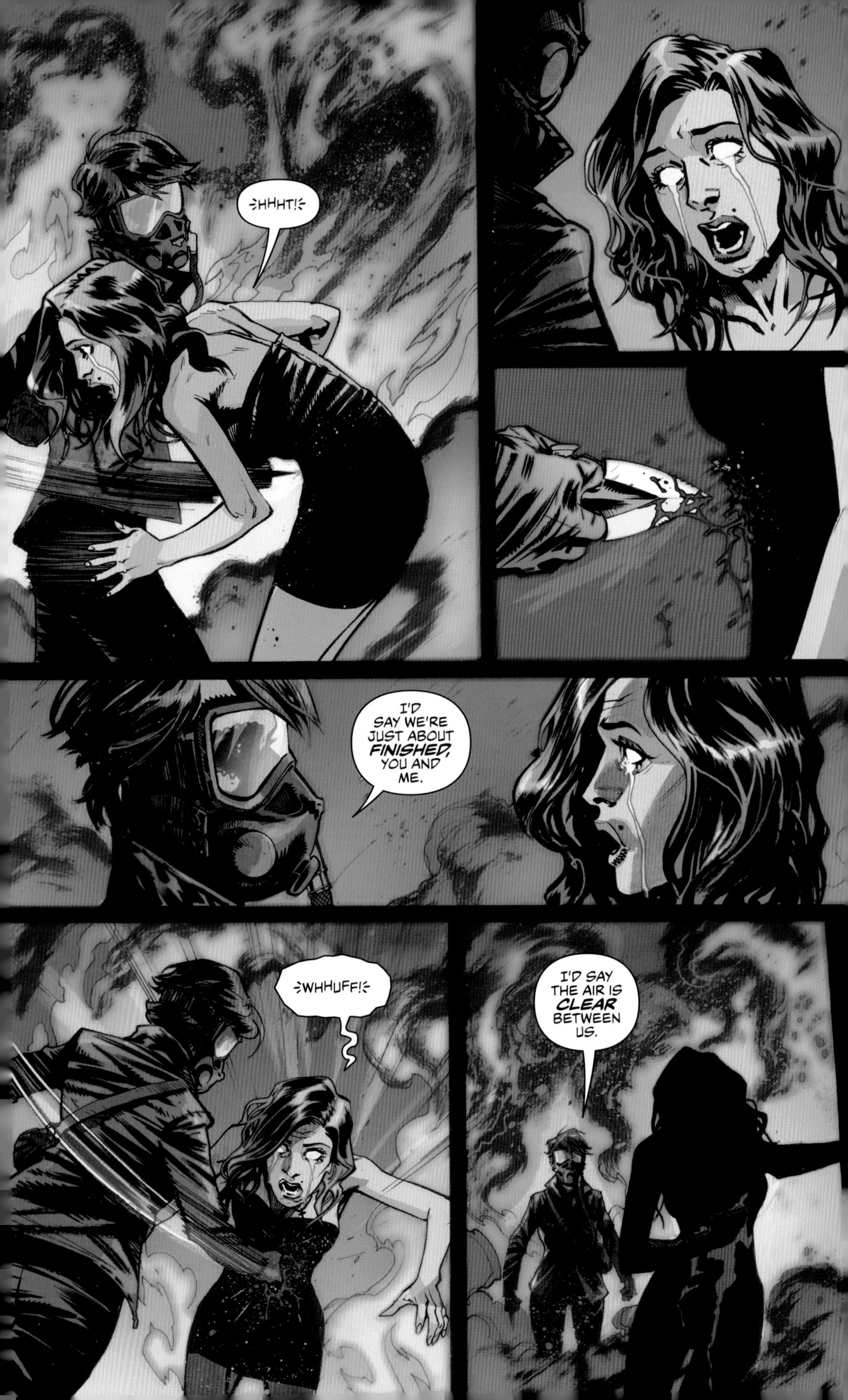
HHHT!
I'D SAY WE'RE JUST ABOUT FINISHED, YOU AND ME.
WHHUFF!
I'D SAY THE AIR IS CLEAR BETWEEN US.

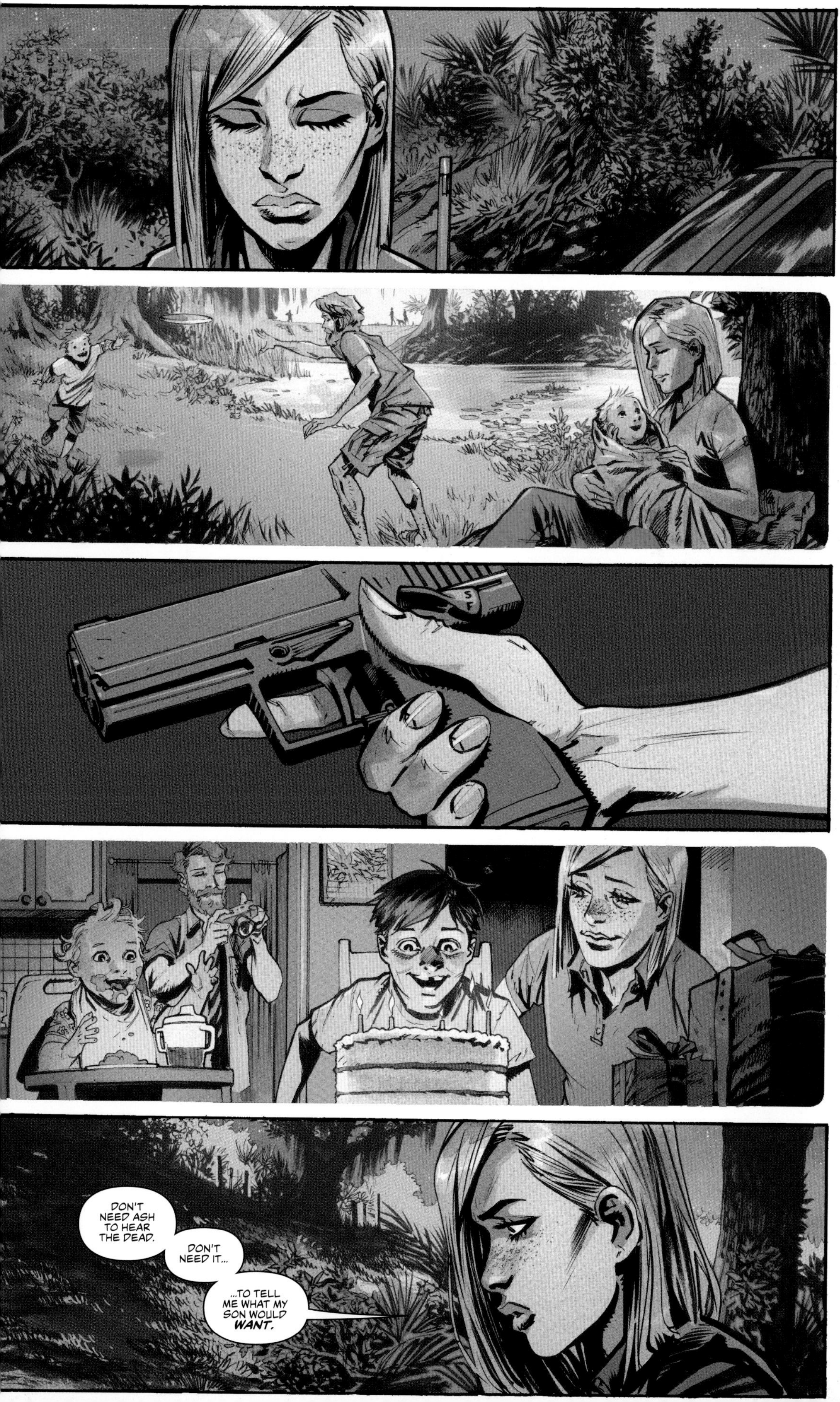

DON'T NEED ASH TO HEAR THE DEAD.
DON'T NEED IT...
...TO TELL ME WHAT MY SON WOULD *WANT.*

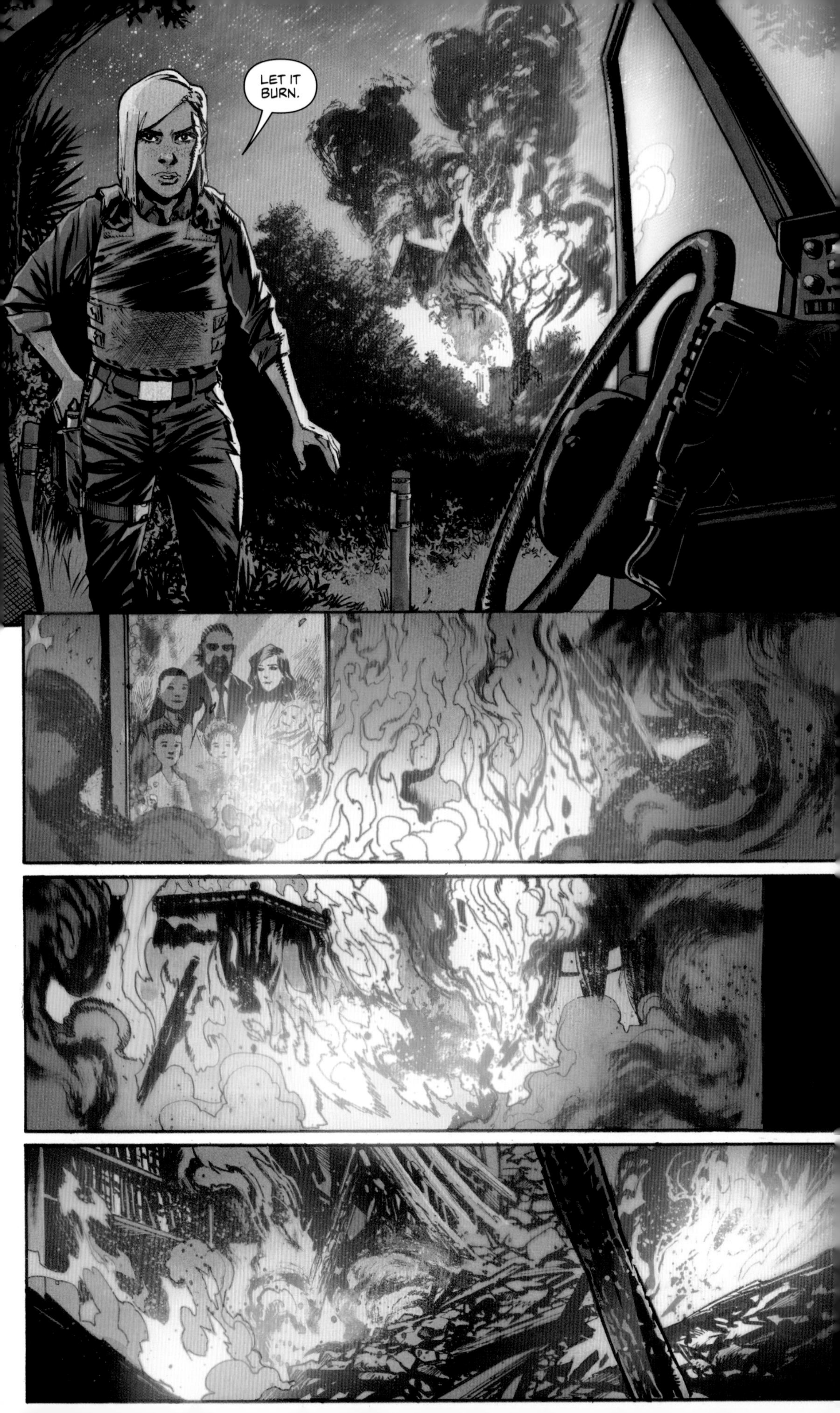
LET IT BURN.

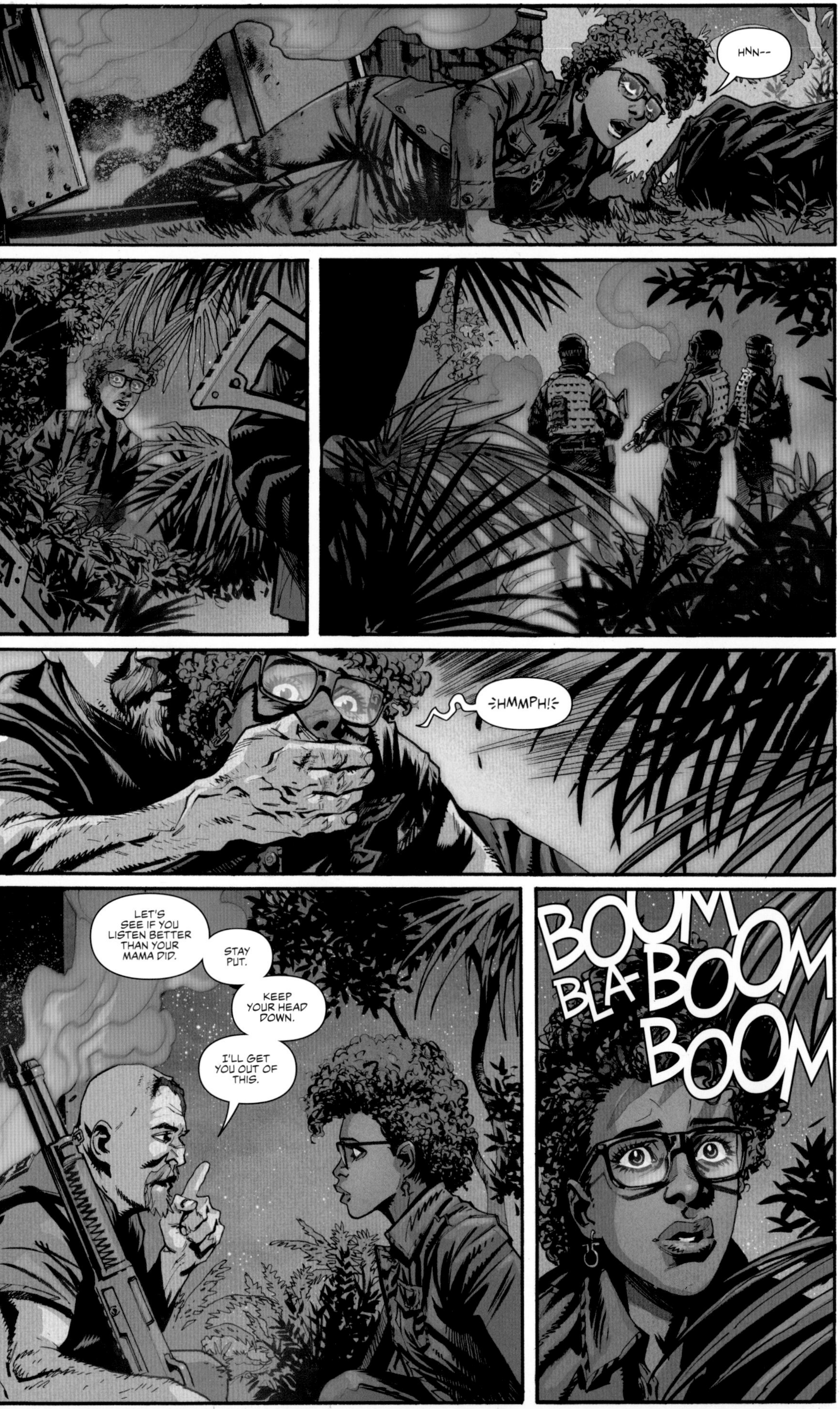
HNN--
HMMPH!
LET'S SEE IF YOU LISTEN BETTER THAN YOUR MAMA DID.
STAY PUT.
KEEP YOUR HEAD DOWN.
I'LL GET YOU OUT OF THIS.
BOOM BLA BOOM BOOM

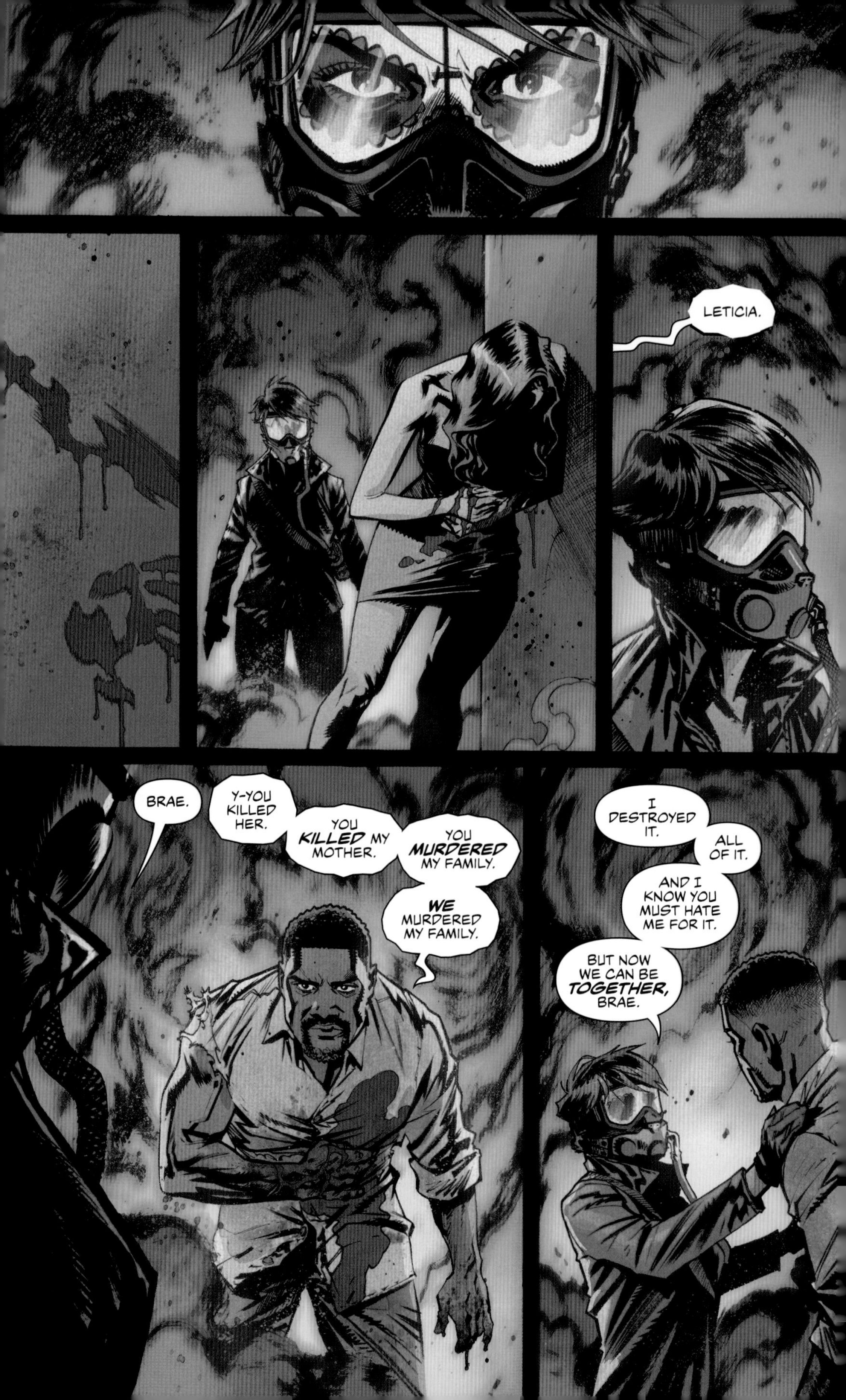
LETICIA.
BRAE.
Y-YOU KILLED HER.
YOU *KILLED* MY MOTHER.
YOU *MURDERED* MY FAMILY.
WE MURDERED MY FAMILY.
I DESTROYED IT.
ALL OF IT.
AND I KNOW YOU MUST HATE ME FOR IT.
BUT NOW WE CAN BE *TOGETHER,* BRAE.

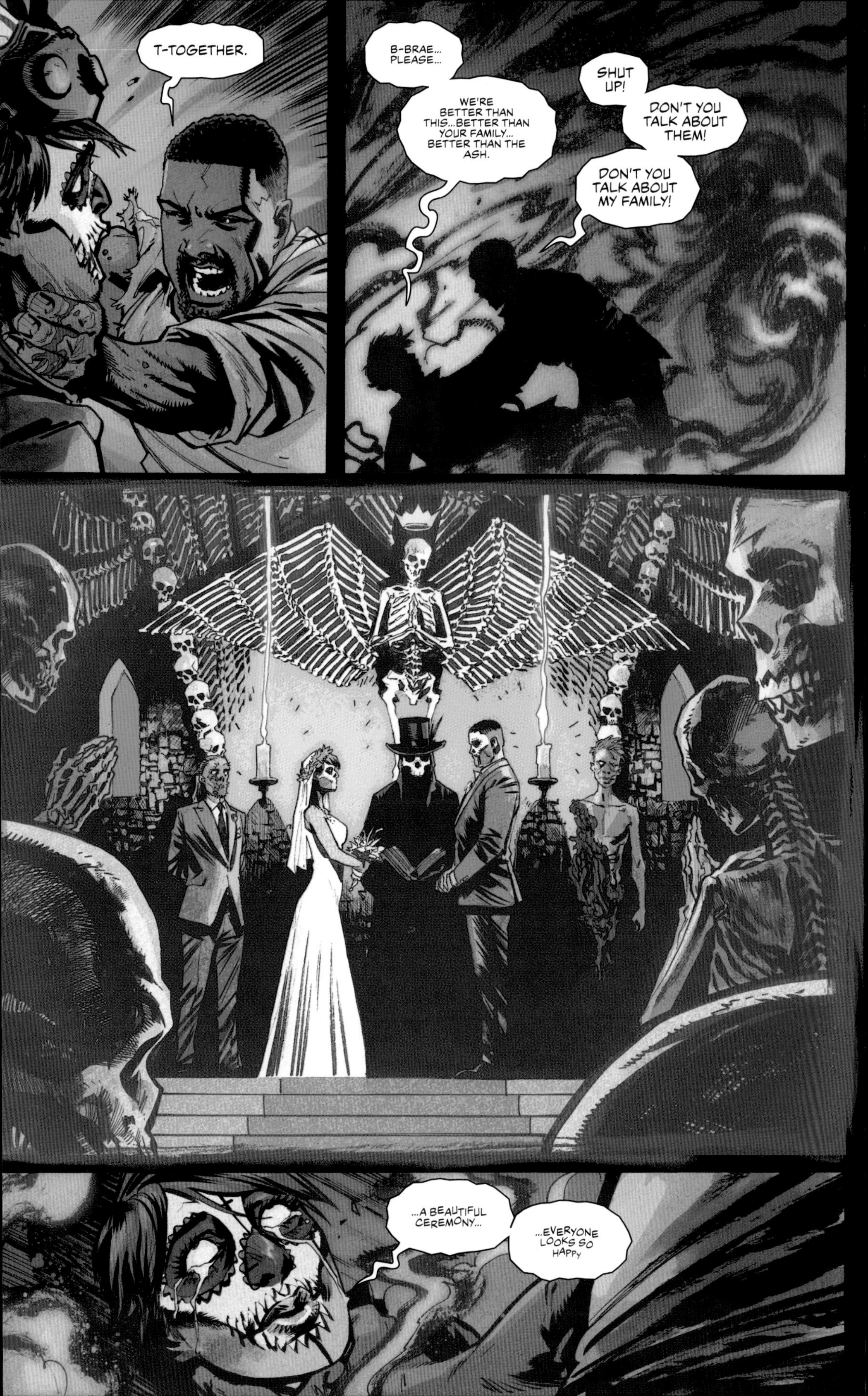
T-TOGETHER.
B-BRAE... PLEASE...
WE'RE BETTER THAN THIS...BETTER THAN YOUR FAMILY... BETTER THAN THE ASH.
SHUT UP!
DON'T YOU TALK ABOUT THEM!
DON'T YOU TALK ABOUT MY FAMILY!
...A BEAUTIFUL CEREMONY...
...EVERYONE LOOKS SO HAPPY

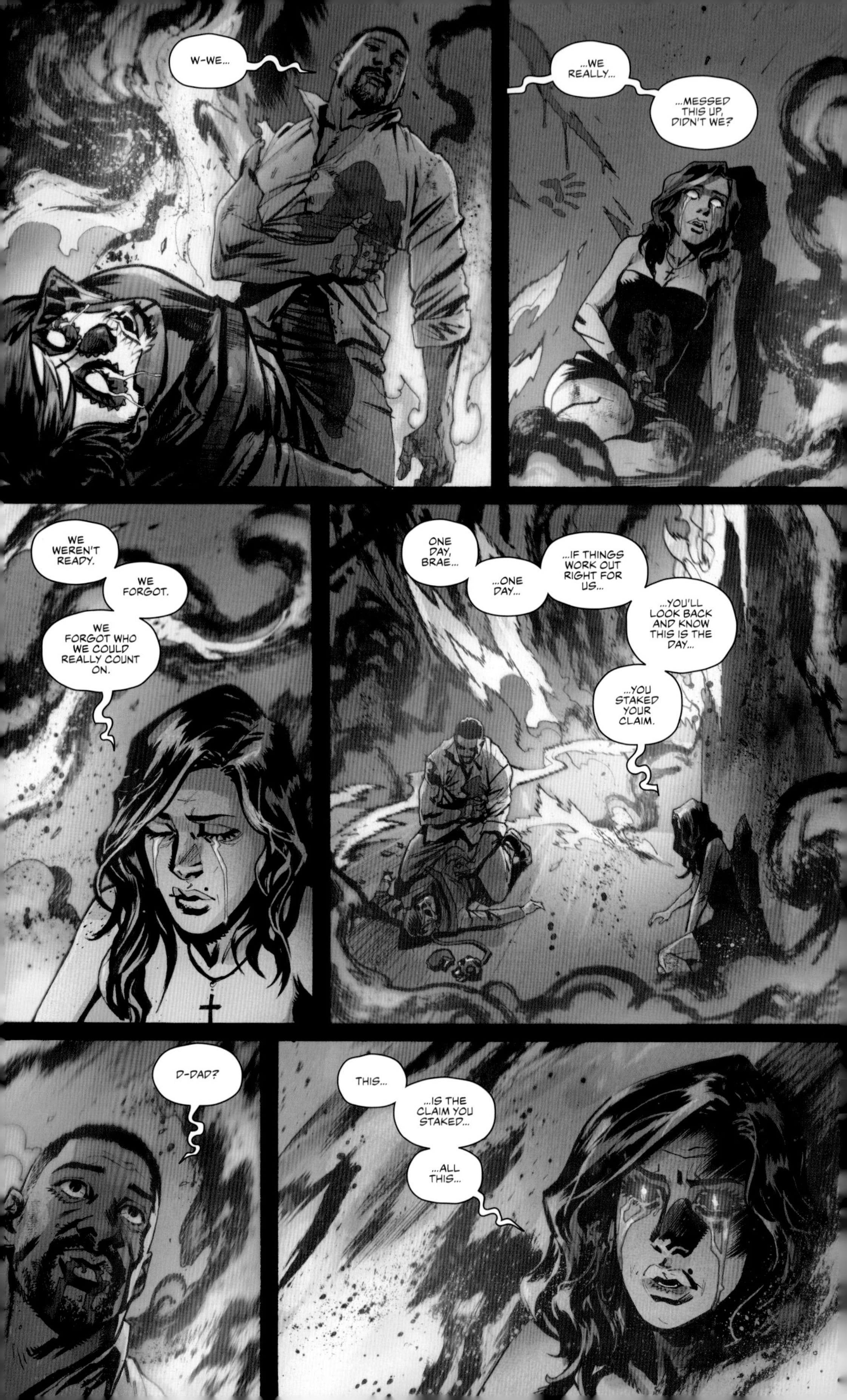
W-WE...
...WE REALLY...
...MESSED THIS UP, DIDN'T WE?
WE WEREN'T READY.
WE FORGOT.
WE FORGOT WHO WE COULD REALLY COUNT ON.
ONE DAY, BRAE...
...ONE DAY...
...IF THINGS WORK OUT RIGHT FOR US...
...YOU'LL LOOK BACK AND KNOW THIS IS THE DAY...
...YOU STAKED YOUR CLAIM.
D-DAD?
THIS...
...IS THE CLAIM YOU STAKED...
...ALL THIS...

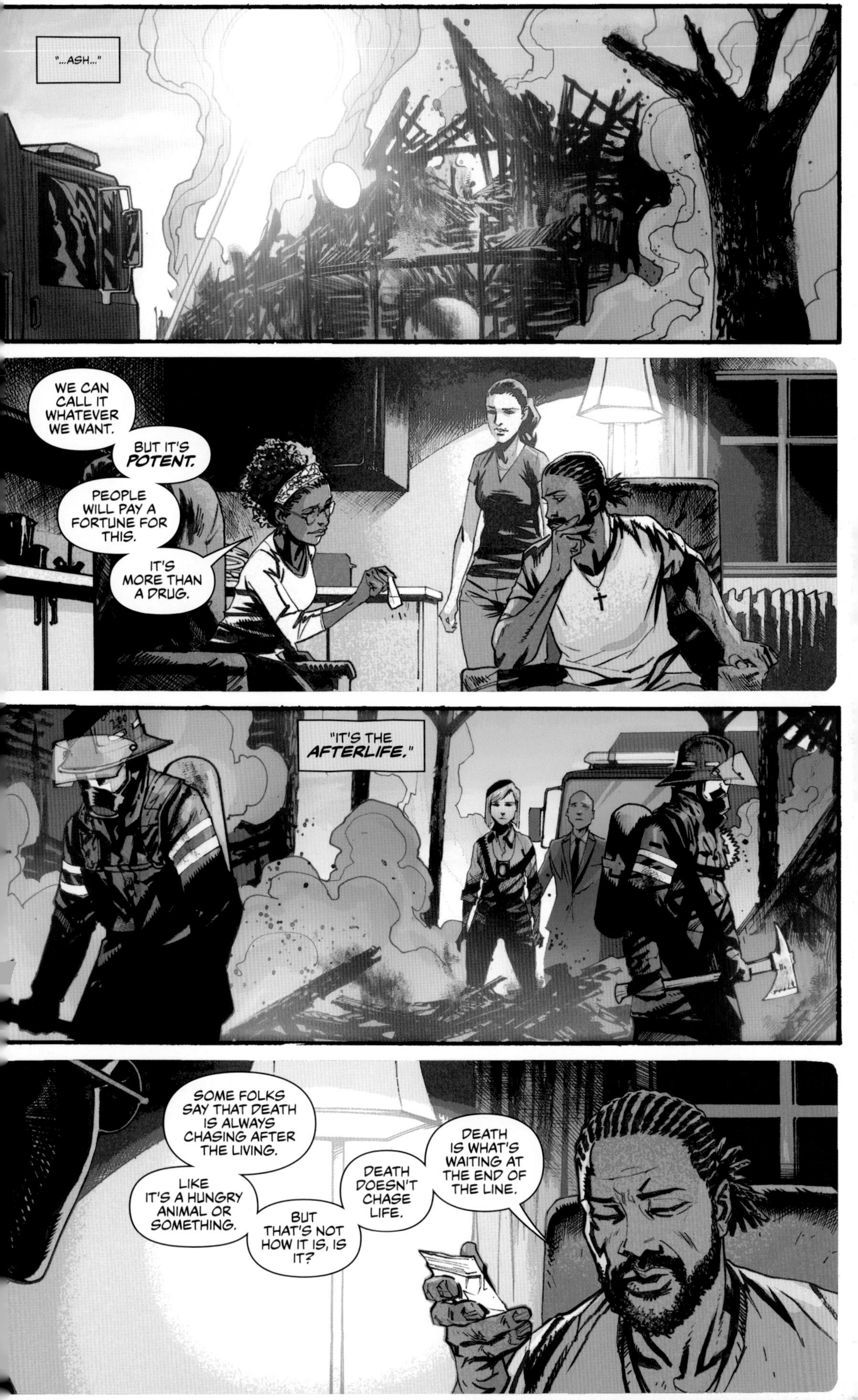
"...ASH..."
WE CAN CALL IT WHATEVER WE WANT.
BUT IT'S *POTENT.*
PEOPLE WILL PAY A FORTUNE FOR THIS.
IT'S MORE THAN A DRUG.
"IT'S THE *AFTERLIFE.*"
SOME FOLKS SAY THAT DEATH IS ALWAYS CHASING AFTER THE LIVING.
LIKE IT'S A HUNGRY ANIMAL OR SOMETHING.
BUT THAT'S NOT HOW IT IS, IS IT?
DEATH DOESN'T CHASE LIFE.
DEATH IS WHAT'S WAITING AT THE END OF THE LINE.

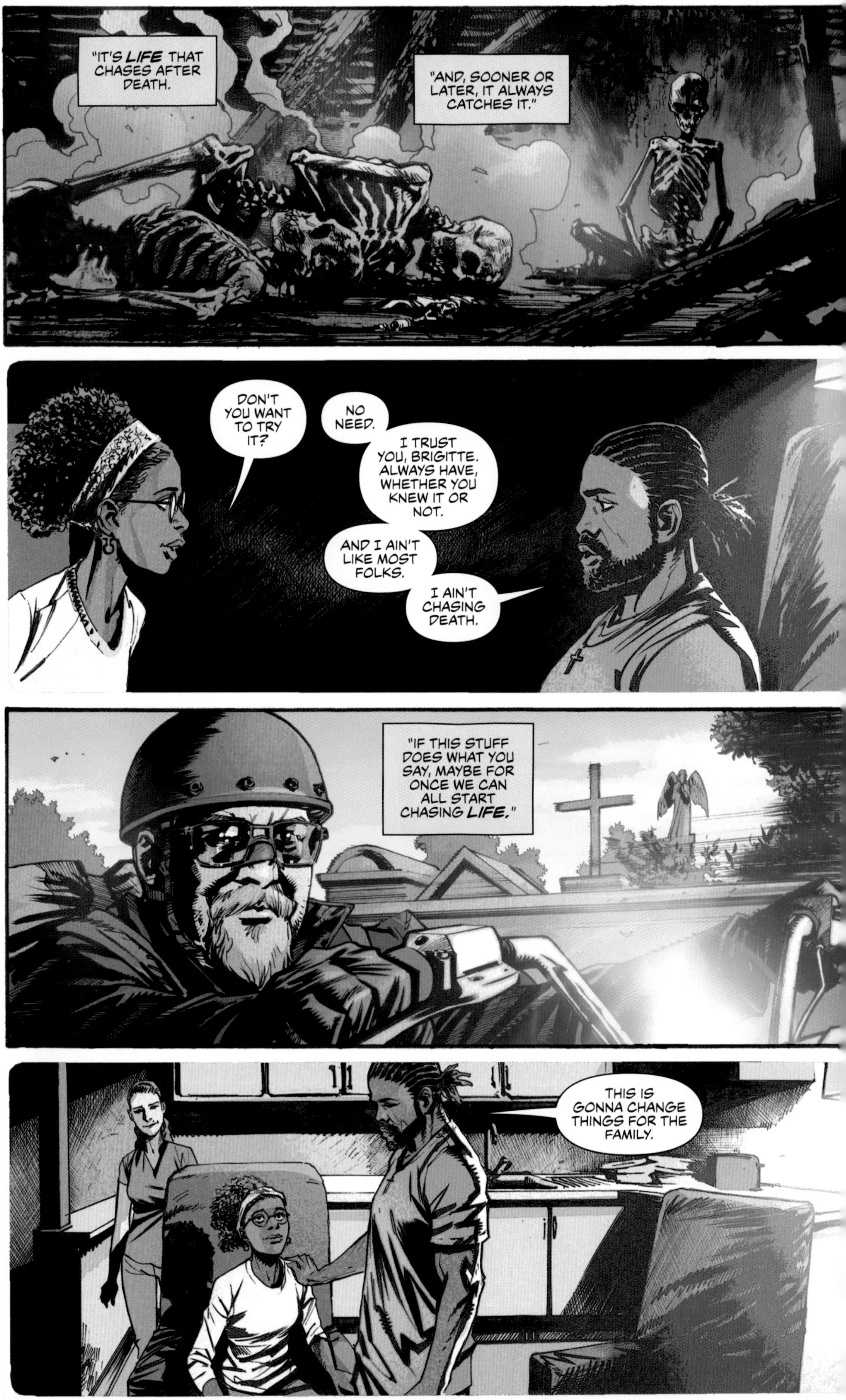
"IT'S LIFE THAT CHASES AFTER DEATH.
"AND, SOONER OR LATER, IT ALWAYS CATCHES IT."
DON'T YOU WANT TO TRY IT?
NO NEED.
I TRUST YOU, BRIGITTE. ALWAYS HAVE, WHETHER YOU KNEW IT OR NOT.
AND I AIN'T LIKE MOST FOLKS.
I AIN'T CHASING DEATH.
"IF THIS STUFF DOES WHAT YOU SAY, MAYBE FOR ONCE WE CAN ALL START CHASING LIFE."
THIS IS GONNA CHANGE THINGS FOR THE FAMILY.

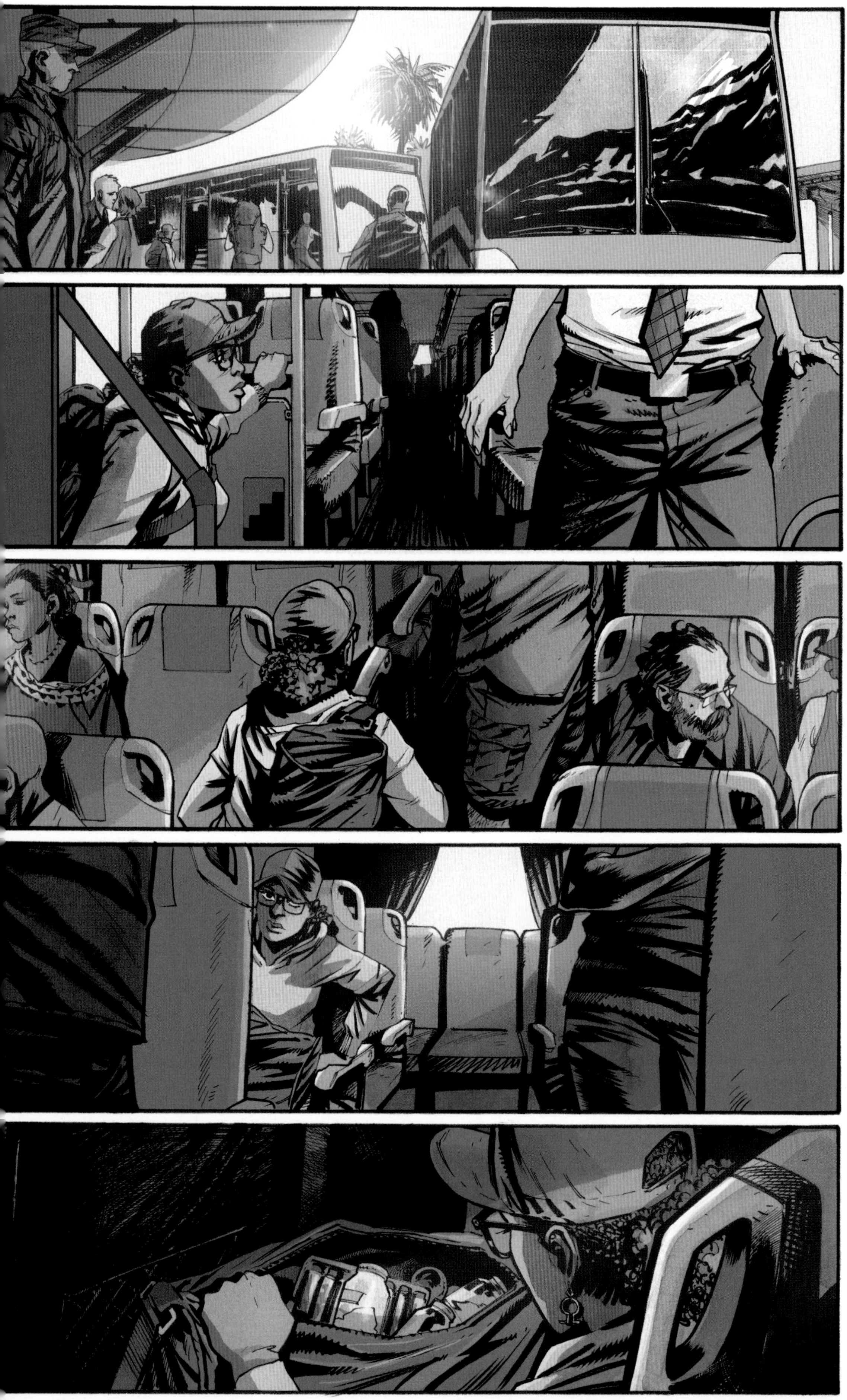

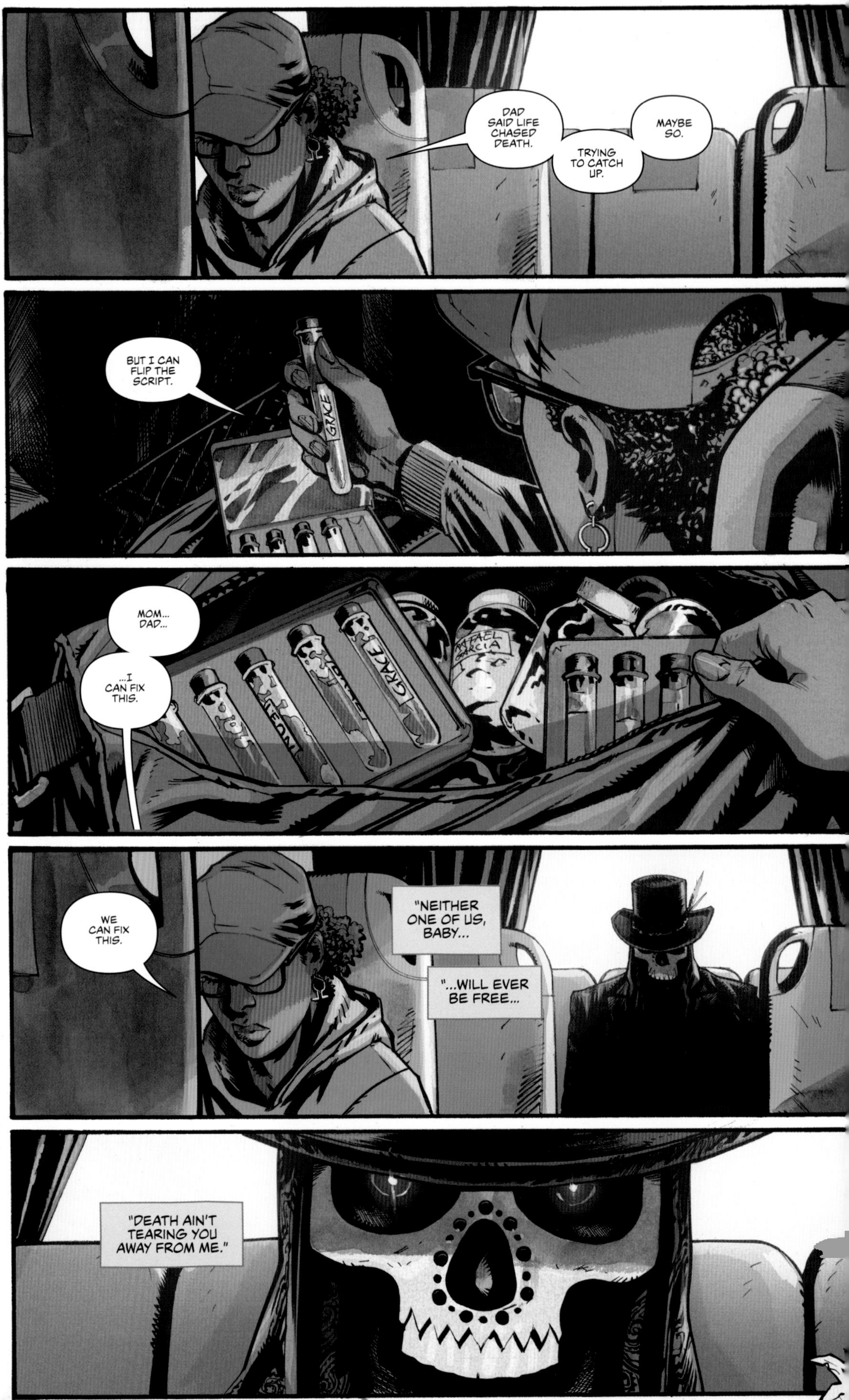
DAD SAID LIFE CHASED DEATH.
TRYING TO CATCH UP.
MAYBE SO.
BUT I CAN FLIP THE SCRIPT.
GRACE
MOM... DAD...
...I CAN FIX THIS.
GRACE
LEON
WE CAN FIX THIS.
"NEITHER ONE OF US, BABY...
"...WILL EVER BE FREE...
"DEATH AIN'T TEARING YOU AWAY FROM ME."

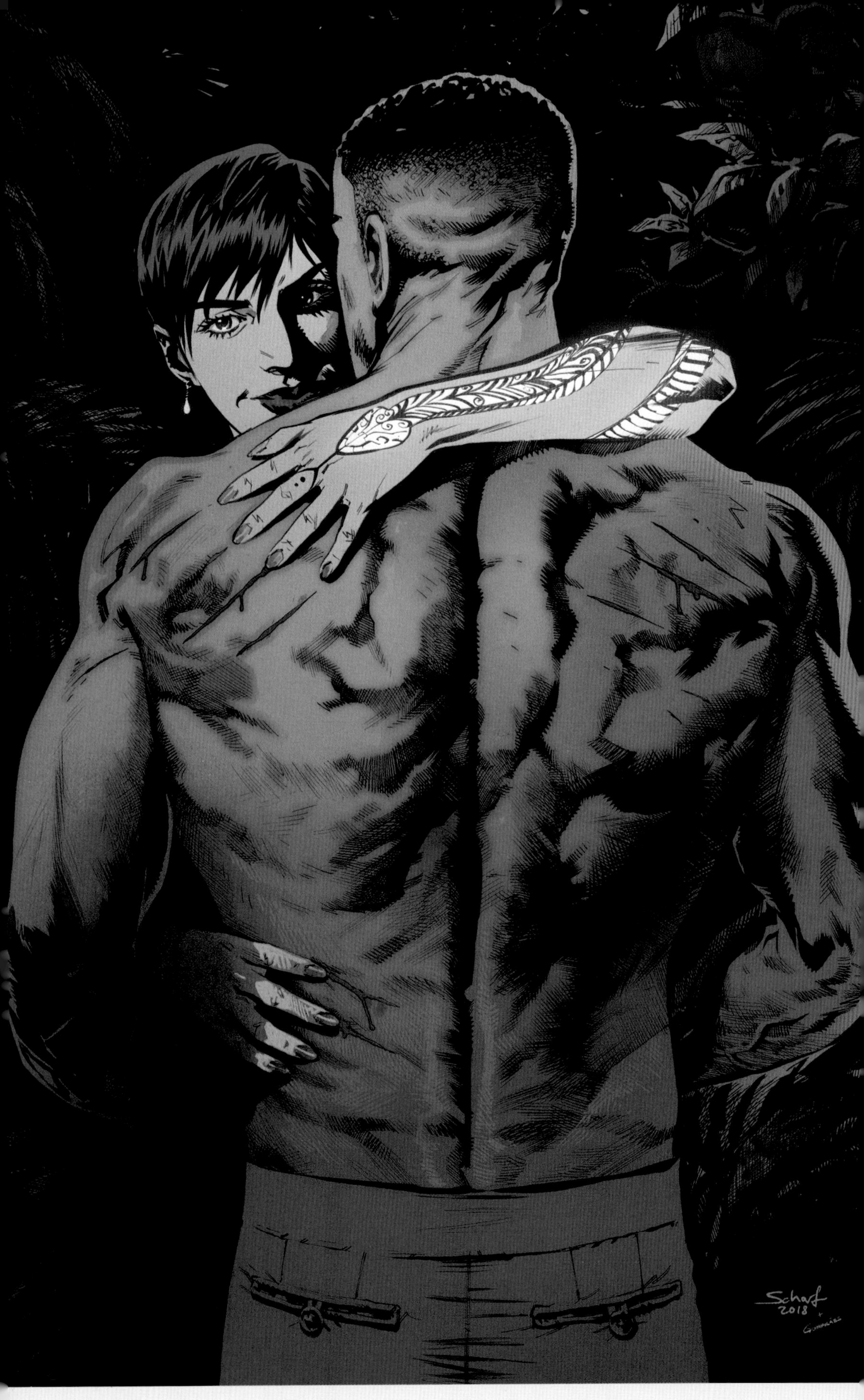
Scharf
2018

Issue Nine Cover by **JONAS SCHARF** with colors by **ALEX GUIMARÃES**

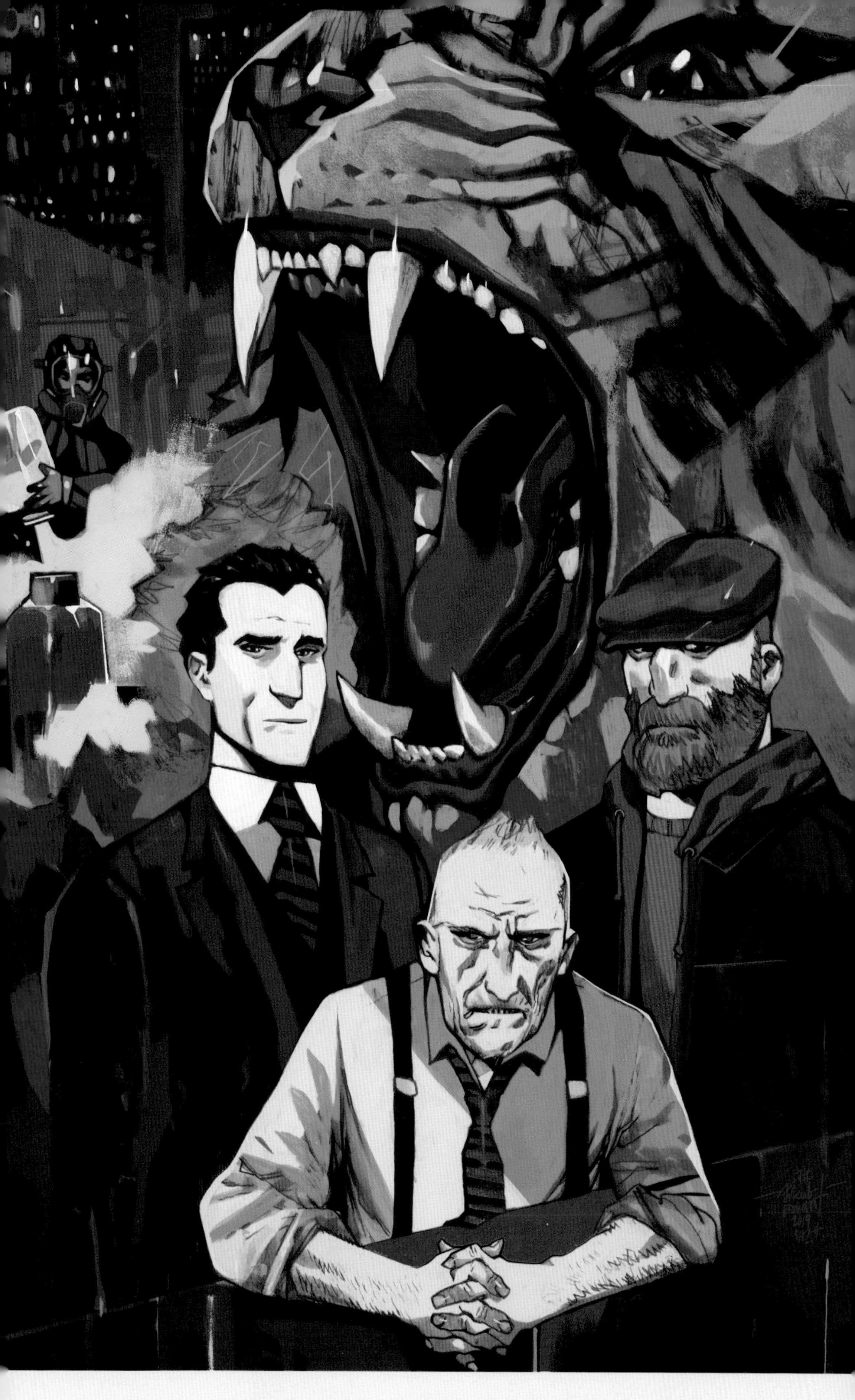

Issue Nine Cover by **JAKUB REBELKA**

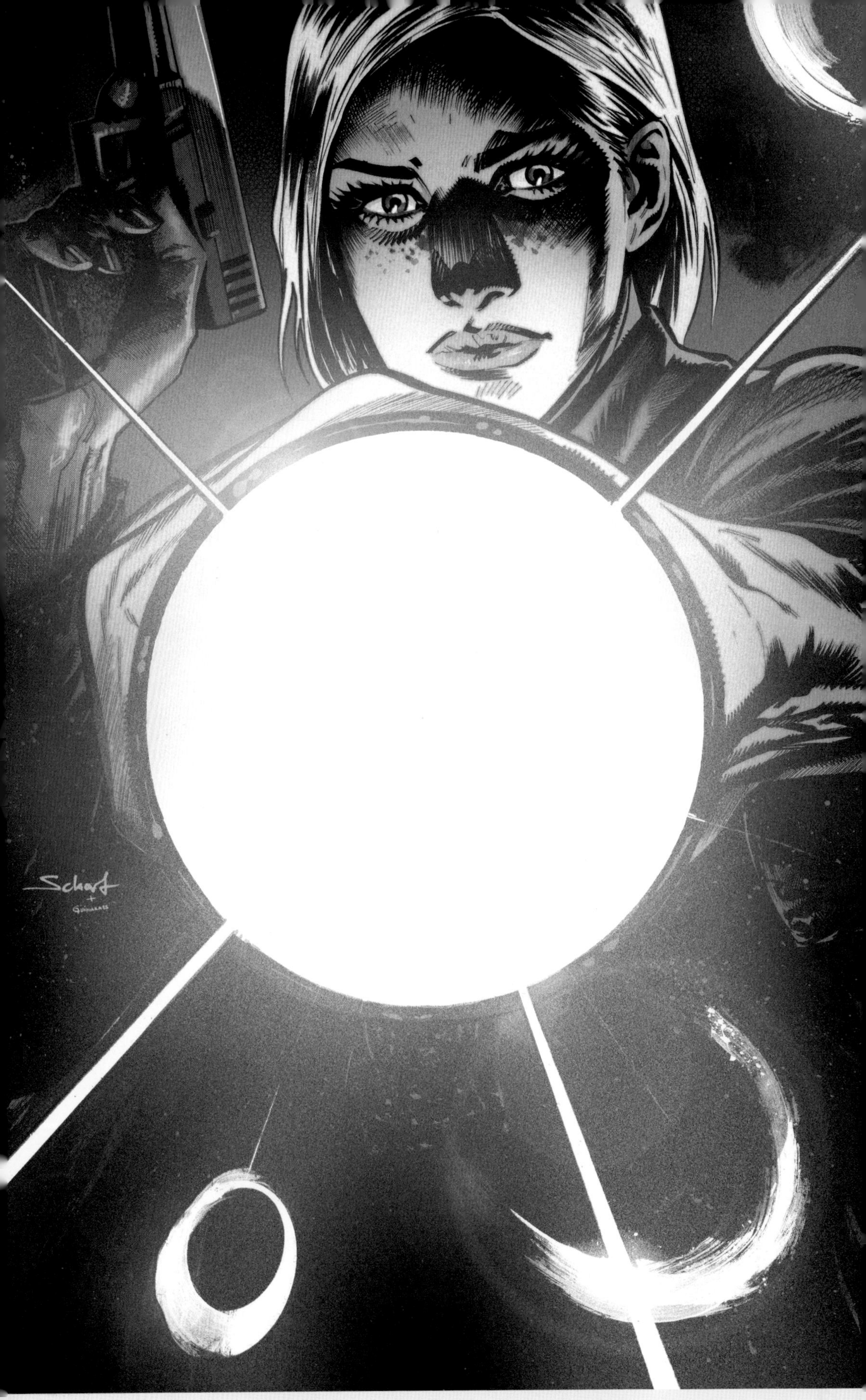
Scharf
+
Guimarães

Issue Ten Cover by JONAS SCHARF with colors by ALEX GUIMARÃES

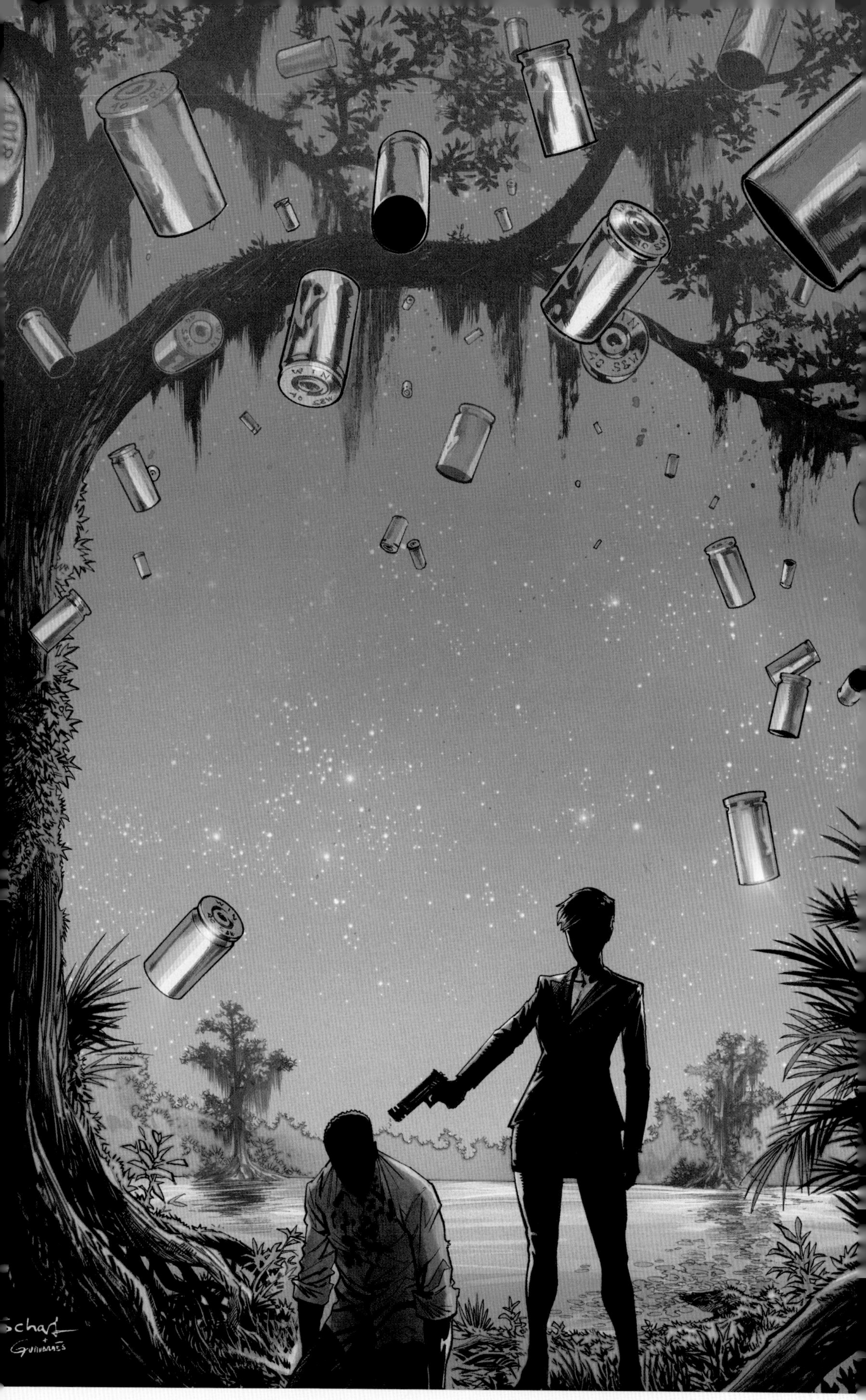

Issue Eleven Cover by **JONAS SCHARF** with colors by **ALEX GUIMARÃES**

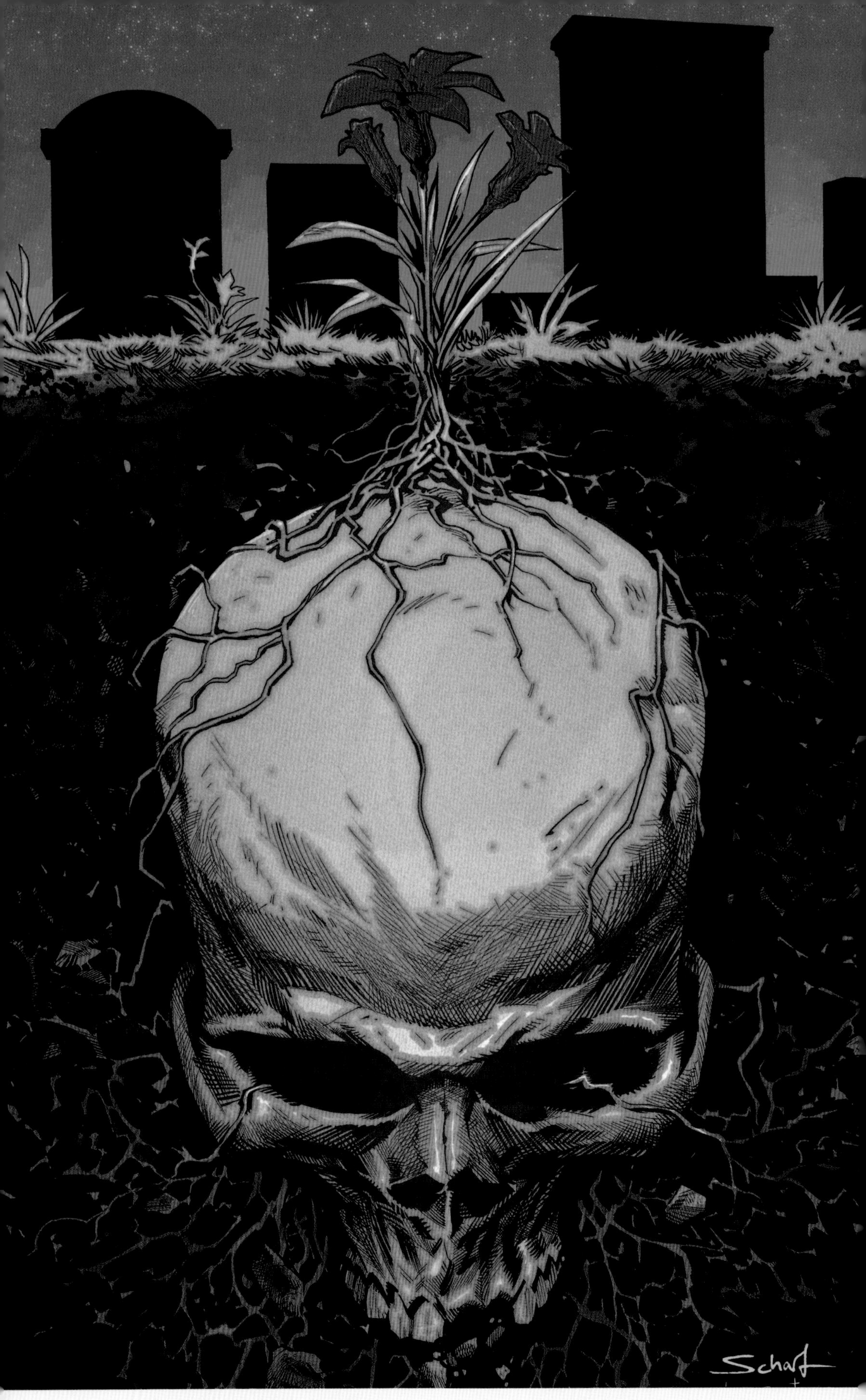
Scharf

Issue Twelve Cover by **JONAS SCHARF** with colors by **ALEX GUIMARÃES**

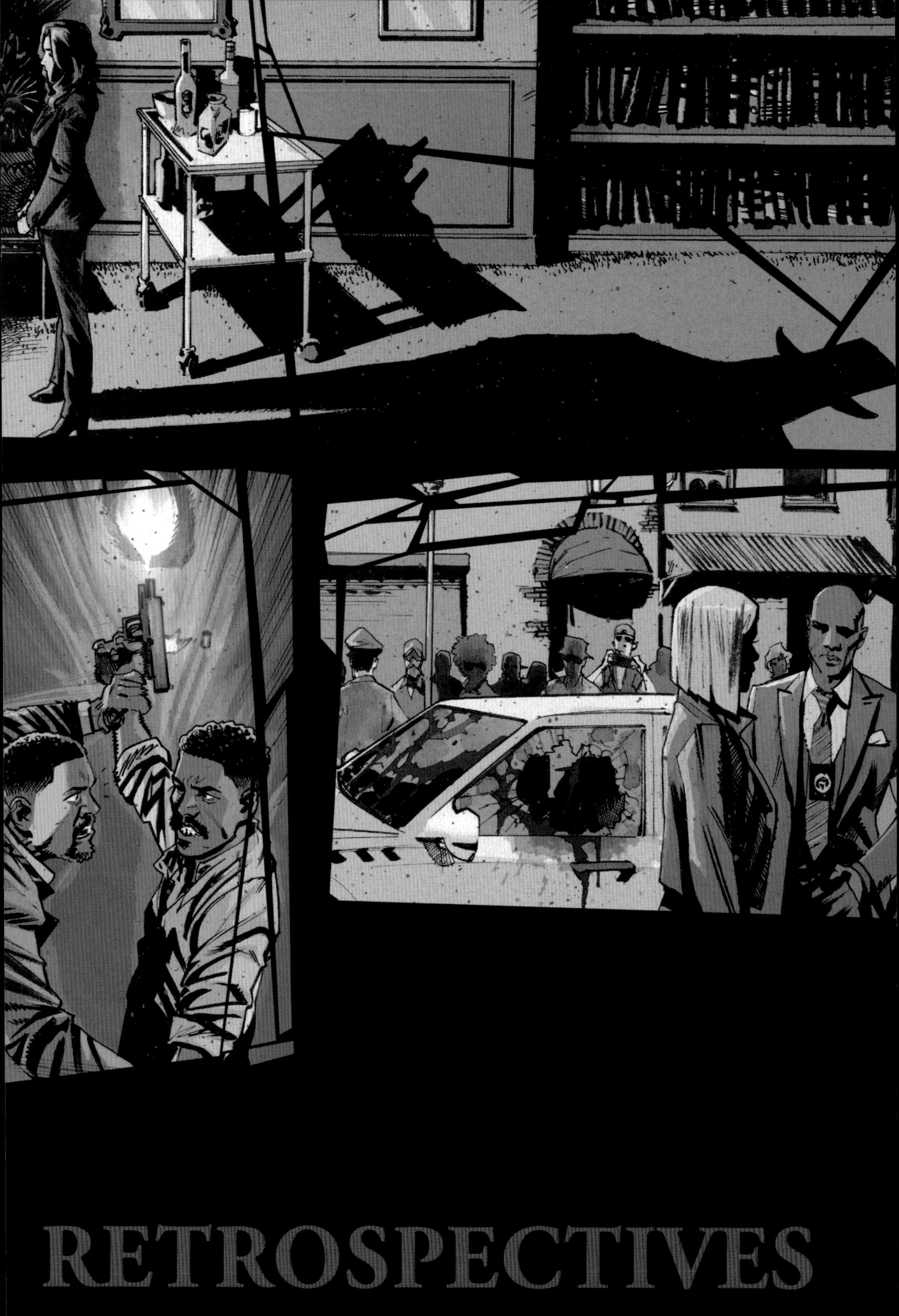

RETROSPECTIVES

I'm gonna let you in on a little secret.

I didn't come up with the idea for *Bone Parish* while lurking around a deserted cemetery. It came to me, years ago, while walking through a grocery store produce section. I don't know what the catalyst was. I don't know that there was a catalyst. There I was, though, looking at strawberries and plums, when—wham!—the idea of people snorting the ashes of others, using them like drugs so they could experience a life that was not theirs, sprang into my head.

The story changed a lot over the years. The initial idea was almost a superhero book, with villains snorting the ashes of ninjas and the like to pull off heists. You still see a hint of that in *Bone Parish*, but my initial approach simply wasn't right. Eventually, I molded the concept into a family crime piece, and it started to feel right.

It wasn't until a few months later, though, after BOOM! had already accepted the book, that it really came together. I was spending Halloween in New Orleans, working early one morning from my hotel room, looking out over the French Quarter. And all of the pieces simply tumbled together. The Winters family came to life. The tone of the story solidified in my head.

I imagined the Winters robbing a New Orleans cemetery. From that point on, nothing else seemed right.

I rewrote the pitch that morning—Halloween morning—and sent it to Eric, my editor. He agreed that this new take on the story, all connected to the mysterious and magical and somewhat sinister undercurrent of New Orleans, was the way to go. It was Eric who, after weeks of trying to figure out the title for the series, suggested "Bone Parish" because it so perfectly reflected both the story and the setting.

Thanks to my collaborators on this book. Jonas, Alex, Ed, Eric, and everyone at BOOM!—I can't express what a pleasure it has been working on this series.

And thank you for reading the series. Thanks for sticking it out with us. I've been so thrilled with the response to this book, and I can't wait to share what we're cooking up next!

CULLEN BUNN

When I read the first script for *Bone Parish*, what really stood out to me was how interesting and complex the premise really is, and how it has applicability well beyond just allegory. It's as much a story about addiction as it is about family. It's about life, death, rebirth, and immortality. It's about the human condition and the ghosts that haunt us; about reality and fantasy.

Those themes stayed on my mind while I was drawing the series and I tried to include little hints, foreshadowing and symbols alluding to those motifs whenever I could, hoping they would pay off along the road. Some worked, some didn't, but that was part of the fun. It was especially rewarding when Alex and Ed then added to the visual storytelling and even expanded on some of those motifs.

As we got more and more comfortable working as a team, Cullen also trusted me with more and more entirely silent scenes. Those proved to be quite challenging, but a great opportunity to be creative with the storytelling and really hammer home those motifs again.

I'm very grateful for the great collaboration I've had with these guys. Eric, our editor, played a huge part in that as well, and I couldn't have done it without his advice and support.

As I'm writing this, I'm only days away from finishing my work on the final issue. These past 15 months really flew by and, although I struggled sometimes, the positive response to the book was a constant reminder of why I love drawing comics.

So I'd like to thank everybody who read, recommended, reviewed or otherwise spread the word about the series.

Thank you for making this all possible.

JONAS SCHARF

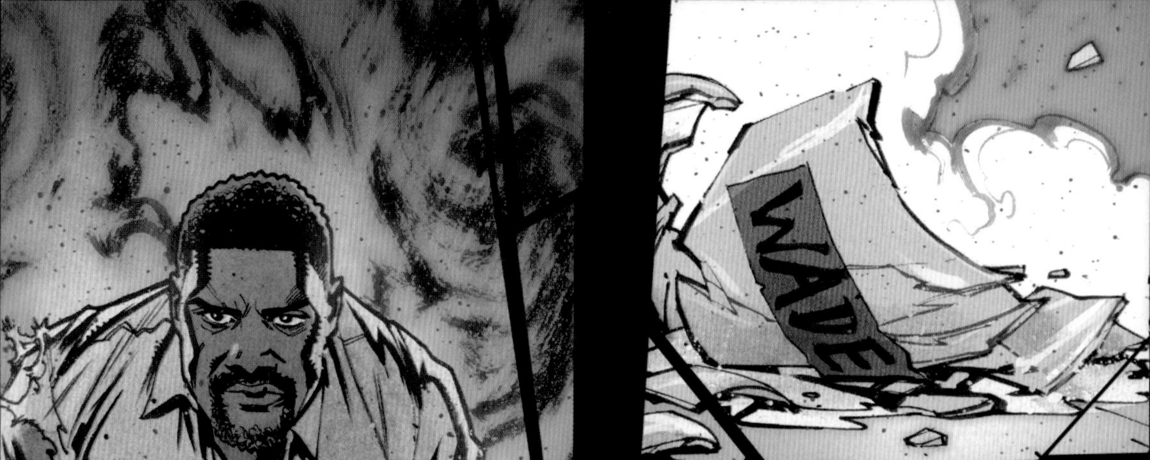
WADE

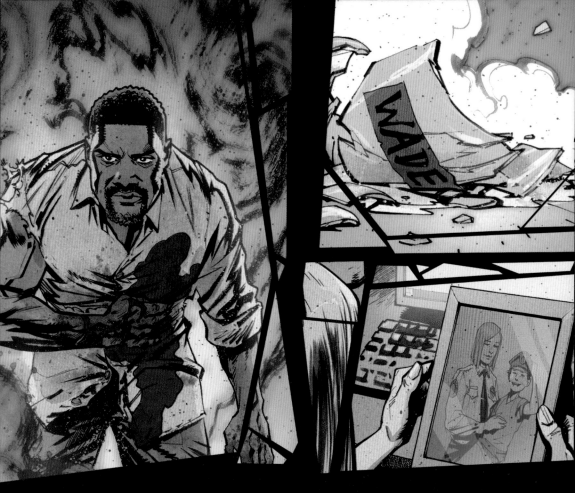

CULLEN BUNN

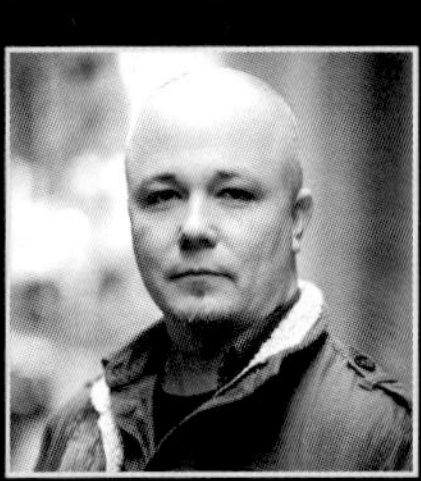

Cullen Bunn writes graphic novels, comic books, short fiction, and novels. He has written *The Sixth Gun, The Damned, Helheim,* and *The Tooth* for Oni Press; *Harrow County* for Dark Horse; *The Empty Man, The Unsound,* and *Bone Parish* for BOOM! Studios; *Dark Ark, Unholy Grail,* and *Brothers Dracul* for AfterShock Comics; and *Regression* and *Cold Spots* for Image Comics. He also writes titles such as *Asgardians of the Galaxy* and numerous *Deadpool* series for Marvel Comics.

JONAS SCHARF

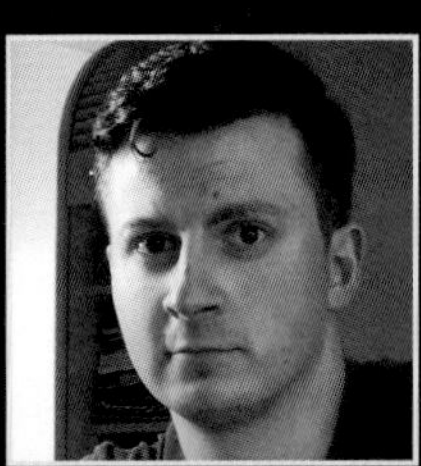

As a kid, young **Jonas Scharf** fell in love with comics and drawing and, being the daydreamer that he was, decided he would one day be a comic book artist. After doing the reasonable thing for a while, getting a solid education and a bachelor's degree, he decided it was time to do the unreasonable thing and pursued a career in comics. In 2016, shortly after his graduation, he was offered his first book and hasn't stopped drawing since. So far he is mostly known for his work on titles like *Warlords of*

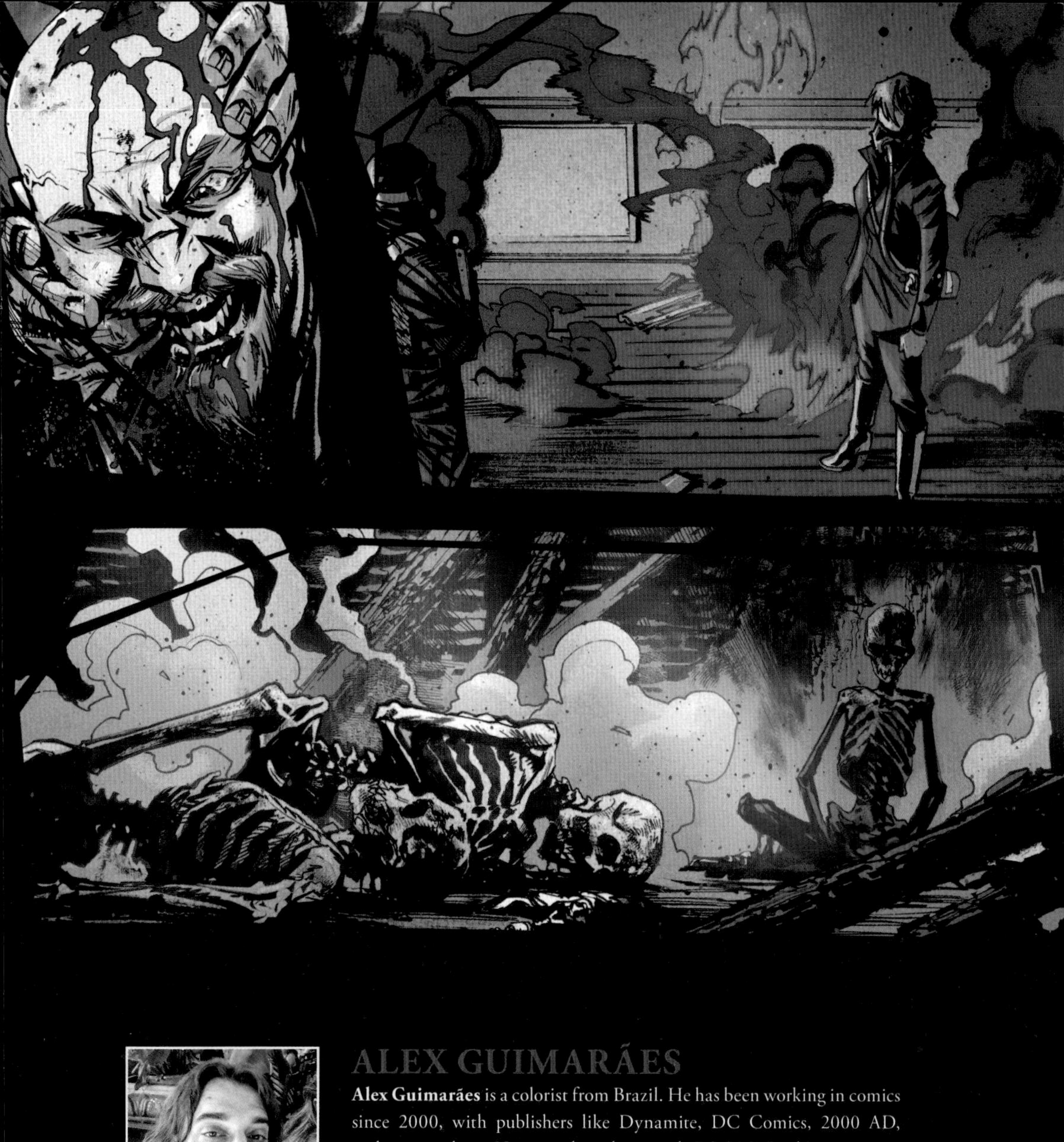

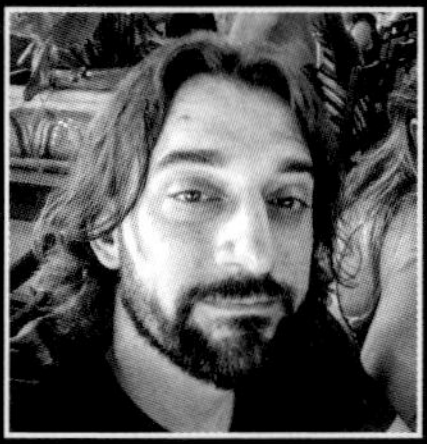

ALEX GUIMARÃES

Alex Guimarães is a colorist from Brazil. He has been working in comics since 2000, with publishers like Dynamite, DC Comics, 2000 AD, and many others. He started working with BOOM! Studios two years ago, and has had a lot of fun with the variety of projects and characters, from *Planet of the Apes* to *Bill & Ted*. He considers *Bone Parish* a career highlight and his best work so far. In addition to *Bone Parish*, he is also currently working on *Invaders* for Marvel Comics.

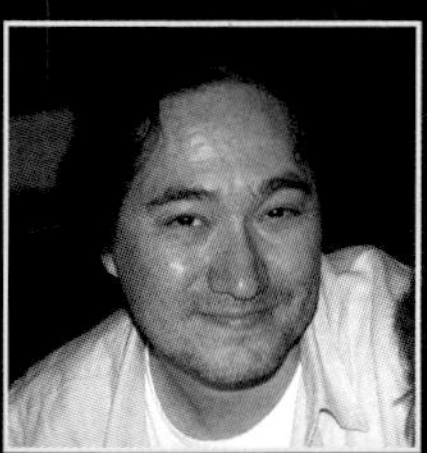

ED DUKESHIRE

Born in Seoul, Korea, **Ed Dukeshire** is a graphic artist and Harvey-nominated comic book letterer who has worked in the biz since 2001. He has lettered titles from mainstream to creator-owned favorites. He also owns and operates the Digital Webbing website, a gathering place for comic creators. And you may even catch him playing video games once in a while.

DISCOVER
VISIONARY CREATORS

THE
WOODS
JAMES TYNION IV • MICHAEL DIALYNAS
VOL. 1
THE ARROW

"The Spire is fantastic! My kind of genre free-for-all."
—BRIAN K. VAUGHAN (Saga)
THE
SPIRE
SIMON SPURRIER
JEFF STOKELY
ANDRÉ MAY

MARK WAID • PETER KRAUSE
IRREDEEMABLE
AFTERWORD BY
GRANT MORRISON

MARK WAID • JEAN DIAZ
INCORRUPTIBLE

MICHAEL ALAN NELSON
DAN MORA
GABRIEL CASSATA
HEXED
THE HARLOT & THE THIEF VOLUME ONE

ABNETT & CULBARD
WILD'S
END
FIRST LIGHT
"IT'S REALLY GREAT!"
JEFF LEMIRE

BOOM! STUDIOS™

AVAILABLE AT YOUR LOCAL COMICS SHOP AND BOOKSTORE

To find a comics shop in your area, visit www.comicshoplocator.com

WWW.**BOOM-STUDIOS**.COM

James Tynion IV

The Woods

Volume 1

ISBN: 978-1-60886-454-6 | $9.99 US

Volume 2

ISBN: 978-1-60886-495-9 | $14.99 US

Volume 3

ISBN: 978-1-60886-773-8 | $14.99 US

The Backstagers

Volume 1

ISBN: 978-1-60886-993-0 | $14.99 US

Simon Spurrier

Six-Gun Gorilla

ISBN: 978-1-60886-390-7 | $19.99 US

The Spire

ISBN: 978-1-60886-913-8 | $29.99 US

Weavers

ISBN: 978-1-60886-963-3 | $19.99 US

Mark Waid

Irredeemable

Volume 1

ISBN: 978-1-93450-690-5 | $16.99 US

Volume 2

ISBN: 978-1-60886-000-5 | $16.99 US

Incorruptible

Volume 1

ISBN: 978-1-60886-015-9 | $16.99 US

Volume 2

ISBN: 978-1-60886-028-9 | $16.99 US

Michael Alan Nelson

Hexed The Harlot & The Thief

Volume 1

ISBN: 978-1-60886-718-9 | $14.99 US

Volume 2

ISBN: 978-1-60886-816-2 | $14.99 US

Day Men

Volume 1

ISBN: 978-1-60886-393-8 | $9.99 US

Volume 2

ISBN: 978-1-60886-852-0 | $9.99 US

Dan Abnett

Wild's End

Volume 1: First Light

ISBN: 978-1-60886-735-6 | $19.99 US

Volume 2: The Enemy Within

ISBN: 978-1-60886-877-3 | $19.99 US

Hypernaturals

Volume 1

ISBN: 978-1-60886-298-6 | $16.99 US

Volume 2

ISBN: 978-1-60886-319-8 | $19.99 US

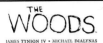

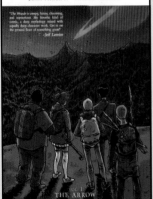

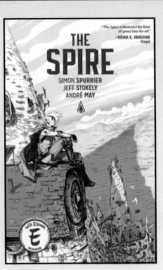

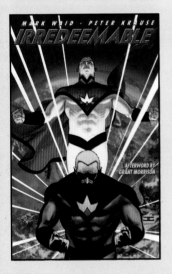

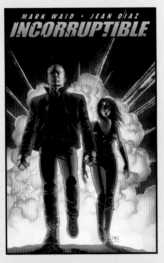

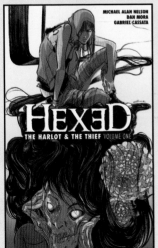

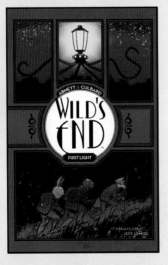

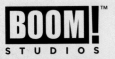